THE
NATIONAL
HOCKEY
LEAGUE

BARNES
&NOBLE
BOOKS
NEW YORK

THE
NATIONAL
HOCKEY
LEAGUE

Edward F Dolan Jr.

This edition published by
Barnes & Noble, Inc.,
by arrangement with Brompton Books
Corporation.

Produced by
Brompton Books Corp.
15 Sherwood Place
Greenwich, CT 06830

ISBN 1-56619-434-2

Printed in Europe

Edward F Dolan Jr is the author of more than 70 non-
fiction books for adults and young people. Among his
works are 21 books on sports history, biography and
instruction. A native Californian, he has been a
newspaper reporter and editor and has written for radio
and television.

Front cover: Mario Lemieux of the Pittsburgh
Penguins.
Photo by B. Winkler/Bruce Bennett Studios.

Back cover:
Top left: Doug Gilmour of the Toronto Maple Leafs.
Photo by J. Wiley/Bruce Bennett.

Top right: Eric Lindros of the Philadelphia Flyers.
Photo by J. Giamundo/Bruce Bennett Studios.

Bottom left: Patrick Roy of the Montréal Canadiens.
Photo by Bruce Bennett.

Bottom right: Wayne Gretzky of the Los Angeles Kings.
Photo by B. Winkler/Bruce Bennett Studios.

CONTENTS

CHAPTER ONE

GAMETIME

First Men on The Ice

On 22 November 1917, a group of troubled Canadian sportsmen from Montréal, Québec, and Ottawa, Ontario, gathered at the Windsor Hotel in Montréal. Born that date of their sometimes angry conversation (for reasons that we'll see in due time) was what would become the world's premier professional ice hockey organization – the National Hockey League. Assigned to it were five teams – the Montréal Canadiens, the Montréal Wanderers, the Ottawa Senators, the Québec Bulldogs, and the Toronto Arenas. As directed by the circuit's president and secretary-treasurer, Frank Calder, they went into action against each other for the first time about three and a half weeks later – on 17 December 1917.

At the time, ice hockey was little less than three-quarters of a century old in Canada. As a sport, no one really knows where it came from. All that can be said with certainty is that, unlike baseball, it was not a deliberate invention but, like American football, a game that evolved from others. There have long been two bodies of opinion on its origins. One holds that it is an outgrowth of the traditional Irish game of hurling, with the other claiming that it is a northern European descendant of the ancient stick-wielding field hockey.

Should the former ever prove to be the case, then ice hockey comes from a game that dates back centuries in Ireland and has long been recognized as that country's national pastime. Originally a communal riot, called *iomain* in Gaelic, it once pitted the teams of rival villages against each other. The rules – what there were of them in those long-ago centuries – set no limits of the number of players per team. The competing villagers crowded onto a grassy field, battled to pick up a brass ball, stone or dried cow pad with their sticks, did their best to keep it balanced on the stick as they ran towards the enemy goal and then tried to score by flinging the thing between two boughs of stripped wood bent into a bow. The game was not simply played for the honor of the village. Some pretty high betting stakes were also on the line. And, at times, even the lives of the players. There are some historical reports of the members of losing teams being excuted.

Hurling, which is mentioned in the oldest of Irish manuscripts and is depicted in bas-reliefs of the fifteenth century, died out at one time. It was revived in 1884 and turned into an organized sport by the Gaelic Athletic Association. Today, looking like a cross between field hockey and lacrosse, hurling is played by fifteen-man teams. The object remains as always: the players are to pick up the game ball on their three-foot long sticks and, whipping it from one man to another, work it upfield and send it into the enemy goal. At no time may any player throw or kick the ball.

At present, there are more than 2000 hurling clubs in Ireland. Competition leads to county, provincial, and national championships. Hurling is also played in other countries with Irish

Right: The ancient game of field hockey.

Page 1: Mark Messier of the Edmonton Oilers and Darryl Sutter of the Chicago Black Hawks.

Page 2-3: A goal mouth mixup between the New York Islanders and the Vancouver Canucks.

Pager 4-5: Wayne 'The Great' Gretzky advances on the goal.

Page 6: The American Indians had a game similar to hockey.

populations, among them the United States. At times, games are played between US and Irish national teams.

If ice hockey, however, evolved from field hockey, then it can, at least indirectly, trace its lineage back to an ancient Persian stick game that was apparently passed on to the Greeks who, in their turn, handed it on to the Romans. Field hockey's early history is, as is true of so many other sports, lost in the mists of time, but one point can be made for certain. Some form of the sport was known in Athens at least 500 years before the birth of Christ. A bas-relief by Themistocles (c. 514-449 BC) was uncovered by archaeologists in 1922. It depicts six young men brandishing sticks in what is unmistakably a hockey-like game. Two of the players are crouching in what seem to be face-off positions.

Nor, since it has never been particularly difficult to dream up games involving sticks whacking balls, was the sport limited to the Persians, Greeks and Romans. Thanks to local inspiration, it took shape just as readily elsewhere. An ocean beyond the Pillars of Hercules, the ancient Aztecs of Mexico played a similar game and left traces of its equipment for archaeologists to dig up centuries later. And there is archaeological evidence to show that the North American Indians – in both the later Canada and United States – participated in several stick-and-ball games. In Western Europe, field hockey was known, in one primitive form or another, by the Dutch, the French and the British prior to the sixteenth century.

The very name of the game suggests its international origins. Several early forms of the sport can lay good claim to inspiring that name.

The French, for instance, played their early game with a curved shepherd's crook that was known as an *hoquet*. The Mohawk Indians of the northeastern United States (or, according to some sources, the Iroquois of the St Lawrence River Valley) christened their game *hoghee* – for a word of theirs whose sound resembles *hockey* and whose meaning indicates the stick and ball's still-persistent habit of making contact with some part of an opponent's anatomy: *it hurts*. Those who support hurling as the ancestor of ice hockey can point to their curved stick as the source of the name. It was – and still

Above: The ladies of London's Wimbledon Skating Club try their hands at playing hockey – 1893.

Top: The championship Québec Bulldogs hockey team of 1912-1913.

is – called a *hurley*. The game itself is often called by the same name.

Both field and ice hockey, especially when informally played, have long had the nickname 'shinny.' It can be traced to a Western European (most likely British) form of the sport that flourished in the nineteenth century and was so christened because of the players' talent for banging one another on the shins with their sticks. The game was played with a worn tennis ball or a small block of wood. The idea was to hit the ball into a goal formed by two stones placed about four to six feet apart on the grass. Play was informal, with the contestants getting together on a Sunday afternoon, picking two captains, and then manning the teams with everybody who showed up. It was common practice to field teams of 30 or more players each.

Somewhere along the line, someone had to figure out that it might be fun to transfer field hockey (or hurling) to the ice. Who first ventured onto a frozen pond or river with stick and stone is anybody's guess. All we really know –

Below: Hockey games attract huge crowds of spectators at Davos, Switzerland, the site of Europe's largest (seven and a half acres) ice rink.

because of an engraving by the Dutch artist Romein de Hooghe – is that his countrymen of the seventeenth century were happily going at each other in a game that, depending on the historian you happen to read, was called *kalv* or *kolven*. They strapped animal bones to the bottoms of their feet, armed themselves with sticks or tree branches measuring about chest high, and then whacked and chased a flat rock along their ice-sheeted canals in wintertime.

From there, especially with the mid-nineteenth century development of the strap-on

steel skate, the ice game spread to other northern European countries where the winters are harsh. Formless in the beginning and with a single intent – the scoring of goals – it gradually took on specific rules dreamed up in various nations and, in time, emerged as the distinct sport known as ice hockey. Later, with the coming of the artificially iced rink in the early twentieth century and the simultaneous establishment of the International Ice Hockey Federation in 1908 (with Belgium, Bohemia, France, Great Britain and Switzerland as the original members), it developed into a world-wide amateur favorite. And still later, it split itself into an amateur and a professional sport, with the birth of Canada's National Hockey League in the twentieth century establishing that country as the seat of the professional game.

By whatever name it was then called – in all likelihood, shinny or hurling – the ice game first took shape in Canada sometime in the second quarter of the nineteenth century. Credited with giving the game its start there were the British soldiers sent out from England to man Her Majesty's Canadian garrisons.

Above: Winter sports action in Banff, Alberta, Canada. In foreground is a curling match.

Above: The Ottawa Club of 1893 – senior champions of the Ontario Hockey Association. Top row, left to right – P D Ross (president), H Pulford, G P Murphy (vice-president), D Walters. Middle Row – J F Smellie, A Smith, W C Young, C T Kirby. Bottom row – H Westwick, F C Chittick, H Y Russell.

Those who had tried whacking a ball along the ice back home found the weather conditions – freezes that gave the nation's countless rivers, ponds and lakes a solid ice sheeting underfoot from early autumn to late spring – perfect for their get-togethers of informal mayhem. And those who had never tried the game before started cutting sticks from trees and getting out on the ice because there wasn't much else around to break the long winter monotony.

The result: wherever you found an icy surface, you found the soldiers slithering along, whipping their sticks in any direction that came to mind, slipping as often as not and routinely swearing, all the while being watched by a local populace that was, in turns, fascinated and befuddled by the wild action. The next step came as no surprise. Soon the young bucks among the locals were themselves venturing on to the ice. By the 1860s, the game was beginning to challenge lacrosse, which had been inherited from the Indians, as Canada's number-one sports pastime. The challenge became even greater after that decade's invention of the strap-on steel skate. Thousands of new players and spectators were attracted to the ice.

But, as popular as it had become, the game remained its old formless self, with everyone, as had always been the case, getting together to choose up teams of any size (again, squads of 30 or more players were common) and not being

the least bothered when one side outnumbered the other. Whatever the rules might have been, they were ill-defined and differed from locale to locale. Of the rules, only three seem to have been widely recognized. The first was 'shinny for your own side,' meaning that players – in a moment of whimsy or annoyance at being on the losing squad – could not switch teams during a match and always had to shoot at the opposition's goal. The second called for non-stop action, with play being suspended only when the game ball – by now called the puck (and aptly derived from the Old English word meaning *demon*) – shot out of the playing area and plunged into a snowbank, disappeared into the underbrush, or went skittering a few hundred yards up the river ice. The third held that games could last as long as the players wanted to continue. Games were not usually called off until everyone was exhausted and in need of a warming drink or until the winter sun disappeared and sent everyone home to dinner.

The equipment was just as primitive. Sticks ranged from barrel staves, broomsticks and canes to strips of wood fashioned from oak and ash saplings, with the wood usually being hacked from the base of a tree or the roots so that the handle would merge into the stick face at the proper angle. Used as pucks were tin cans, rubber balls, pine cones, tree knots and barrel bungs. There were no such things as uniforms. Heavy trousers, sweaters, woolen scarves and stocking caps did the job. Newspapers or pages torn from mail order catalogues served as protective gear when they were wrapped around the arms and shins with rope and, later, large rubber bands cut from tire inner tubes.

Though an ice-covered pond or river, with trees looming on all sides, could be a thing of beauty, the playing surface was anything but conducive to easy skating and concentration on the action. The players had to be on the constant look-out for humps in the ice, rough and slick areas and, in particular, weak spots. The goals also had to be closely watched because they weren't the easiest things in the world to see. They usually consisted of a couple of rocks placed a few feet away from each other at either end of the playing areas. Sometimes, if everyone wanted to take the time before playing, the teams would set up the goals by chopping holes in the ice and shoving branches into them. Some of the better maintained areas had one- to four-foot-high wooden borders around them to keep the puck from sailing in among the spectators and, if not bruising someone, then burying itself in the snow.

TAYLOR PREMIER QUALITY HOCKEY GLOVES

No. G. Taylor "GOALIE" Goal Keeper's Gloves. Cream colored horsehide with tan leather knuckle patches. Hair filled pads. Padded palms with canvas web between fingers. Seven-inch reed cuffs. Used by all the leading goal tenders. Pair 18.00

No. GK. Taylor "GOALIE TOP NOTCH" Goal Keeper's Gloves. Same as No. G, but have extra heavy felt padding on entire back. Pair........................ 21.50

No. GC. Taylor "LEAGUE" Goal Keeper's Gloves. Tan horsehide with mahogany colored finger pads, tan cowhide padded palms with web fingers. Hair filled pads. Six-inch cuffs reinforced with reeds. A popular school team glove. Pair.......................... 9.50

No. FHL. Taylor "PRO" Hockey Gloves of cream colored horsehide with tan leather knuckle patches. Hair filled pads. Seven inch reed cuffs, extra well padded. Large size. Ideal glove for better players. Pair......... 13.50

No. G

No. FH. Taylor "RANGERS" Hockey Gloves. Cream colored horsehide, tan leather knuckle patches. Hair filled pads. Seven-inch reed cuffs. Extra well padded. Pair 12.50

No. PH. Taylor "ROYAL" Hockey Gloves of golden tan horsehide with tan knuckle patches. Light weight. Hair filled pads. Six-inch reed cuffs. Excellent all around glove. Pair 12.00

No. FH

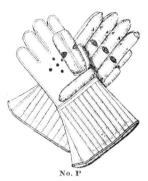

No. P

No. P. Taylor "REGAL" Hockey Gloves of tan and mahogany colored horsehide, tan cowhide palm. Hair filled pads, six-inch cuffs reinforced with reeds. Light in weight. Pair 8.00

No. Y. Taylor "TIGER" Hockey Gloves. Tan cowhide leather palm, imitation leather back and cuff. Padded fingers, five-inch cuffs reinforce with reeds. Ideal for boys. Pair 4.50

TAYLOR "OFFICIAL" HOCKEY PUCKS

OFFICIAL WEIGHT, SIZE AND QUALITY

No. O. Taylor "OFFICIAL" Hockey Pucks. Each.... .50

No. P. Taylor "PRACTICE" Hockey Pucks. Each.... .35

TAYLOR PREMIER QUALITY HOCKEY SUNDRIES

No. CHG. Taylor "CHAMPIONSHIP" Hockey Goal, constructed under specifications of star players of American Hockey League. Constructed of tubular steel with flat steel base fitted so as to spike into the ice. Will not shift. The net is of official diamond mesh construction, made of heavy twine. Price for pair complete......................... 100.00

No. HN. Taylor "DOMINION" Official White Twine Hockey Goal Nets (separate). Pair.... 42.50

As the popularity of the game spread through the 1860s and 70s, manufacturers became aware of its profit potential. They began to turn out highly polished sticks (costing 25 cents each) and pucks. To their list of equipment they added baseball's catcher's mitt for the goalie – plus cricket's leg and arm pads – when the puck, which had always slithered along the ice, was finally lifted into the air and started to blacken eyes, remove teeth and bruise various parts of the anatomy. Contrary to widespread popular belief, the puck was not first sent airborne by the natural and long-used forehand shot but by a later evolving shot – the backhand.

The story of the puck's development into its present form is an interesting one that began with the hockey-playing students at Montréal's McGill University in the 1880s. Sources differ on how the puck got started there, with some historians saying that the young men devised a square, flat rubber block that was eventually reshaped into today's circular affair. Other sources – and theirs is the interesting version –

Above: A page from an early sports equipment catalogue showing hockey gear.

Far left: Dr Joe Sullivan, the goaltender on the Canadian Olympic team in the 1928 winter games in St Moritz, Switzerland.

Opposite left: Bill Touhey of the Ottawa Senators.

Opposite right: Bill Burkley (left) and Summer Randall of the Massachusetts Institute of Technology team.

Below: The Oxford University team plays the Davos (Switzerland) hockey club in 1924. In the center of the picture is Clarence Campbell.

hold that the students came up with a wooden square and then, when it shredded quickly from the moisture in the ice and the constant stick punishment, turned to the hard rubber ball used in lacrosse. The rubber ball remained on the scene until the arrival of the first indoor rinks, with its career abruptly ending on the night that it sailed into a balcony, bounced here and there, smashed several windows en route, and did about $300 in glass damage before finally deciding to stop. The arena owner, understandably annoyed, hacked the ends of the ball away and left the players with the flat circular center and the forerunner of the modern puck.

The initial development of another basic piece of equipment provides a story almost as interesting. The goal cage as we know it today was born when a player, whose identity is unknown, visited a coastal village and saw the fishermen there mending their nets. Struck with a idea seeming so obvious today that it strikes us as strange that no one had earlier thought of it, he purchased a stretch of netting, suspended it between two posts, and ended for all time the problem of the puck sailing out of the playing area on passing through the goal.

By the time these and other developments came along, hockey had evolved from a let's-get-together-and-choose-up-sides game to an organized amateur sport. The roots of this transformation can be traced back to the small city of Kingston, Ontario. A place of fierce winters, its civic records indicate that a very primitive form of the ice game was played there as early as the 1830s. Further evidence shows that Kingston could boast organized teams by the 1850s, outfits made up of players from an

army regiment stationed at the local Tete-du-Pont Barracks – Her Majesty's Royal Canadian Rifles. The teams operated each winter out on the ice in the city's harbor.

From there, the organized game spread away in various directions, especially westward as the country inched towards the Pacific Coast and made its way onto the western prairies where the winters were especially harsh. Springing up throughout the 1860s and 1870s were teams formed by schools, military units and sports and social clubs. Though organized as teams, they all played by the ill-defined rules that still governed the game. Historians generally agree that the first game to be played by specific rules – and thus the game that can be said to have been the first 'official' hockey match – took place in 1879 on the campus of Montréal's McGill University. Pitted against each other were two student teams, each manned by 30 skaters.

Because of that game, Montréal has long thought of itself as the birthplace of today's ice hockey, a claim that Kingston, with its soldier teams of the 1850s, disputes. The Montréal claim is also disputed by the city of Halifax on the grounds that the McGill game was organized by a student named J G A Creighton. Creighton was a native of Halifax, which thinks that it may well have originated ice hockey in a form still recognized today because Creighton was bringing to Montréal a sport long known in his home town.

Though the McGill match was played according to a firmer set of rules than had been known in the past, the subsequent months saw the adoption of what can be called hockey's first genuine rules. The credit for the work done

Above: Lord Stanley of Preston, the governor general of Canada who donated the Stanley Cup – the symbol of world professional hockey supremacy.

ston Hockey Club and the Kingston Athletics. Queen's University took the infant league's first championship.

Eighteen eighty-five saw a group of hockey enthusiasts meet in Montréal and form the country's first truly influential hockey body – the Amateur Hockey Association of Canada. The Association fielded five teams: a unit each from Québec and Ottawa, and three from Montréal – the Crystals, Victorias, and Montréals. The Association also altered the team size, reducing it from Robertson's nine men to seven. Manning each squad now were two defensemen (the point and cover point), three forwards, the goalkeeper and the rover, who divided his time between offense and defense as playing situations dictated. The game was now one man away from its present configuration which calls for six-men teams.

The next years saw leagues – among them the Montréal Amateur Athletic Association, the Victoria Hockey Club of Winnipeg, and the Eastern Canada Amateur Hockey Association – spring up throughout the country. By 1895, there were more than 100 clubs involved in league or individual play in the Montréal area alone, while an estimate of the day held that not a Canadian town or village could be found without a hockey club. The AHA, however, remained the strongest of the leagues until 1899 when, as the result of internal turmoil, it was disbanded. A group of its officials then formed the Canadian Amateur Hockey Association, which remains the country's principal amateur organization to this day.

The final decade of the nineteenth century and the opening years of the twentieth century saw three developments that capped off hockey as an organized sport. First, in 1893, the governor general of Canada – Lord Stanley of Preston – invested ten guineas ($48.63) in a silver mug that was to be awarded to the country's top amateur team after a championship series at the close of each season. The Stanley Cup, which immediately became (and has continued to be) the premier prize in hockey, fired the imagination of fans across the country and rendered an already popular sport immeasurably more popular, a fact made clear by the mob – a record hockey crowd for years to come – that turned out in 1894 to watch Ottawa and the Montréal AAA vie for the Cup (in 1893 the Cup had been awarded to the winner of the AAA regular season title, Montréal). Further, since there was at the time nothing equivalent to it in baseball, soccer or the infant American football, the Cup endowed hockey with a prestige that ensured that it would endure as a sport. So important has the Stanley Cup been to the game, that it will have a chapter to itself later in this book.

Second, the ice game moved southward across the border to the United States. Until the 1890s, Americans – even in the iciest of the country's eastern regions – knew little or nothing of hockey, with football (the US child of soccer and rugby) and baseball occupying their attention. However, sometime during that last decade of the century, ice hockey made an appearance at two American universities – Yale at New Haven, Connecticut, and Johns Hopkins

here belongs to a McGill student, W F Robertson, who visited England in 1879, saw a field hockey game there, and wondered if its rules could be adapted to the shinny-like ice game played back home. On his return, he got together with a fellow McGill student, R F Smith, and the two of them came up with rules that the McGill teams began to use in 1881. They were rules drawn not only from field hockey but from lacrosse, soccer and hurling as well. Perhaps the most significant of their number called for the game to be played by nine-man teams. The rule set hockey on the way to its present six-men teams. It rid the ice of army-size squads, made the sport more popular by giving individual players a better chance to display their skills, and gave the fans a better chance to see these skills displayed.

By 1885, organized play had become so popular that Canada saw the formation of its first leagues. Kingston wrote another page in the game's history book by establishing the first, a four-team circuit made up of two school outfits – Queen's University and the Royal Military College – and two city squads, the King-at Baltimore, Maryland. Yale recalls that the game came to its campus after two student tennis stars, Arthur Foote and Malcolm Chace, traveled to Canada for a series of tennis matches, saw a hockey game, fell in love with the action and returned home to introduce the new-found fun to their fellow students. Johns Hopkins reports that a Canadian student, C Shearer of Montréal, formed a team at the Baltimore campus and brought in a Canadian squad to play the students. First played by Canadian students, the game soon was winning a following among their American counterparts. From these beginnings, hockey fanned out from the schools to the country's northeastern and midwestern regions and, by the dawn of the twentieth century, was catching on in Boston, Chicago, Cleveland, New York, Philadelphia, Pittsburgh and Washington, DC. New York City alone could boast three enthusiastic leagues by 1902.

The Americans can lay a claim to the next two developments, the first of which was the indoor rink with artificial ice. For a number of years, the Canadians had tried their hand at indoor rinks to increase fan attendance by drawing those who enjoyed some degree of comfort while watching the action. They had built the rinks around natural playing surfaces and had illuminated them with oil lamps. The Americans took the indoor rink a major step forward and, as had been planned, increased fan attendance by establishing the rink equipped with an artificial ice surface. By 1908, there were artificial ice arenas in Chicago, New York, Philadelphia and Pittsburgh, all of them drawing good crowds. Canada had yet to try its hand at artificial ice.

And the fourth development? It came just after the dawn of the twentieth century. It was the birth of the professional game, a birth that brings us to our next chapter.

Above: W G Rollins, the captain of the Columbia University hockey team during the 1920s. The team played at the 181st Street Ice Palace in New York City.

Left: The Yale University hockey team of 1934.

CHAPTER TWO

FACE-OFF

The Pro Game Takes Shape

Operating in the British tradition, the Canadians of the 1800s were amateur players and took pride in being amateurs – lovers of the

There was a good reason for Portage Lake's success. It was manned with the best Canadian skating talent that Gibson could lay his hands

The tradition of amateurism, however, did not present a problem in the United States – at least, not for Dr J L Gibson, a dentist practicing in the Michigan copper-mining town of Houghton. A hockey enthusiast and a man of entrepreneurial bent, Gibson introduced unabashed professional play to the game in 1903 when he formed a barnstorming team and christened it the Portage Lake Hockey Club. Portage Lake spent its first season touring the surrounding area – including a venture over the Canadian border – and taking on any squad that cared to challenge it in any town with fans willing to pay Gibson's admission charge. In all, the team played twenty-six games that season and won all but two. Among its victims was a powerful Canadian amateur squad that would claim the Stanley Cup in another two years – the Montréal Wanderers

who remained at home and took money under the table did not suffer the stigma so widespread today when an amateur is discovered playing for pay. They lost neither the respect that traditionally goes with amateurism (at least, among the purists) nor their amateur status.

With a highly successful maiden season under his belt, Gibson in 1904 spearheaded the formation of hockey's first professional circuit, grandly calling it the International Pro Hockey League. Consisting in the beginning of Michigan teams, it was joined within a few months by a squad from Sault Ste Marie, Ontario. The newcomer was Canada's first acknowledged pro unit.

While Gibson's league was flourishing south of the border, the tradition of amateurism continued to die to the north. The demise was

Previous page: A close-up view of a face-off before the puck is dropped.

Below: The 1907 Wanderer Hockey Club of Montréal.

Wanderer Hockey Club and Executive of Montreal.
—Winnipeg, 1907.—

hurried along by a steadily growing number of Canadian fans who, because a superior brand of action could be expected, were showing themselves willing to pay their way into games featuring known professionals and semi-professionals. Semi-pro play was widespread in Canada by 1907. In 1908, a group of hockey entrepreneurs got together and formed Canada's first truly professional body – the Ontario Professional Hockey League. A year later, the well established Eastern Canada Amateur Hockey League turned professional. For several years, the League had straddled the amateur-pro fence by fielding two amateur outfits and four admittedly pro units. The two amateur teams withdrew in 1909 and left the league with no choice but to drop the word 'Amateur' from its name and become a truly play-for-pay organization.

Then, also in 1909, yet another organization took shape – the National Hockey Association (NHA). The newcomer, which in time would evolve into today's National Hockey League, started with five teams. Three came from cities around Montréal – Cobalt, Haileybury and Renfrew, with the last being a town of such mining wealth that its team was christened the Millionaires. The remaining two units were headquartered in Montréal itself – the Wan-

Above: The Portage Lake Hockey Club of 1904. Dr J L Gibson, the dentist entrepreneur, is center top row.

Far left: Ernie 'Moose' Johnson of the Montréal Wanderers. Johnson was elected to the Hall of Fame in 1952.

21

derers and Les Canadiens (just as widely known as Les Habitants), with the first, the former amateur powerhouse that had met Gibson's

the cut was intended to save on club salaries, but it seems to have been the result of an abrupt action taken in a face-off during a game back in

Right from its start, the infant league changed the complexion of hockey and took it another step along the way to being the game that we recognize today. For openers, the NHA reduced team sizes from seven to six men, doing so by eliminating the offense-defense rover position. Some hockey historians suspect that

periods. The periods were extended to three, each to last 20 minutes.

Business proved good for pro hockey, with the NHA, the Ontario League, Gibson's International League, and several minor operations drawing nice crowds throughout eastern Canada and parts of the northern US. But, with-

Below: The champion Cobalt Hockey Club of 1910.

Left: The Haileybury Hockey Team of 1910 – called 'the highest-priced team in the world.' The team received over $5,000 for one game, in addition to mining claims.

Below: Frank Patrick when he played for the Vancouver team of the Pacific Coast Hockey League – 1912. Patrick was elected to the Hall of Fame as a builder in 1958.

in three years of the NHA's formation, the circuits faced a challenge from the far west. By the end of the twentieth century's first decade, the Pacific Coast from British Columbia in the north to California in the south was well settled. Amateur hockey was proving to be a solid favorite in British Columbia and was becoming an attraction over the border in Seattle, Washington and Portland, Oregon. Behind the challenge were two brothers – Lester and Frank Patrick – who, after starring for a season with the NHA's Renfrew Millionaires, had put their skates aside in 1910 and moved to Vancouver, there to joint their father, Joseph, in establishing what was to become a highly successful lumber business. But, on arrival, the brothers decided that they had stumbled upon an area ripe for professional play. It was a decision that resulted in the formation of the Pacific Coast Hockey Association (PCHA).

But the Patricks did more than simply establish a new pro circuit that would begin play with three franchises – Victoria, Vancouver and Westminster. Realizing that hockey would surpass its present popularity if it could be played indoors for customer comfort, they borrowed 300,000 from Joseph and set about building two arenas equipped with articial ice – a 10,500-seat facility at Vancouver and a 3,500-seat affair at Victoria. The arenas were ready for play by 1912; the league went into business on 2 January at Victoria, followed by a Vancouver opening three days later.

That the brothers had been right on the mark in thinking British Columbia ripe for professional play and in deciding to build their indoor rinks was more than established on those two nights. The Victoria match, Canada's first hockey game on artificial ice, packed the 3,500-seat arena to capacity. Three nights later, more than 10,000 fans paid their way into the Van-

Above: The 1912-1913 Victoria Aristocrats of the Pacific Coast Hockey League. Lester Patrick, who was elected to the Hall of Fame in 1945, is seated in the front row, third from left.

couver facility. In the eyes of many hockey historians and buffs, the Patrick arenas, described as 'magnificent' affairs by the players who took to the ice out west, deserve the credit for eventually turning pro hockey into a major spectator sport.

The PCHA was off to a rousing start and went on to be even more successful. In great part, the Association's success was due to the inventiveness of the Patrick brothers. To help the fans more easily identify the skaters, the two put numbers on their players' backs, an unheard-of practice that would soon be adopted by teams in all sports. To swell the league coffers, the brothers dreamed up the idea of selling game programs. And, to make the PCHA game itself more interesting, they changed its anatomy in a variety of ways.

For example, after viewing a soccer match while on a visit to England, they inaugurated hockey's penalty shot. They invented the assist as a scoring recognition for the player who, while not actually posting a tally himself, sets up the situation leading to a goal. The deferred penalty system, which dictates that there may be no fewer than four men — including the goalie — on the ice at one time, was another of their innovations. So was the change in the

traditional rule that had always limited the goalkeeper's actions. Hitherto, the goalie had been required to stand up while accepting the shots that came his way, with a penalty being exacted if he threw himself to the ice to block a score. But now the Patricks let him sail out flat on the ice. It was a rule adjustment that has since given the game some of its most exciting moments.

The Patricks did, however, stick to one rule that had been discarded by the National Hockey Association. The PCHA kept the rover position and operated with seven-man teams.

Both brothers were excellent players. The tall and stately Lester — nicknamed 'The Silver Fox' in later years when his mop of curly hair turned gray — is the better remembered player of the two, while Frank has the reputation of having been the greater innovator. The pair divided the management of their arenas between themselves, with Lester handling the Victoria facility and Frank taking care of the Vancouver installation. Lester, a superb defenseman, is credited with being the first of his kind to take the puck on offense and move it deep into enemy territory, a maneuver that predated the aggressive Bobby Orr style of play in the late 1960s and early 1970s by more than 60 years.

Lester began playing with the Montréal Wanderers in 1903 and was team captain in 1906 when the Wanderers took the Stanley Cup from what looked to be an unbeatable Ottawa Silver Seven. The Ottawa squad went into the competition with three consecutive Cup wins to its credit – in 1903, 04 and 05 – but dropped the two-game series, 12-10. Because it ran for just two games and thus could not be decided on the majority of games won, the series was awarded on a total-goal basis, with Lester scoring Montréal's eleventh and twelfth goals. Once the PCHA was formed, Lester owned, managed, coached and played for his Victoria franchise, the Cougars. In later life, he etched out a notable career as manager and coach of the NHL's New York Rangers. We'll talk more of him in upcoming chapters. In all, The Silver Fox is said to have been to professional hockey what Connie Mack was to baseball and Knute Rockne to football.

In the east, the NHA and its fellow leagues watched the PCHA's rising star with a mixture of feelings that ranged from annoyance to outright anger. There was annoyance at the close of the PCHA's maiden season when the Patricks, in a move that the easterners saw as a burst of youthful audacity, invited the NHA to send its championship team out to British Columbia to meet their number-one outfit in a series of games to decide a national title. The NHA refused.

The annoyance continued into the next year and was this time centered on the Stanley Cup playoffs. Though originally intended for amateur outfits, the Cup playoffs by 1910 were being increasingly invaded by professional teams. At the end of the 1913-14 season, the PCHA felt entitled to compete for the Cup. The NHA objected, was over-ruled by the Cup's trustees, and reluctantly sent its championship team to face the PCHA's Victoria in a playoff series. Victoria took the series, only to have the NHA refuse to surrender the Cup.

The series, however, did lead to another Patrick invention – perhaps the most significant ever devised by the brothers. At the time, a player was penalized for being offside if he received a pass while skating ahead of the puck-carrier. It was a rule that, earning much noisily-expressed anger from the spectators, saw the action stopped 15 times during the first five minutes of one of the games. When the Patricks launched their next season, the PCHA ice was divided into three zones by means of two blue lines painted across the width of the rink about 30 feet to either side of center ice. Forward passing was permitted in the area between

Below: The Montréal Wanderers of 1905. Lester Patrick is standing in the second row at the center of the picture.

the blue lines. It was an innovation that speeded and opened up the game, so much so that forward passing – with specific controls – was

But when the NHA, obviously trying to protect its teams against humiliation at strong PCHA hands, objected to US participation in the playoffs and argued that the Cup was a Canadian award and should remain so, the cup trustees disagreed. They held that, with the Americans now in the game, the Cup should be an international prize. In a move that simultaneously welcomed the American teams to the playoffs and took the Cup another step away from its amateur status, a deal was worked out in which the champion PCHA and the NHA outfits would face each other at the end of each season to decide hockey's ultimate title for the year.

The Portland franchise – the Rosebuds (an unlikely hockey name if there ever was one) – took the PCHA's 1914-15 championship and went against the Montréal Canadiens in the Cup playoffs, losing three games to two, to the accompaniment of much nationalistic relief. In 1916-17, Seattle's Metropolitans earned the playoff berth. But, before departing for the championship series, the Seattle troop outraged the NHA. Remembering Victoria's experience, they refused to entrain unless the NHA guaranteed to surrender the Cup should they win. A tight-lipped promise was given, the Metropolitans swept into Montréal for a meeting with the NHA's Canadiens, won the championship series in four games (walloping the Canadiens 9-1 in the final game), and became the first American unit to bring the Cup out of Canada.

Seattle's Stanley Cup win and the PCHA's expansion south into the United States were more than enough to rankle the NHA. But there was something worse. It was a matter bound to rankle most of all because it hit the NHA in a spot where businessmen most hate to be hit – in the pocket.

Right from the moment they launched their league, the Patricks showed themselves more than willing to pay their players top salaries and, as a result, quickly began to drain off some of the NHA's best talent. The case of Edouard 'Newsy' Lalonde, the early great center (and, at times, defender) who tallied 441 goals in a 365-game career, provides an

LOUIS BERLINGUETTE   AMOS ARBOUR   JACK LAVIOLETTE

S. NEWSWORTHY   SKENE RONAN

THE STANLEY CUP HOLDERS

example of the Patricks' largesse. In 1912, when the brothers lured him away from the Canadiens and installed him at Vancouver, Lalonde was paid $6000 for 12 games – a king's ransom by the standards of the day. Lalonde himself figured that his paychecks boiled down to ice time at $8 a minute.

Another example of the talent enticed to the

Above: The Stanley Cup Champions – The Montréal Canadiens of 1915-1916.

U.P. BOUCHER President

NAP. DORVAL Secr.

DIDIER PITRE

COUPE STANLEY

BERT. CORBEAU

GOLDIE PRODGERS

HOWARD McNAMARA

GEORGES VEZINA

1916

E.V. POULIN

A. OUIMET

COUPE O'BRIEN

CHAMPIONS OF THE WORLD

MONTREAL CANADA

west: the Vancouver club of 1915 sported the following lineup: goalkeeper Hugh Lehman, defensemen Frank Patrick (Lester's brother) and Silas (Si) Griffis, rover Fred (Cyclone) Taylor, center Duncan (Mickey) Mackay and wings Russell (Barney) Stanley and Frank Nighbor. Each of these men would later be inducted into hockey's Hall of Fame.

Though the PCHA recruitment irritated the NHA and forced the league owners to open their pocketbooks wider to keep their stars in the fold, this is not to say that the NHA was itself innocent of similar practices. The league functioned in an every-man-for-himself era and behaved accordingly. It grabbed players from the Ontario and Eastern Canada circuits, plus the

Right: The
Vancouver
Millionaires – the

Far right: Edouard D
'Newsy' Lalonde, the
Hall of Famer of the
Montréal Canadiens.

lesser leagues. It talked defectors to the PHCA, among them Lalonde, into returning home. It saw its own teams pirate players from each other.

And just who were the players being so eagerly sought? They were among the best that the game has ever seen, with many of their number, as was true of the entire 1915 Vancouver squad, later winning entry to hockey's Hall of Fame. Here, beginning with a name already mentioned, are three examples of the very best:

Edouard 'Newsy' Lalonde

This former lacrosse star got his nickname because of his brief tenure in a newspaper pressroom as a young man. After playing for a time as an amateur, Lalonde joined the Montréal Canadiens in 1910. His first season saw him take the honors as the NHA's leading scorer, tallying 38 goals in 11 games. The youngster, however, was shifted to the Renfrew Millionaires near season's end, a move that had nothing to do with a drop in his skills. Rather, the transfer was due to the fact that, despite his presence, the Canadiens were sitting in the league's cellar while Renfrew was vying for the championship spot. The Canadiens sent him to Renfrew to help tie down things, a gesture that seemed to be the soul of generosity on the part of Canadien owner Ambrose O'Brien – that is, until you remember that O'Brien also owned the Renfrew club.

Left: Joe Hall poses for a picture in 1917, two years before this Canadiens' Hall of Famer died of flu.

Below: The Seattle Metropolitans— Stanley Cup winners in 1916-1917.

Holmes. Rowe. Seattle World's Hockey Champions 1917. Carpenter. Walker. Foyston, capt. Muldoon, Mgr. Riley.

Hockey has always been a rough sport, perennially capable of generating mayhem in any 60 minutes of playing time. It was particularly who played for the NHA's Québec Bulldogs. With tempers of equally short fuses, the two could always be counted on to delight the

wing who would stay with the team for sixteen years, play in 654 regular season games, 54 post-season matches, and eventually join Lalonde in the Hall of Fame – Aurel Joliat.

The trade stunned Montréal fans. It was one that saw Lalonde first play for and then coach the Saskatoon team. And it was one that ended in 1932 when he returned to the Canadiens as a coach. He remained with the team until his retirement in 1934.

Fred 'Cyclone' Taylor

'Newsy' Lalonde is remembered as the Canadien's first superstar. But to Fred Taylor goes the credit of being the pro game's first superstar. He was a man so fast on the ice that appropriately descriptive nicknames dogged him for a quarter century, from his first amateur days to his retirement at age 36. As a youngster playing at Listowel, Ontario, he was dubbed 'Thunderbolt,' then 'Tornado' during a stint in Manitoba, and then 'Whirlwind' when he joined the International League. Finally, the Ottawa press hit upon 'Cyclone' during his first season with the NHA's Ottawa Senators. It was the name that stuck and remained with him for the rest of his career.

The name was invented on a night that saw Ottawa up against the Montréal Wanderers. Taylor, though a defenseman, flashed along the ice and scored five of the goals in an 8-5 Ottawa win. It was a splendid achievement in a time when, as would be the case for years to come, defensemen concentrated principally on what they were designed to concentrate on – defense. In carrying the puck deep into enemy territory for scores, Taylor was continuing the style of play that Lester Patrick had inaugurated and that would bring Bobby Orr fame years later.

So far as fame is concerned, Taylor had all of it that he could handle. His reputation as a daring and exciting speedster was so widespread that he was even a favorite in the United States, a country that, regardless of the International League and a growing number of minor circuits, had yet to embrace hockey wholeheartedly. When, for several years, Taylor led a team on a barnstorming tour of the northeast US, he packed the houses wherever

Left: Fred 'Cyclone' Taylor – the fastest man on ice. This Ottawa Senator was elected to the Hall of Fame in 1945.

Opposite: Hall of Famer Joe Malone when he played for the Québec Bulldogs.

he went – except on those occasions when it was announced that he would not play. Knowing the effect that his absence would have on the gate receipts, the promoters simply cancelled the games.

Adding to Taylor's crowd appeal was his ability to skate backwards, a talent that resulted in a legend still heard today – that he once posted a goal after skating backwards through an entire team. The story first began to take shape when Taylor left Ottawa to join the Renfrew Millionaires for a $4000 bonus (a stunning award in those days) and an equally stunning pre-season salary of $5250. The defection infuriated the Ottawa fans and they heaped such abuse on Taylor that, in a moment of understandable impatience he promised to skate backwards through all his former teammates and score a goal when next they met. He did just that – or almost just that – on the appointed night. His actual feat: a five-yard trip past several Ottawans before a wicked backhand shot into the net.

When the Patrick brothers launched the PCHA, Taylor was among the first players recruited westward. He joined Vancouver and served as a team mainstay until his retirement. Taylor remained in Vancouver for the rest of his life, residing there and following the hockey scene until his death in 1979 at age 93.

Joe Malone

Playing at center and occasionally at the right wing spot, Malone ranks as one of the greatest scorers – if not the greatest – that the pro game has ever seen. Born in 1890, Malone was a Québec native who enjoyed a career that ran from 1909 to 1924 and saw him play for his home city's Bulldogs and then the Montréal Canadiens. In the 1917-18 season, he posted 44 goals in 20 games for the Canadiens, a record that has not been matched to date. In that same year, he became the only NHL player thus far to average more than two goals per game in a season.

Later record scorers – Maurice Richard, Mike Bossy and Wayne Gretzky – tallied a greater number of goals, yes. But not one of them did so in a 20-game span. Both Richard and Bossy tallied 50 goals in 50 games. Gretzky put 50 across in 39 games.

On yet another count, Malone, to date, stands alone in the NHL record book – this time for a remarkable seven goals in a single game. They were scored on a winter night in 1920 during a performance that, unfortunately, was seen by a mere 700 people. Most fans stayed at home that night and Malone never blamed them for doing so. The temperature outside was ranging between 20 and 25 degrees below zero.

Popular though hockey had always been, the NHA was in trouble by 1916, both at the gate and within the league. World War I was at its height and can be blamed for the money problems. The league's most ardent fans, all the youngsters who had been raised on hockey, were in uniform and away in camp or overseas. Further, the country had its fair share of men who were avoiding the service, and the police

Above: The Renfrew Millionaires team of 1909-1910. In the center row are Fred Taylor (third from left), Lester Patrick (fourth from left) and Frank Patrick (third from right). Newsy Lalonde is in the bottom row center.

Right: Cyril Denneny, elected to the Hall of Fame in 1959.

Opposite: Joe Malone while he was with the Montréal Canadiens.

had taken to raiding NHL games in search of them. It was a tactic that plucked many an able body from the stands but kept many another from going anywhere near the arenas. On top of all else, the fact that some of the best players themselves had gone off to war had severely reduced the game's drawing power.

Within the league, the teams were bickering as they vied with each other for the best of the available talent. Hurting at the box office, some units dropped out of the circuit, either temporarily or permanently. There were salary arguments, with players suddenly switching to other teams when the front office would not meet their demands. When Art Ross, who would later win lasting fame as a coach and general manager with the Boston Bruins, faced a salary cut at Haileybury, he threatened to quit the team and form a league of his own. (Though some astronomical salaries — for that day, at least — were being paid, it must not be thought that every hockey player was becoming a rich man. Joe Malone, at the height of his career, received about $1000 a season from the Canadiens, a stipend so meager that he never traveled to away games, staying home so that he could hold down a needed daytime job.)

The league's problems all came to a head in the 1916-17 season. The trouble began with a nationwide scandal involving one of the several hockey teams that the Canadian Army had formed to boost morale. The unit, composed of top professionals, was so good that it applied for and received a NHA franchise. It competed in the 1916-17 season until the word got out that it was recruiting further players with the understanding that they would never be sent to the fighting. The public reacted with such righteous anger that half the squad was immediately sent to France, while the NHA was widely criticized for its connection to the scandal. The dispatch of the players triggered a change in the league standings and, to straighten things out, the circuit had to divide the season into two halves, with the first-half leader to go against the second-half leader in a playoff series for the NHA championship at season's end. Everything ended dismally when the Canadiens, after taking the playoffs from the Ottawa Senators, suffered their humiliating Stanley Cup loss at the hands of the Seattle Metropolitans.

But, before that dismal end rolled round, there was a salary argument that came close to sending the NHA players out on strike. The argument centered on Cy Denneny, the Toronto Arenas' fine left wing and a future Hall of Famer. Denneny, who had just made his home in Ottawa, told his Toronto boss, Eddie Livingstone, that he wanted to be transferred to the Senators there so that he could be with his family during the season. When the request was turned down, he refused to get into uniform and was handed a suspension. At the end of two months, Denneny was still idle and sympathetic colleagues throughout the league were saying it was time to fight front office high-handedness with a player union and a strike. Frightened by the idea, the NHA owners descended on Livingstone and urged Denneny's release. Livingstone at first gave them a deaf ear, but finally relented and traded Denneny to Ottawa for a goalie and $750. At the time, it was a record payment for a trade.

All the trouble finally led to a November 1917 meeting of NHA owners. Representing the Canadiens, the Wanderers, the Québec Bulldogs, and the Ottawa Senators, they gathered at Montréal's Windsor Hotel with a radical plan in mind: the creation of a new league. They were tired of the NHA's problems and especially weary of Livingstone, whom many saw as a continuing source of trouble. The basic idea was to be rid of the Toronto boss and the only apparent way to do so was to establish a circuit that would refuse his club membership. It was an idea that infuriated NHA president Major Frank Robinson. He wanted nothing to do with it, nor with the presidency that the owners offered him. But it was an idea that nevertheless went through. Born on 22 November 1917 was the National Hockey League.

In time, it would become the world's premier professional hockey league, with its teams playing in both Canada and the United States. Between the moment of its founding and our time, it would divide its history into three eras — a struggling infancy, the golden and, simultaneously, dark years of youth and the growth to today's adulthood.

We turn now to the first of those eras.

CHAPTER THREE

FIRST PERIOD

The Infant Years

The NHA's president, Major Frank Robinson, was infuriated at the plot to drop Livingstone. Robinson's anger was such that he refused the

Though launched with five teams, the NHL played its first season with just four. The reason: The Québec Bulldogs had been losing money in the recent difficult years and the owners, deciding that enough was enough,

RICHARD CARROLL
COACH

JACK

CH

THE O'BRIEN CUP

Above: Eddie Gerard of the Ottawa Senators – elected to the Hall of Fame in 1945.

Page 36: Action around the goal mouth.

elected to suspend operations for the time being. They distributed their players among the other teams, with the scoring great, Joe Malone, going to the Canadiens, much to the delight of Montréal's French-Canadian fans. Also going to the Canadiens – and, again, to Montréal's delight – was one of hockey's genuinely talented brawlers, Bad Joe Hall, for years now Newsy Lalonde's most publicized on-ice enemy. Soon after the distribution was made, the Québec owners had a change of heart

and reactivated the Bulldogs for play in the league's third season.

The NHL's infant seasons ran from 1917-18 to 1924-25. They were to be years marked by financial pains, instances of superb play, the establishment of one as-yet unbroken record and a moment of terrible sadness in Stanley Cup play. In this chapter, we'll look at each of those seasons in turn.

But a note before we begin. The Stanley Cup results will be given for each season, but the

CKEY CLUB OF TORONTO

PIONS OF THE WORLD

THE STANLEY CUP

Cup games themselves will not be described. Accounts of what are considered by hockey aficionados to be the best of the Cup games through the years are to be found in Chapter Six. For quick reference, a list of Stanley Cup winners since the award's inception is included in Chapter Six.

1917-18
After deciding to play a 22-game season, the National Hockey League went into action for the first time on 19 December 1917, sending the Montréal Wanderers against the Toronto Arenas at the Montréal Arena. The Wanderers came away winners, 10-9, in a game that attracted only 700 fans – despite the fact that men in uniform were admitted without charge. The meager crowd left no doubt that pro hockey, even under a new banner, was still suffering from the army scandal, the NHA's old bickerings and the absence of the big draws who were away in the service.

and then professional outfits came to an end. The Canadiens, who had shared Westmount with their rivals, finished out the season at the

was left undermanned and overmatched. The Canadiens redeemed themselves with a 4-3 win in the second match – but to no avail. Since the series was being decided in two games, the winner was judged on total goals. Toronto had picked up 10 to the Canadiens' seven and was judged the NHL's first champion.

The Arenas, coached by Dick Carroll, went on to win the year's Stanley Cup from the PCHA's Vancouver.

1918-19

The NHL continued to suffer bad times in its second season. Crowds remained sparse, even though the league tried to elicit interest by adopting the forward-passing rule that the Patricks had invented for their PCHA and that was proving especially popular with West Coast fans. The Arenas suffered a disaster when they finished in the cellar in both halves of the season and closed out the year with an embarrassing record of 5 wins and 13 losses. The season was cancelled after each team had played 18 games, following Toronto's 9-3 loss to Ottawa on 20 February.

The Canadiens defeated Ottawa in the league playoffs and set off to meet the Seattle Metropolitans for the Stanley Cup. The Cup matches – which featured a fourth game that went into an hour and forty minutes of overtime play – ended in tragedy. Canada was in the midst of a lethal epidemic of influenza that, touching the Cup teams, sent the Canadiens' Bad Joe Hall to the hospital, where he died six days later. The competition was called off. For the first and only time in its history, the Cup was not awarded.

1919-20

The year saw three developments. First, with the war over and all the young hockey enthusiasts who had been in uniform returning home, business promised to improve in the coming months and so the league elected to try a 24-game schedule. Second, the Toronto Arenas, humiliated by their lame showing in the previous season, decided that a change of name was in order. They became the Toronto St Patricks, a name that they retained until the

Above: Hall of Famer Cecil 'Babe' Dye of the Toronto St Pats.

Opposite: The Hamilton Ontario Tiger Hockey Club – champions of the Ontario Hockey Association, 1918-1919.

The season was to be one of triumph and disaster – triumph for Joe Malone, who pounded home his 44 goals in 20 games for the Canadiens and established a scoring record that stands to this day. On the disaster side, the Montréal Wanderers lost their home rink when the Westmount Arena burned to the ground in early 1918. The Wanderers had not drawn good crowds during the season and, with the arena lost, the owners decided to call it quits. What had long been one of Canada's finest amateur

H. THOMAS, Exec.

H. CHILMAN, Exec.

AUDLEY MORDEN, Exec.

W. R. TOPE, Exec.

W. T. GREEN, Forward

W. DUNCAN, Forward

M. R. ROACH, Centre

T. E. McCARTHY, Forward

S. BURGOYNE, Coach

W. HEDDLE, Trainer

Jos. MATTE, Defence

L. REISE, Defence

H. REAUME, Goal

R. SMITH, Defence

J. D. CHILMAN, Sec.-Treas.

B. L. SIMPSON, Pres.

C. C. MORIN, Vice-Pres.

F. ROBBINS, Rep. to O.H.A.

HAMILTON TIGER HOCKEY CLUB
SENIOR CHAMPIONS O.H.A. 1918-1919.
HOLDERS of the ALLAN CUP ~ CHAMPIONS of CANADA

Above: Hockey was so popular in Canada that the Bank of Montréal even sponsored a ladies hockey team in 1920-1921.

mid-1920s when they rechristened themselves the Maple Leafs.

Third, the circuit grew by one unit. Québec returned to the fold with its Bulldogs. The stay, however, proved to be a short one.

On the return, the Bulldog management insisted that, to be competitive and thus have a chance at good attendance, they must have back some of the personnel that had been given away in the league's first season. The league agreed and several players were handed back, among them the one man they really wanted – Joe Malone. Malone served the team well, scoring 38 goals in the 24-game route. The season also saw him post his seven goals against the St Pats, a single-game record that, in common with his 44-goal accomplishment, stands unbroken to this day in the NHL. He followed that night's feat by tallying six goals against the Ottawa Senators in the season closer.

But, despite Malone's presence in the lineup, the year was an unhappy one for the Bulldogs. They relegated themselves to the NHL cellar in both halves of the split season, posting the exact same record in each half – two wins against ten losses. En route to those statistics, the team watched its fans depart in droves, with the result that at season's end, the management, though receiving offers of financial help from

fellow owners, decided to call it quits again, this time for good.

Ottawa's Senators emerged as the circuit's powerhouse unit, so formidable that they eliminated the necessity of a league championship series by winning both halves of the split season. Their overall 1919-20 record: 19 wins and five losses. They then bested the Seattle Metropolitans for the Stanley Cup.

1920-21

Despite Québec's collapse and departure, the NHL fielded four teams this season. Replacing the Bulldogs were the Hamilton Tigers, a deplorably weak outfit made strong enough for competition by the arrival of Joe Malone from the deceased Bulldogs and several players provided through the largesse of the Toronto St Pats. It was a largesse that quickly evaporated when the Pats realized that they had given up a slender wingman who was not only good but great.

The player in question was twenty-two-year-old Cecil (Babe) Dye, who was just entering his second year of league play. A slightly built youngster who could nevertheless uncork blazing shots, he had done well in his rookie year with Toronto and was marked as a future star but was considered expendable because of the St Pat depth. However, the Toronto management changed its mind when Dye skated out on the ice with the sadly overmatched Tigers for the season opener and attacked with a 5-0 shutout. Dye himself slammed in two of the five tallies. Toronto immediately called him home and sent the Tigers a goalie in his place.

Though criticized for an obviously selfish move, the Toronto management delightedly watched Dye take the season's scoring championship with 35 goals. From there, the young man, who had learned his first hockey from his mother (Dye was an infant when his father died) went on to play eight more years, carving out for himself one of the most illustrious careers in early NHL history. It was a career that saw him play for the Chicago Black Hawks and the New York Americans as well as Toronto, and that saw him earn several spots in the NHL's record books. For openers, he led the league in scoring in 1923 and 1926, posting 26 goals and 11 assists in 1923 for 37 points, and 38 goals and six assists in 1925 for 44 points. (Combining goals and assists, points are used in NHL statistics to provide an overall picture of a player's performance. One point is awarded for each goal, and one for each assist.)

Next, Dye's sizzling shots won him a slot on the league's all-time list of highest goals-per-game averages (career averages among players with 200 or more goals). With a .738 average posted between his 1919-20 rookie year and his retirement at the end of the 1928-29 season, he stands in fifth place. Ahead of him at present are Pittsburgh's Mario Lemieux (.826 for 1984-85 through 1992-93); Mike Bossy of the NY Islanders (.780 for 1977-78 through 1983-84); the St Louis Blues' Brett Hull (.775 from 1985-86 through 1992-93); and Ottawa Senator Cy Denneny (.767 for 1917-18 through 1928-29).

Above: The great goalie for the Montréal Canadiens — Georges Vezina — in a publicity photograph. Note that the Hall of Famer is wearing his street trousers.

Left: Joe Malone when he was in the Hamilton Tigers.

Far left: Cecil 'Babe' Dye of the Toronto St Pats commemorates their Stanley Cup championship of 1922-1923.

Dye also stands in the fifth spot on the league's list of longest goal-scoring streaks, tied at 11 games with Marcel Dionne and Pat

Far right: Clint Benedict of the Ottawa Senators – 1923. He was elected to the Hall of Fame in 1965.

Below: Frank Nighbor when he was with the Senators. Nighbor made the Hall in 1945.

1917-18 (23 goals) and Lumley in 1981-82 (15 goals).

Hot though he was in that 1920-21 season, Dye could not get Toronto into the Stanley Cup competition. He and his teammates met the Ottawa Senators in the league playoffs and fell victim to two shutouts, 5-0 and 2-0, in great part because of Clint Benedict's splendid goaltending. Benedict took Ottawa on to play against Vancouver and came back with the Stanley Cup.

Vancouver may well have envied Ottawa for the win, but the NHL could not help but envy the PCHA's game. Some 51,000 British Columbia fans turned out for the five-game series: the largest crowd ever to attend a Canadian hockey series to that date.

Goalkeeper Benedict, along with the likes of Georges Vezina, George Hainsworth, Terry Sawchuk, Tony Esposito and Jacques Plante, has gone down in NHL history as one of the finest goalies ever to step out on the ice. In an eighteen-year career that ran from 1913 to 1930, the muscular and handsome six-footer played in 42 Stanley Cup games. He was a member of four Cup-winning teams.

In the NHL's listing of goaltending records, Benedict stands twelfth among the all-time shutout leaders, posting 19 while with Ottawa and 39 later on with the Montréal Maroons, for a total of 58. He occupies fifth place in the rankings for ten or more shutouts in a season. As a Maroon, he posted 13 in the 1926-27 season. He is tied in the fifth spot with Hainsworth (1927-28), John Roach (1928-29), Roy Worters (1927-

28 and 1928-29), and Harry Lumley (1953-54). Hainsworth leads the list, with 22 shutouts posted for the Canadiens in 1928-29, a 44-game season, and holds down the third-place spot with 14 for the Canadiens in 1926-27.

Long before the Patrick brothers allowed PCHA goalkeepers to block shots by falling on the ice, Benedict had defied the traditional stand-up-and-take-them-as-they-come rule and was much responsible for its eventual demise. Early in his career, to the annoyance of the opposition's fans (who would deride him with shouts of 'Get your bed, Bennie'), he became famous for his crashes to the ice – and for his acting ability at such moments. He always (or, at least, usually) managed to avoid penalties by making his tumbles look as if they were accidents.

Benedict was inducted into the Hall of Fame in 1965.

1921-22

Here was one of the wildest seasons in the NHL's infant history. It was highlighted by incidents involving Sprague Cleghorn, Francis (King) Clancy and Babe Dye.

For Cleghorn, an aggressive defenseman, it was a season of vengeance. Though he had helped to win them the 1920-21 Stanley Cup, his Ottawa Senators traded him to the Canadiens, apparently having had enough of his rough and tumble style of play, a style that earned him four penalties, including a match penalty, during the Cup series. Angry at the exchange, Cleghorn vowed to take revenge on anyone he met in a Senator uniform. He kept his promise one night when, with his brother Odie, he put three of the Senators' top performers out of commission. The gentlemanly Frank Nighbor, one of the league's all-time fine centers, got knocked to the ice and sustained a damaged elbow. A rap with a Cleghorn stick opened a cut above forward Eddie Gerard's eye that took five stitches to close. And Cy Denneny bloodied the

ice when he took a stick in the eye. The three-some did not return to action for the next three games. Under today's league policies, Cleghorn would have likely faced a stiff fine or even suspension. As it was, he got off with a $15 fine, a match penalty, and a warning from president Frank Calder to cease such displays of annoy-ance or face suspension for a season.

For Clancy, a 5-foot, 9-inch 185-pound rookie who would go into the Hall of Fame after a long and splendid career, 1921-22 was the season that saw him become one of the select few ever to score a goal on their very first shot to the net in

Art Gagne

Charlie McV

Jack Asseltine

Puss Traub

"Red" McCusker

Amby Moran

"Duke" Dutkowski

major league play. In itself, that was enough to cause a stir in the press. But Clancy's shot earned him an extra stir. Here is what happened.

Wearing a Senator's uniform, Clancy spent most of the season on the bench. It was not until an overtime period in a late-season match with the Hamilton Tigers that he was sent onto the ice. He took the puck a few seconds after the face-off and passed it to a teammate. When the puck came sailing right back to him, Clancy set aside his role as a defenseman and headed for the Tigers' goal, ending his journey with a smash at the net. Though the goal judge signaled a score and put Clancy into the record books, there was a lasting doubt concerning his right to be there. The angry Tiger goalie insisted that the puck had entered the goal cage through the side of the net and thus could not be counted.

There may have been some doubt about the legitimacy of Clancy's goal. But there was none whatsoever about his playing ability. Clancy starred in the league for 16 years and, in the 1923 Stanley Cup playoffs, won a spot for himself that completely overshadowed his first-goal feat. In the final game of the series, with five of his fellow Ottawa stars sidelined because of injuries, Clancy played every position on the team, including the goalie's spot.

For Toronto's Babe Dye, 1921-22 was the season of his never-forgotten 'mystery shot.' The shot came during Cup competition against Vancouver when he sailed up the rink and fired so hard for a tally that neither the crowd nor the Vancouver goalkeeper saw where the puck had gone until a second or so after it had arrived in the cage. The goalie was still looking for it when the crowd began pointing to the rear netting in astonishment. The shot broke Vancouver's back for the night, ended a tie of two games each in the series, and gave Toronto the Cup.

While the likes of Cleghorn and Dye were exciting the fans, the league officials were looking west with interest. A new loop—the Western Canada Hockey League (WCHL) had opened shop and was in business at Calgary, Edmonton, Regina and Saskatoon. Just how its box offices would fare was anybody's guess.

There was no guessing, however, about what the newcomer circuit did to the Stanley Cup playoffs. It changed their schedule completely. By agreement with the Cup trustees, the PCHA and WCHL champions faced each other in what was called a semi-final round for the right to advance to the Cup competition. As for the NHL, it dropped its split-season arrangement and staged a semi-final match between its first and second place units. The semi-final winners from east and west then met to decide the Cup in a best-of-five-game series.

In the PCHA-WCHL matchup, Vancouver downed Regina, which fielded a surprisingly tough outfit for a maiden season. Toronto's St Patricks knocked the Ottawa Senators aside in the NHL and then went against Vancouver, taking the Cup, 3 games to 2.

1922-23

The big news of the year centered on the Canadiens. Sportsman Leo Dandurand took over as the team's owner. In the next years, though

the Canadiens had always been a formidable unit, Dandurand built it into one of hockey's greatest dynasties. But he started out by infuriating the Montréal fans. The reason: unable to get along with Newsy Lalonde, he traded the superstar off to the WCHL's Saskatoon Sheiks for a diminutive (5 feet 6 inches tall and listed at 146 pounds) wingman named Aurel Joliat.

It didn't take long for the twenty-one-year-old to make his new city forget Lalonde. He proved to be one of the fastest skaters in the business, so fast that Toronto's Babe Dye, after putting up with him for a night, told the Canadien management that, if they would place Joliat at center and then set mirrors to his either side, they'd have the fastest line in hockey.

Joliat, who was to spend 16 seasons in the NHL, all of them with the Canadiens, was as respected for his backhand shots as his speed. Whenever he hit the blue line, the fans could expect a sudden and deft backhand pass to a teammate. And, of even greater spectator delight, there was what he called his 'shuttle play.' It would come as he scooted the puck across the front of the goal. In the instant that he seemed about to sail beyond the cage, a sudden backhand would send the puck sizzling past a startled goalie and into the netting.

Adding to his fan appeal was the fact that Joliat was on the eccentric side, especially where a personal item of headgear was concerned. He always wore a black baseball cap while on the ice. When the cap flew off or was otherwise dislodged, Joliat would forget the action until the thing was retrieved and placed back where it belonged.

Though he performed beautifully in his NHL

Above: A 1932 photograph of Frank Calder, the National Hockey League's president from its inception in 1917 until his death in 1943.

Opposite: The 1923-1924 Regina Capitols of the Western Canada Hockey League.

Right: A 1922 photo
of Aurel Joliat of the
Montréal Canadiens.

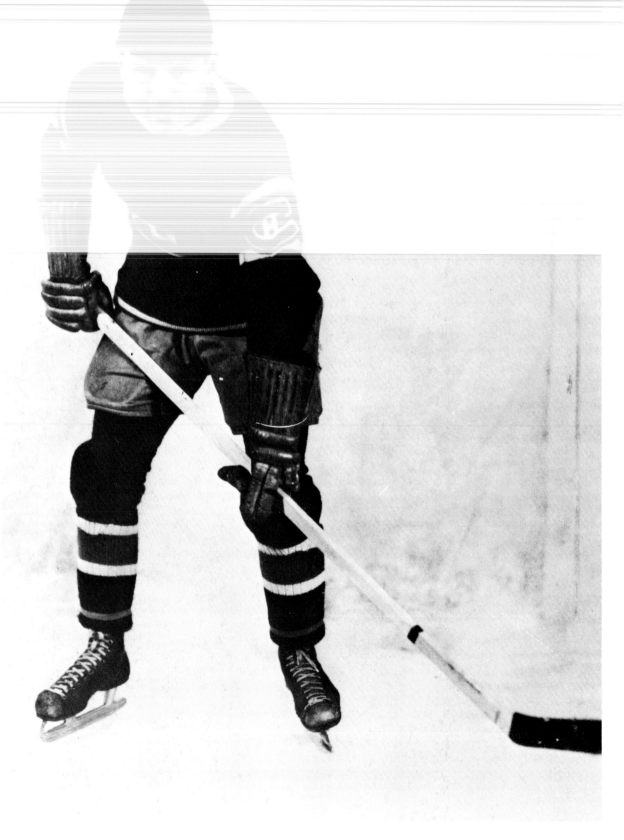

rookie year, Joliat really came into his own
when a young center of equally blazing speed —
Howie (The Stratford Flash) Morenz — joined the
Canadiens in the 1923-24 season. They immediately formed an excellent partnership and
close friendship, operating so well together
that, when the league inaugurated the annual
practice of naming first and second All-Star
teams in 1930, both Joliat and Morenz were

placed on the first team. Morenz was named to
the first team in 1931-32, while Joliat made the
second team that season and also in 1933-34
and 1934-35.

Their partnership was improved when
Johnny (The Black Cat) Gagnon donned a
Canadien uniform in 1930. From 1930-31
through 1933-34, the threesome comprised one
of the finest lines in Canadien history. The com-

bination was shattered when Morenz, now past his zenith, was traded to the Chicago Black Hawks during the 1934-35 season. The new linesman assigned to replace Morenz did not work out and the veteran returned in 1936-37, putting the old (in age as well as point of service) Joliat-Morenz-Gagnon line back in business. Though not quite their former flashing selves, the trio worked well until the night that Morenz took a hard but legal body check and went flying into the sideboards, embedding a skate there and breaking a leg. Sent to the hospital, Morenz, for reasons that have never been fully understood, died several weeks later (the feeling is that, realizing his career was over, he lost the will to live). Joliat, now past his own prime and dispirited by the loss of his friend, retired two years later.

As befitted two long-time partners, both Joliat and Morenz were inducted into the Hall of Fame in the same year – 1945.

Ottawa ended the 1922-23 season as the NHL's champion and undertook a new – and what proved to be a passing – Stanley Cup schedule. The Senators met and defeated the PCHA's Vancouver in semi-final play and then advanced to take the Cup by downing the WCHL's Edmonton in finals action. The Senators won the semi-final matches 3 games to 1, and the finals round 2 games to 0.

1923-24

This was the season that saw the close of several memorable early careers. After playing in the league since its inception, the Ottawa Senators' fine right wing, Jack Darragh, retired. He would go into the Hall of Fame in 1962.

The Senators also lost forward Eddie Gerard, who underwent surgery for a growth in the throat. Gerard planned to be away temporarily, but never returned as a player. He spent the rest of his life in the front office, as coach-manager for the Montréal Maroons, and as general manager for the New York Americans. Dying of his

long-endured throat problem in 1937, Gerard was inducted into the Hall of Fame in 1945.

Though Gerard spent his entire NHL playing career with the Senators and though they participated in three Stanley Cup competitions, he managed to play in four. The reason: he was 'borrowed' – a perfectly legitimate tactic at the time – by the Toronto St Patricks to lend them a hand in the 1921-22 Cup series.

The season's departures were capped off by the retirement of Joe Malone.

In 1923-24 Stanley Cup action, the Montréal Canadiens dropped the PCHA's Vancouver in the semi-finals and then topped the WCHL's Calgary in the championship series. Montréal took both the semi-final and championship rounds by margins of 2 games to 0.

Management spent a goodly part of the 1923-24 season looking in two directions – west and south. To the west, the Patrick brothers and their PCHA were in financial difficulty, a problem that had been growing through the years. At the base of their troubles were their fine arenas. Though the facilities were packed with fans during the season, there were not enough off-season events to cover the costs of their

Above: George 'Buck' Boucher of the Ottawa Senators – 1925. Boucher was elected to the Hall of Fame in 1960.

Far left: Howie Morenz of the Montréal Canadiens. Morenz was elected to the Hall of Fame in 1945.

maintenance; such activities as conventions and automobile and boat shows were yet things of the future, with hockey being the day's prime indoor entertainment. Worsening matters were the high salaries that the Patricks continued to pay their players. Such was the financial pinch that the brothers closed down their championship Seattle franchise and then merged with the Western Canada League to share facilities and

thus reduce expenses. These maneuvers failed to pay dividends. In a matter of months, Lester and Frank went out of business. Both then moved on to illustrious coaching and management careers in the NHL.

Management's southward look fastened the NHL's eyes on the United States. As usual, though the gates had been improving over the years since its birth, the league was working on

shaky financial ground because attendance figures, even with good crowds, remained low. At the core of the problem here were the circuit's woefully inadequate facilities. It was an ironic situation, considering the fact that the Patricks were in trouble out west because of their top-notch arenas while the eastern circuit was suffering because most of its rinks continued to be primitive affairs offering meager seating capacities and few customer comforts. Money was needed to maintain the teams and make possible the construction of new arenas. Well, there was money – and, apparently, plenty of hockey enthusiasm – down in the United States. The time had come to extend the NHL's operations south over the border.

At hand was the step that would carry the league over the bridge from infancy to youth.

Sunday sports enthusiasts on London's Wimbledon Common Pond in 1930 – a crowded way to play hockey.

CHAPTER FOUR

SECOND PERIOD

Youth

The expansion into the United States came close on the heels of the NHL's look southward. The Boston Bruins became the league's first

players then being absorbed into the new ownership's US and Canadian units. Just as the Patricks were folding up, they let two of their teams go intact at $100,000 each to businessmen establishing NHL franchises. The Portland Rosebuds went to Chicago and were renamed the Black Hawks, while the Victoria Cougars became the Detroit Cougars.

The NHL's growth in this period did not limit itself to the US. Boston was not alone in being granted a franchise in 1924. One also went to Montréal so that an English-speaking team could take over where the Wanderers had left off. The new unit: the Montréal Maroons.

Page 53: The race toward the goal.

Below: Harold 'Mush' March, the great right winger for the Chicago Black Hawks in the 1930s.

All the additions brought the NHL's strength to ten clubs. To avoid any unwieldy playing structure, the league divided itself into two seg-

NEW YORK RANGERS
PITTSBURGH PIRATES

Of the ten teams that began that 1926-27 season, six were to flourish. Still at play today, they are: the Boston Bruins, the Chicago Black Hawks, the Detroit Red Wings, the Montréal Canadiens, the New York Rangers and the Toronto Maple Leafs. The Americans, the Maroons, the Pirates and the Senators — all would collapse before the league's youth was a thing of the past.

All but one of the unfortunates would be out of business by the 1938-39 season, causing the league to drop its divisional arrangement. Divisions would not return to the scene until the expansion years of the late 1960s.

In this chapter, we'll follow the ten teams through the league's youth, which ran from the 1924-25 season through the Depression years of the 1930s. We'll look first at the teams that fell by the wayside.

THE FALLEN ONES

THE MONTRÉAL MAROONS
Formed by James Strachan and Donat Raymond, who paid $15,000 for the franchise, the Maroons were formed to attract Montréal's English-speaking fans and thus to help business along at the newly constructed Forum Arena, where the Canadiens played. Though manned with excellent talent, the Maroons were destined to remain on the NHL scene for just 14 years. They fell victim to the Depression, a time in which no one could fill the Forum. Because there were more French- than English-speaking fans in the city, the Maroons were dropped from the league so that the more cherished and popular Canadiens could survive.

In its 14 years, however, the club did itself proud. It consistently fielded top-notch personnel. In uniform over the years were the likes of wingman Harry (Punch) Broadbent; goalie Alex Connell who, as an Ottawa Senator in

1926-27, had set a not-equaled-to-date goal-tending record — 461 minutes and 29 seconds without a single tally against him; Nelson (Nels) Stewart, who became the first player in NHL history to score 300 goals in a career. With Reginald (Hooley) Smith and Oliver (Babe) Seibert, Stewart formed the Maroons' famous 'S Line' of the late 1920s and early 30s.

A year after being formed, the Maroons won the first of their two Stanley Cups, defeating the PCHA's Victoria, three games to one, in the 1925-26 action. The five-game series was the last Cup meeting to involve a team outside the NHL, with the western league closing down a few months later. The Maroons' second Cup came in the 1934-35 series. For the win, they dropped Toronto, 3 games to 0. In the interim, the Montréal outfit consistently made its way to the Cup battles, only to be eliminated somewhere between the quarter-final and final rounds.

THE NEW YORK AMERICANS
The Americans played their first game on 15 December 1925, going against the Canadiens in the recently built second Madison Square Garden. Mayor-elect James J Walker, the marching band from West Point and 17,000 fans were on hand to celebrate the occasion, supplemented by a contingent of red-uniformed Canadian Foot Guards.

With such a send-off and as New York City's first NHL competitor, the Americans might have been expected to etch a noble history for

Above: Goalie Davey Kerr of the New York Rangers slides on his back after coming out of the net to turn back one of the 49 Boston Bruins point drives in a game on 24 November 1935.

Left: Nelson Stewart of the Montréal Maroons. This Hall of Famer was the first player in the history of the league to score 300 goals in a career.

Above: Roy Worters, the goalie for the New York Americans, who was elected to the Hall of Fame in 1969.

Opposite: Dave Schrier of the New York Americans.

The Americans skated along in their mediocre fashion until the 1941-42 season when they switched allegiance and became the Brook-

themselves. But the score of that first outing was a more accurate omen of things to come – a 3-1 victory for the Canadiens – as was the Americans' lineage. They were the always financially troubled and sometimes inept Hamilton Tigers, purchased by US bootleggers Bill Dwyer and brought south for a change of name. Once ensconced in New York City, they proceeded to write a page of mediocrity in the NHL record book, never once finishing in their division's first place and not once winning the Stanley Cup, though they found themselves in Cup action on five occasions, losing three times in the quarter-finals and twice in the semi-finals.

Despite their sad performance, the Americans sent some superb players onto the ice. To name just a few, there were linemen Harvey (Busher) Jackson and Charles (The Bomber) Conacher, and defensemen Eddie Shore and Clarence (Hap) Day, of whom all were future Hall of Famers. But the problem was that the Americans brought them in at the close of their careers.

At one point in its history, the team suffered the rumor that owner Dwyer was using it for some dishonest wagering. The betting, so the talk went, came in 1933 when Dwyer set one of his cronies up as goal judge for a game with Detroit and then ordered him to signal a tally for any New York shot that came anywhere near the cage. No one can say for certain whether there was any truth to all this, but it is interesting to note that Detroit's goalie, Alex Connell, swept around the cage after one especially obvious non-goal and knocked the judge to the ice.

Throughout its lifetime, Ottawa fielded some of the game's finest players. In the pre-NHL days, there were such greats as defenseman Cyclone Taylor and goalie Percy LeSueur. In the NHL's infancy and youth, center Frank Nighbor spent 12 seasons with the club; wingman Cy Denneny was there for 11, defenseman King Clancy for nine, goalie Alex Connell for eight, and wingman Punch Broadbent for seven. Two of the Boucher brothers – center Frank and forward George – also wore Senator uniforms. Frank spent the 1921-22 season at Ottawa before going on to the PCHA's Vancouver for four seasons and then to the New York Rangers for a spectacular career as player and then coach. George Boucher spent 12 of his 15 years in the league with the Senators, moving to the Montréal Maroons and then the New York Americans at the close of his playing days.

Despite the high quality of its play, the club spent much of its time on shaky financial ground, especially with the dawn of the Depression. The nature of the city of Ottawa itself lay at the core of the problem. As Canada's capital, it was principally a civil service town, and so there was always difficulty finding enough fans with enough income left over to spend on hockey games. In 1931-32, the club temporarily dropped out of the league in the hopes of retrenching financially. In 1934-35 it shifted to St Louis, Missouri, and was renamed the Eagles. Even though it brought most of its players south and its caliber of play remained high, the club was unable to survive. It disbanded for good in 1935.

THE PITTSBURGH PIRATES

Considering its personnel, the Pirate outfit should have been a success. It went into its first season – 1925-26 – with the tough and competent Odie Cleghorn as player-manager and then manned its roster at one time or another with such greats as wingman Harold (Baldy) Cotton, defenseman Lionel Conacher and goalie Roy Worters. But the fact is that the team, owned for much of its history by the Americans' bootlegging Bill Dwyer, did nothing but post a sad on-ice record and encounter one front office difficulty after another, chief among them

overdue bills, plus a bouncing check for railroad fare that once almost left the players stranded on the road. Up against such head-

but controversial figures — Arthur (Howie) Ross, the Haileybury defenseman who once threatened to depart and form his own league

his mind, however, when he attended a Stanley Cup series in Montréal and got a look at the competition's packed houses. Home he went to found the team that would become the NHL's first American representative.

Adams started the ball rolling by hiring as his manager one of the NHA's most accomplished

ingly pinched financially. The best of those purchased was the battling forward, Emory (Spunk) Sparrow.

In that 1924-25 season, the Bruins proved themselves to be as inadequate as they looked. Winning only two of their first 15 games and enduring an 11-game losing streak at one

Below: Arthur 'Howie' Ross (center), the first general manager of the Boston Bruins.

point, they posted the worst seasonal record ever seen in the league — 6 wins against 24 losses.

The team's fortunes, however, began to improve in the next seasons. The tough Sprague Cleghorn came in from the Canadiens to lead the defense in 1925-26. One of the Ross amateurs, goalie Charles Stewart, paid off the coach's faith by permitting an average of 2.3 goals per game. Two other Ross amateurs — forwards Carson Cooper and Jimmy Herberts — did themselves proud in the scoring department, with Cooper placing second in the league, and Herberts third. Then, taking 13 of 18 games in the season's second half of the 1926-27 season, the Bruins went to their first Stanley Cup playoffs. They knocked over the Chicago Black Hawks in the quarter-finals and then downed the New York Rangers in the semi-finals for a spot opposite the Senators in the championship round. Ottawa claimed the Cup, 2 games to 1 (with 2 ties).

For the next years, the Bruins went nowhere but up. After placing second in the American Division in 1926-27, they then took the divisional title four years in a row and their first Stanley Cup at the end of the 1928-29 season when, with Cy Denneny as coach and Ross as manager, they beat the Canadiens 3 games to 0 in the semi-finals and then the New York Rangers 2 games to 0 in the championship round.

Much responsible for the team's on-ice success in those years was Eddie Shore, a battling defenseman who joined the club for the 1926-27 season and who remained for 13 seasons, becoming a hockey legend along the way. The son of a ranching family in Saskatchewan, he had played out west with Regina, Victoria and Edmonton before being picked up by Ross when the western league folded and its best performers were absorbed into the NHL. The Bruins picked up Shore — along with Frank Boucher — in a seven-player deal that cost owner Adams $50,000. It was a major purchase (by today's standards, the outlay was equivalent to $5 million), but Shore alone was worth every penny of it.

Why? Because Boston, though a hotbed of amateur hockey, was only mildly interested in the Bruins at the time, with too many fans, despite the team's improvement, still remembering the sad 1924-25 showing. Though a defenseman, Shore brought with him an aggressive style of play that, in the tradition of Lester Patrick and Cyclone Taylor (and later Bobby Orr), made him always a threat as a puck handler. He immediately captured Boston's imagination, attracted an ever-increasing number of fans, and made the franchise one of the most profitable of the NHL's youthful years.

On top of all else, Shore brought with him a reputation for unadulterated courage and then, to the delight of the fans, proceeded to build on it throughout the years. He hadn't been in the league for long when the opposing teams realized that the only way to stop Boston was to stop Shore, and, from then on, he was subjected to one assault after another, enduring and resisting them all stubbornly and stoically.

For example, there was the night when every

Above: Defenseman Eddie Shore of the Boston Bruins — 1934. Shore made the Hall of Fame in 1945.

man on the Montréal Maroons seemed intent on incapacitating Shore. One player's stick cut his chin open. Another opened his cheek. Still another caught him full in the mouth and knocked him to the ice with a broken nose, three broken teeth, a deep cut over his left eye and two blackened eyes. Carried off the ice, Shore was done for the night. But he was back and suited up for the Bruins' next game.

All this, however, is not meant to say that Shore was always the victim. He himself instigated some fine battles. One was staged during the 1938-39 Stanley Cup playoffs with the New York Rangers. It began when, charging up the ice, Shore took out Ranger center Phil Watson with such energy that he drove Watson into the boards and left him stunned. The maneuver so irritated Ranger Fred (Muzz) Patrick, a former Canadian amateur boxing champion and the son of Lester Patrick, that he barreled into Shore and ignited a swinging match that left Shore with a broken nose.

Another Shore battle, this one staged early in his pre-NHL career with a player who would one day be a Boston teammate – John (Red) Beattie – delighted the fans and eventually became a basic staple of hockey lore. The two began hammering at each other so hard one night that they were both ejected from the game. A few weeks later, the press reported that Shore and his wife had two special guests for Christmas dinner – the Red Beatties. It turned out that the two couples, regardless of whatever mayhem occurred out on the ice, were the closest of friends.

Endearing Shore to the Boston fans even more was his obvious dedication to the game, an example of which was seen on a January night in 1929 when a traffic tie-up kept him from catching the train on which the Bruins were to

travel to Montréal for a meeting with the Maroons. Knowing that he would be sorely needed because a fellow defenseman was on the injured list, Shore engaged a friend's chauffeured car and headed north through a blizzard that finally caused the chauffeur to quit driving, at which point his passenger took over the wheel. In the next hours, the car slipped off the road five times, on the last occasion becoming so firmly stuck that it could not be forced back onto the pavement. Shore trudged away through the wind and snow, located a farmhouse, talked the owner into hitching up a team of horses and pulling the car free, and continued on his way. At the end of a night- and day-long journey, a thoroughly frozen Shore pulled into Montréal at 6 PM and, two hours later, was in uniform and on the ice. He played a full 60 minutes – except for two minutes in the penalty box – and scored the night's only goal, to give his Bruins a 1-0 win.

But, topping Shore's list of endearing characteristics to fans and teammates alike was his exceptional on-ice ability. In the nine years between their inception in 1930-31 and the 1938-39 season, he missed being on the annual All-Star teams just once – in 1936-37. He was named to the All-Star first team in 1930-31, 1931-32, 1934-35, 1935-36, 1937-38 and 1938-39. Shore was on the second team in 1933-34. During the same period, he won the league's Most Valuable Player honors four times – in 1932-33, 1934-35, 1935-36 and 1937-38.

At the close of his career, Shore went to the New York Americans in the 1939-40 season. He retired a year later and was inducted into the Hall of Fame in 1945.

Shore may have been the Bruins' stellar attraction during the NHL's youthful years, but he was far from being alone out there on the ice. Ross in those years put together two unforgettable lines. 'The Dynamite Trio' worked from the late 1920s through the early 30s. Making up the unit were center Cooney Weiland, left wing Norman (Dutch) Gainor and right wing Aubrey (Dit) Clapper, the first man to carve out a 20-year career in the NHL. The 'Dynamites' were followed in the mid-1930s by the 'Kraut Line,' consisting of Milt Schmidt at center, Bob Bauer at right wing and, across the ice at left wing, Woodrow (Woody) Dumart. In 1940, the three led the league in scoring, with Schmidt in first place, Dumart in second and Bauer bringing up the rear in third.

And let's not forget goalkeeper Cecil (Tiny) Thompson, who joined the squad for the 1928-29 season and remained in a Bruin uniform for ten-and-a-third seasons. In the 1928-29 Stanley

Opposite: Boston Bruin Eddie Shore being congratulated by manager Art Ross on his return from an accident on the ice in 1934.

Far left: Ralph 'Cooney' Weiland of the Boston Bruins, who was elected to the Hall of Fame in 1971.

Below: Tiny Thompson, the Boston Bruins goalie who won the Vezina Trophy in 1929-1930, 1932-1933, 1935-1936 and 1937-1938. He was elected to the Hall of Fame in 1959.

Cup action, he recorded two shutouts against the Canadiens in the semi-finals and one against the New York Rangers in the championship round. Four times the winner of the Georges Vezina Trophy for goaltenders (see Chapter Seven), Thompson ranks fifth among the NHL's all-time shutout leaders, posting 74 in 467 regular-season games with the Bruins, and seven in 85 games during little more than a season with the Detroit Red Wings at the close of his career. His grand total: 81 in 552 games.

The Bruins won the Stanley Cup in 1938-39, defeating the Toronto Maple Leafs 4 games to 1. Another Cup came their way at the end of the 1940-41 season when, coached by Cooney Weiland and managed by Ross, they blanked the Detroit Red Wings 4 games to 0.

There was no way of telling at the time, but the Boston unit, by the opening of the 1940s, had come to the end of its first great period. The team's on-ice fortunes went downhill, with Ross setting aside his coaching duties in 1945, to be followed by a succession of coaches who were unable to lift the team back to its former greatness. Things would not improve until the close of the 1960s. By then, the Bruins had failed to make the Cup playoffs no fewer than 11 times.

THE CHICAGO BLACK HAWKS

Until reaching their first glory years in the late 1960s, the Black Hawks wrote one of the oddest pages in the history of the NHL. The team came into being in 1926 when wealthy Chicago sportsman, Major Frederic McLaughlin, purchased the Portland Rosebuds from Lester Patrick's financially troubled western league for $100,000 and renamed the unit in honor of his World War I outfit. With Pete Muldoon

coaching and with four major stars in the line-up – wingman Babe Dye, forward James (Dick) Irvin, wingman George Hay and goalkeeper Hugh Lehman – the Hawks worked their way up to the American Division's third place in their maiden season, with Irvin placing second in league scoring, right behind champion Bill Cook of the New York Rangers. But, except for a year here and there, the next decades were to be marked by one disaster after another.

There is little doubt that many of the team's problems stemmed directly from owner McLaughlin, a man with little hockey experience but an abundance of impatience. The two factors drove him to hire what seemed to be an unending succession of coaches over the years. He dropped Muldoon after a successful first season and then fired Muldoon's replacement – Barney Stanley – before the man was able to complete a full season. Dick Irvin, with his playing days over because of an injury, took on the coaching job in 1928 and hung on until the end of the 1929-30 season. In 1931-32, the team enjoyed the services of two coaches. The 1932-33 outing posted a coaching record – three. By the time the Hawks took their first Stanley Cup at the close of the 1933-34 season, they had worked under no fewer than ten coaches. After the Cup win, coach Tommy Gorman was released. Three years later, in the wake of the Hawks' second Cup win, coach Bill Stewart was fired.

But the club's headaches went beyond McLaughlin's 'revolving door' policy for coaches. Despite the presence of Dye, Irvin and company in the initial lineup, McLaughlin had the habit of choosing players who, while of pro caliber, were simply not up to the league's competition.

On top of all else, there was the fact that the Hawks gave every indication of being a 'bad luck' team, with many fans saying that it was for years the victim of the 'Muldoon Curse'. A legend that may well have been a sports writer's fancy on a day when good copy was not to be had, the curse was supposedly handed out by Pete Muldoon on the occasion of his firing. The deposed coach reportedly intoned, 'The Black Hawks will never finish first', and then continued (so the legend goes) to repeat it through the coming years. Whether by coincidence or psychic force, the team lived up to the hex. It did not finish at the top of its division for four decades.

And, whether by coincidence or psychic force, there is no denying that the Hawks did suffer more than their fair share of misfortune in their early seasons, with one of the worst being the 1927-28 campaign. For openers, Babe Dye broke his leg in a pre-season practice session and, because of the injury and the fact that he was nearing the end of his career, he was sent to the New York Americans; he posted a disappointing season there, retired, entered the construction business, and resided in Chicago until his death in 1962.

Next, goalkeeper Hugh Lehman turned 40 during the 1927-28 season and found that he could no longer handle the physical strains that went with his job. After leading the league in ice time in 1926-27 (2797 minutes), he played but 250 minutes and retired.

Putting the frosting on the cake of misfortune was Dick Irvin's injury. During a game in Montréal, he crashed into the Maroon's defenseman Mervyn (Red) Dutton, hit the ice and lay there with a fractured skull. On recovering after a hospitalization of several weeks, Irvin was refused permission to play for the remainder of the season by a concerned Frank Calder, the league president. He came back for the 1928-29 competition, participated in a few games, and then was appointed coach. It marked the beginning of one of the more illustrious coaching careers in the history of the pro game. We'll talk more of it in a later chapter.

But it must be said that the Black Hawks' early years did not consist only of bad luck and the fruits of erratic management. There were two developments that ran contrary to the team's history of the day. First, during Irvin's tenure as coach, McLaughlin ordered the use of rapid line changes, bringing in fresh troops whenever a line seemed to tire. The idea was based on a theory that McLaughlin had learned in the army – that fresh troops always have the edge over a fatigued army. It was a strategy that has since become basic to the game.

Second, in sharp contrast to the team's usual hiring practices, McLaughlin brought in goalkeeper Charlie Gardiner to replace the retired Lehman. Gardiner looked to be anything but a star during his first four performances, but then did a sudden about-face and went on to become one of the finest goaltenders ever seen in the NHL. He played for only seven years, with his career ending tragically in 1934 when he died soon after undergoing brain surgery. But, in those seven years, he produced 42 shutouts, posted a splendid record of 2.13 goals against

average and won the Vezina Award in 1931-32 and 1933-34. Gardiner was named to the league's All-Star first team in 1931, -32 and -34, and to the second team in 1933. His appearance in the Hawks' 1933-34 Cup victory has long ranked high among the most courageous performances ever seen in NHL play. It will be covered in the chapter on the Stanley Cup.

The 1933-34 Cup competition saw the Black Hawks down the Montréal Canadiens in the quarter-final round and then move to the championship series by defeating the Montréal Maroons in the semi-finals. The Chicagoans took the championship series, 3 games to 1, over the Detroit Red Wings. Four years later, at the close of the 1937-38 season, the Hawks earned their second Cup by handing the Toronto Maple Leafs a 3-games-to-1 defeat after besting the Canadiens in the quarter-finals and the New York Americans in the semi-finals.

In the wake of the successful 1937-38 campaign, the Hawks suffered such a poor season that their fans stayed away in droves. The club, in fact, had come to the threshold of a two-decade experience that would make the problems of earlier years seem like nothing. We'll cover those two decades in Chapter Five.

THE DETROIT RED WINGS

NHL hockey arrived in America's motor center in 1926, when a group of businessmen purchased the Patrick brothers' Victoria Cougars for $100,000 and turned them into the Detroit Cougars. It was a purchase that looked rather unwise in the club's opening season in its new home. Though led by three future Hall of Famers – wingman Jack Walker and centers Frank Frederickson and Frank Foyston – the

Above: Chicago Black Hawk defenseman Clarence 'Taffy' Abel.

Cougars ended in their division's last place, winning a mere dozen of the season's 44 outings. The three linemen, though splendid per-

quarter-finals. A year later, Detroit was again in the Cup battle, this time defeating the Maroons in the quarter-finals, only to drop the

reins at the end of the 1946-47 season) and 35 years as the club's general manager (retiring in 1962). During his tenure, Adams took the club through some of its worst and best times, along the way winning seven Stanley Cups and taking his division's first-place spot 12 times.

Under Adams' tutelage, the unit began a gradual if erratic improvement and, in 1931-32, made its way to its first Stanley Cup competition, losing to the Montréal Maroons in the

on-ice efficiency plunged because there wasn't enough money around to hire some sorely needed personnel.

Yet, despite these problems, Adams managed to make some good trades and acquisitions. Wingman Herbie Lewis came aboard in 1928-29 and remained for 11 years, scoring 148 goals in 483 regular-season games. Fellow wingman John Sorrell arrived in 1930-31 and was on the ice for 347 regular-season games, scoring 96

Below: National Hockey League president Frank Calder with three of his referees.

points, before going to the New York Americans in the 1937-38 season. Undoubtedly, however, the best catch of the day was Ebbie Goodfellow, the superb center who joined the team in 1929-30, performed as a mainstay for 14 years, and went into the Hall of Fame in 1963. Starting in his regular position, Goodfellow was shifted for a time to the defense in an effort to strengthen the team's weakest spot. He performed beautifully in an unfamiliar position, but all in a losing cause because of the poor caliber of his fellow defenders.

Adams performed as well in the front office as Goodfellow did on the ice. The coach-manager pulled every stunt he could think of to better his team's financial fortunes. In 1930, for example, he sought to create new fans by staging an exhibition game for charity, asking only that the spectators pay only what they could afford to get past the box office, with all money after expenses to go to charity. He let it be known that he was always ready to serve as a guest speaker at civic and social club dinners. Just before the 1930-31 season, he launched a contest to find a new name for the club. The name selected: the Falcons.

His energetic work, however, bore little or no fruit. The grandstands remained alarmingly bare through the early 1930s. Detroit's on-ice performance remained poor, because morale was still down and there was the growing possibility that each season might be the team's last.

But all the problems suddenly evaporated just before the 1933-34 season. Behind the change of fortune was the millionaire grain merchant and hockey enthusiast, James D Norris. A former amateur player who had long wanted to own a team of his own and who had just made an unsuccessful bid for the purchase of the Chicago Black Hawks, Norris bought the Falcons, pumped needed money into the club, and – to tie down the idea that it now had a new lease on life – immediately changed its name to the Red Wings.

The story behind the new name provides an interesting sidelight in the club's history. As a boy, Norris had played with an amateur Montréal outfit called the Winged Wheelers. He simply revised his old team's name and adopted its emblem, a wing within a wheel. The wheel symbolized the city of Detroit as America's automotive capital.

Once the purchase was made, Norris placed Adams on a year's probation as coach-manager. The two men, however, soon found that they worked very well together. Adams' career with Detroit was to continue for another two decades.

With salaries up (with payment at last guaranteed), all bills out of the way, and player morale high, the newly christened Red Wings immediately placed first in the American Division and headed into the 1933-34 Stanley Cup competition. There, they dropped Toronto, 3 games to 2 in the semi-finals only to lose to Chicago, 3 games to 1, in the championship round.

As had happened all too often to other units, the Red Wings suffered a poor season in the wake of the Cup appearance, dropping to fourth place in the division. Midway through the

season, Norris tried to improve matters by hiring a brilliant 22-year-old named Syd Howe, obtaining him from the about-to-collapse St Louis Eagles. A professional since 1929, Howe had played for Ottawa, Philadelphia (in the single season that the former Pittsburgh Pirates had spent there), and Toronto before going to the Eagles. For $50,000, Norris acquired his services, along with those of a fine defenseman, Scotty Bowman. The Norris payment was a fantastic one for its day, with estimates saying that the purchase would equal several million dollars today.

But Howe (who was not related to Detroit's later star, Gordie Howe) by himself proved to be worth every penny spent on the deal. Credited with being one of the most versatile players ever seen in pro hockey, he could handle every position on the team. He was especially good at center and left wing and divided his time between the two positions during his years with the Wings, eleven and a half years that ended

Above: James D Norris, the legendary owner of the Detroit Red Wings.

with his retirement at the close of the 1945-46 season.

first to do the job, in 1919-20 and 1920-21, with the Canadiens following suit in 1929-30 and 1930-31). The Wings, however, won the distinction of being the first NHL team ever to take a divisional first place *and* the Cup in back-to-back seasons.

Though their accomplishment was a splendid one, the Wings could not maintain their momentum in the 1937-38 campaign and suffered a poor season. In great part, their mediocre showing was due to the fact that some of their stars, among them Sorrell, were now aging and no longer as proficient as was once the case. Recognizing the problem, Adams took two steps. First, he resolved never to keep a player too long but to trade him away once the ravages of age had begun to show themselves. Second, he instituted a farm system for the club to insure that the team would always have a

fresh supply of youngsters on hand. Adams is credited with being the first hockey executive to

Bruins, 4 games to 0 in the championship round to take home their third Cup.

But the best was yet to come. The Wings' greatest age was fast approaching and would dawn in the mid-1940s, with the retirement of one great star, Syd Howe, and the emergence of another with, oddly, the same last name – Gordon (Gordie) Howe. But this is a story for the next chapter.

THE MONTRÉAL CANADIENS

Playing for the honor of Canada's French-speaking people and with a tradition of never giving up, the Canadiens were a powerhouse team in the first of the NHL's youthful years, at last coming upon hard times in the mid-1930s.

Their power, obviously, was due to an always splendid lineup: the battling Newsy Lalonde until his transfer to the Saskatoon Sheiks in

Below: George Hainsworth, the Hall of Fame goalie for the Montréal Canadiens.

1922; the eccentric and brilliant Aurel Joliat, a mainstay from 1922-23 through 1937-38; the fleet Howie Morenz from 1923-24 until that terrible night in 1937 when he crashed into the boards and ended his career; and the superb goaltender, Georges Vezina, a man whose memory has now served as an inspiration to his counterparts for more than a half-century now.

Born at Chicoutimi, Québec, in 1887, Vezina early showed himself to have the makings of a fine, if somewhat eccentric, goalie – eccentric because of his raw-boned casual manner prior to a game's start and his habit of not wearing skates while at work. The fact is, he did not like the things and finally learned to get about on them just two years before he began professional play in 1910.

His emergence as a professional came about by happy accident. In 1910, the Montréal Canadiens arrived in Vezina's home town to play an exhibition game with his amateur team. From the look of the skaters as they flowed out onto the ice for the face-off, the teams promised to be anything but evenly matched, with the handsome, muscular pros on one side and the rag-tag amateurs on the other. But, thanks principally to Vezina, they turned out to be unevenly matched, but in a totally unexpected way. While the Montréal management watched

Above: Three Hall of Fame players for the Canadiens. Left to right: Maurice 'Rocket' Richard, Elmer Lach and Hector 'Toe' Blake.

Left: Georges Vezina, the legendary goalie for the Montréal Canadiens.

67

Far right: A Montréal Canadien fights with a Detroit Red Wing for

with increasing fascination, the lanky six-footer turned away the visitors' every attack and handed them a 2-0 shutout.

played there since the turn of the century, was still trying to become a truly popular sport. His career, however, was destined to end in tragedy. At some point during his playing days, he developed tuberculosis, a disease that, though he tried to ignore its presence, gradually weakened him until, after he had played a superb first period in the 1925-26 season opener, it felled him. He collapsed on the ice and, as a hushed and shocked crowd watched, was carried to the dressing room. Vezina never returned to action. He died on 24 March 1926.

Immediately after his death, the Canadiens presented the Vezina Trophy to the league. Until the 1981-82 season, it was awarded annually to the goalkeeper who allowed the fewest enemy goals. Since then, it has gone yearly to the man judged by NHL managers to be the season's 'outstanding goalkeeper.' The winners of the trophy since its inception are listed in Chapter Seven. Vezina himself was inducted into the Hall of Fame in 1945.

With an obvious talent for picking goalies, the Canadiens filled Vezina's post with a 31-year-old veteran of the defunct Western Canada Hockey League – George Hainsworth. Though small for the position (five feet, six inches at 150 pounds), Hainsworth immediately demonstrated his talent by winning the Vezina Trophy in his first three seasons. In that trio of years, he posted, respectively, 14, 13 and an amazing 22 shutouts. Hainsworth remained with the Canadiens until being traded to Toronto in 1933. He returned to Montréal in 1936-37, retiring at the end of that season. In his combined Canadien-Toronto career, he was in the crease for 465 regular-season games, posting 12,415 minutes of ice time, 247 wins, and 94 shutouts. In the NHL's listing of all-time shutout leaders, he stands second to Terry Sawchuk, who recorded 103 shutouts between 1949 and 1970.

The Canadiens picked up another top player in the mid-30s – the superb wingman Hector (Toe) Blake. He came to the club in 1935-36 after a two-year stint with the Montréal Maroons, performed well for the rest of the decade, and then enjoyed his best years in the 1940s when, on the left side, he formed one-third of the awesome 'Punch Line' with Maurice (The

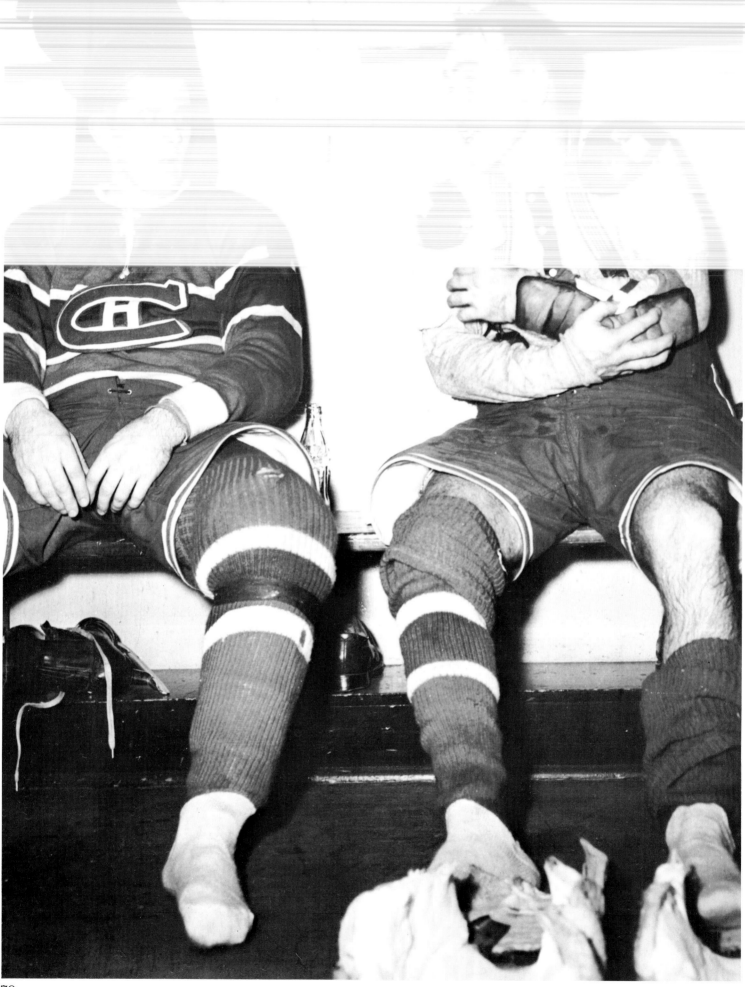

Rocket) Richard at right wing and Elmer Lach at center. Starting as a pugnacious and flamboyant competitor, Blake matured into one of the game's most sportsmanlike and effective performers. In all, he skated in 578 regular-season games for the Canadiens, scoring 235 goals and 292 assists, before the January night in 1948 when, as the result of a strong bodycheck, he suffered a shattered ankle that ended his playing days. He then went on, as we'll see later, to a 13-year coaching career with the Canadiens. Blake was inducted into the Hall of Fame in 1966.

Led by Blake and Hainsworth, the Canadiens fared well at the start of the 30s, taking the Stanley Cup in 1929-30 with a 2-games-to-0 win over Boston, and then reclaiming the prize in 1930-31, with Chicago their victim this time, 3-games-to-2. But life turned sour for the club at mid-decade, both at the gate and on the ice. The Depression struck Montréal hard, so damaging were the Forum's box office receipts that the city's English-speaking Maroons were closed down to enable the more popular Canadiens to survive. Apparently disheartened by the sad financial picture, Les Habitants placed first in the team standings only once between the 1934-35 season and 1939-40. That first-place finish was achieved in 1936-37 and was followed by a disappointing loss in the Cup competition – a 3-games-to-2 defeat at Detroit's hands in the semi-finals. Otherwise, the club managed to advance no higher than third place in the standings and suffered quarter-final losses in the 1934-35, 1937-38 and 1938-39 Cup action. In 1935-36 and 1939-40, for two of only three times in their history, the Montréalers found themselves so far down in the standings that they failed to make the Cup playoffs.

But better days were to come in the 1940s. They would begin to show themselves in, 1942-43 with the arrival of Joseph Maurice (The Rocket) Richard.

THE NEW YORK RANGERS

Here is a team that stands as a sports rarity. It is one of the very few expansion outfits in any sport ever to win a divisional first place in its initial year of play.

Millionaire sportsman Tex Rickard, the president of the new Madison Square Garden, formed the Rangers in 1926. Though not an avid hockey fan, Rickard was an astute businessman who quickly saw the game's financial possibilities while watching the New York Americans play their first season at his Garden. He rented the facility to the Americans and decided that he must have an outfit of his own, one that would give the Garden an additional attraction while simultaneously handing him a nice profit as team owner.

The Rangers' immediate on-ice success was anything but an accident. Hired aboard were four fine veterans from the Patrick brothers' defunct western league – the battling defenseman, Ivan (Ching/Ching-a-Ling Chinaman) Johnson; the brother wingmen, Bill and Frederick (Bun/Bunny) Cook and center Frank Boucher. Johnson was to remain with the club for 12 seasons, in that time playing in 435 regular-season games and then winning admission to the Hall of Fame in 1958. The Cook brothers scored 47 goals their first season, with Bill accounting for 33 of that number and taking the league's scoring honors; the two donned Ranger uniforms for ten years, with Bill being named a Hall of Famer in 1952.

Of the four players, there is little doubt that Frank Boucher etched the most impressive career. Twenty-six years old at the time he joined the Rangers, Boucher had already put in a year with the Ottawa Senators and had starred for the Patricks' Vancouver club. The rest of his career was to be spent with the Rangers as a player and then a coach. As a player, he appeared in 557 regular-season games – scoring 161 goals and 262 assists – before retiring at

Opposite: Maurice 'Rocket' Richard (left) and Hector 'Toe' Blake of the Montréal Canadiens relax after a hard night's work.

Below: A tense moment around the New York Ranger goal.

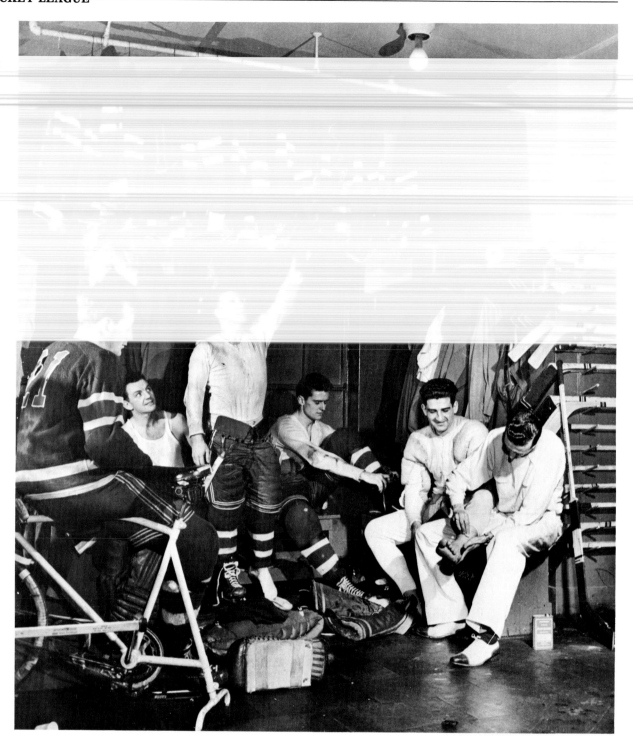

the end of the 1937-38 season. At that time, with the front office having long ago recognized his leadership abilities, he was assigned to coach in the Rangers' farm system. He came to the parent club as coach in the 1939-40 season and put in 11 years on the job.

A stylish and gentlemanly player (Frank Nighbor had been his boyhood idol), Boucher won the Lady Byng Trophy (see Chapter Seven) for sportsmanship seven times in the eight seasons from 1927-28 through 1934-35, a feat that caused the trophy to be given to him in perpetuity while another was fashioned for future recipients. Additionally, Boucher was named to the NHL's All-Star team three times during his playing career – once to the second unit (1930-31) and twice to the first squad (1932-33 and 1933-34). He went into the Hall of Fame in 1958.

Inventive as well as stylish, Boucher early joined his fellow linemen, the Cook brothers, in dreaming up the drop pass. The maneuver

would begin as Bill Cook herded an enemy puck-carrier over to Boucher. Frank would hook the puck away and pass it to Bun Cook. In turn, Bun would head for the blue line and, on arrival, draw a defenseman to him by faking a shot. The puck was then left for Boucher as he came sailing up behind Bun. More of Boucher's inventiveness will be seen when we come to his years of coaching.

Responsible for bringing Boucher, the Cooks and Johnson to the Rangers was the team's first coach-general manager, the young Conn Smythe, who was hired because of his great success with a number of Canadian amateur units. Just before the team went into its first practice sessions, however, Smythe was dismissed for reasons that remain matters of debate to this day – with some fans believing (as Smythe himself claimed) that owner Rickard and club president Colonel John S Hammond wanted a more experienced hand at the helm, while others hold that the firing came about because Smythe ignored Hammond's orders to hire the now aging wingman, Babe Dye. Whatever the case, Smythe departed and Lester Patrick came in from the west to replace him and to serve as coach-general manager until he himself was replaced by Boucher at the close of the 1930s.

Looking awesome, the Rangers posted a record of 25 wins, 13 losses, and six ties in their first season to take the American Division's top spot. They went to the Stanley Cup competition with the hope of now becoming the first NHL expansion team to take home the coveted Cup in its maiden year – a hope that was shattered in semi-final play when they lost to Boston, 3 goals to 1.

From that initial season through the 1939-40 campaign, the Rangers never placed below third in their division and never failed to make their way to the Stanley Cup competition. In those 14 seasons, they won the Cup three times – in 1927-28, dropping the Montréal Maroons 3 games to 2; in 1932-33, downing Toronto 3 games to 1 and in 1939-40, again beating Toronto, this time 4 games to 2.

The 1939-40 Cup was won with Frank Boucher in his first season as coach – the season that saw his inventive mind introduce the Rangers' soon-to-be-famous 'box defense.' It called for the players to form themselves into a rectangle on their side of the ice when one of their teammates had been banished to the penalty box. So positioned, they were able to protect all their corners.

Boucher also introduced the idea of replacing the goalie in the final moments of a game in which his team was trailing by a goal. Onto the ice in the goalie's place came a forward to give the Rangers a sixth attacker and an improved chance of tying the score and sending the game into overtime.

The Rangers suddenly encountered bad times with the dawn of the 1940s. In great part, the problems centered on the fact that their ranks were decimated with the coming of World War II and the loss of so much of their manpower to the armed forces – more than half of their starters. They were not to return to greatness until the late 1960s.

THE TORONTO MAPLE LEAFS

The Toronto St Patricks became the Toronto Maple Leafs in February 1927. The change of name was the work of one of the club's new owners – Conn Smythe, the amateur hockey genius who had been hired that year as the New York Rangers first coach-general manager and then had been fired before the Rangers began their first practice sessions. Smythe, one of Canada's most ardent boosters and patriotic citizens, picked the name because the maple leaf was the country's national symbol. And, perhaps not coincidentally because he was also an astute businessman, he felt that the name would inspire a strong following for his team.

After winning the Stanley Cup in 1921-22, Toronto had fallen on difficult playing times. For the next four seasons, the club failed to win a spot in the Cup competition. The franchise went on sale in 1926 and was snapped up for

Above: Conn Smythe, the major force behind the Toronto Maple Leafs and the building of the Maple Leaf Gardens.

Left: Frank J Selke, part owner of the Toronto Maple Leafs.

$135,000 by Smythe and several businessmen, chief among them his longtime friend and fellow hockey enthusiast, Frank J Selke. With Smythe as its new president and general manager, the club skated out for the 1926-27 season and ran smack into disaster – a fifth-place divisional finish and yet another miss at the Cup playoffs. Smythe then named himself coach, a job that he held for the remaining three seasons of the decade. In that time, the Leafs made the Cup battles just once – in 1928-29 when they were knocked out of the semi-finals by the coach's former team, the formidable Rangers, 2 games to 0.

Life in Toronto improved abruptly in the 1930-31 season, however, thanks to Smythe's front-office astuteness. For openers, he wisely stepped aside as coach and handed the job to Art Duncan for little more than a season and then gave it to Dick Irvin for the remainder of the decade while he himself concentrated on the work for which he seemed best suited, the selecting of top players. He had already demon-strated that skill by bringing aboard three superb young linemen – 21-year-old Joseph (Gentleman Joe) Primeau in 1927, followed by 18-year-old Harvey (Busher) Jackson and 19

through 1936-37, being named to first team four times. Conacher made the first team three times and was twice placed on the second unit.

From the look of the NHL record book alone, Primeau seemed to have been the weakest member of the Kid Line. In nine years with

from 1929-30 through 1935-36 – as the un-forgettable 'Kid Line.'

In that time, the trio amassed 792 points in regular-season play and 71 in playoff action, for a grand total of 863. Of the three men, Conacher at right wing scored the most goals, leading the league in scoring for five years. He posted 31 goals in 1930-31; 34 in 1931-32; 32 in 1933-34; 36 in 1934-35 and 23 in 1935-36. It was an especially remarkable feat because Conacher was prone to being hurt. More times than not, he was unable to play a full season because of an injury.

Working at right wing, Busher Jackson took the league's point-scoring championship in 1932-33, collecting 53 for 28 goals and 25 assists. With Conacher, he made the All-Star team five times in the six seasons from 1931-32

award in 1931-32.

The 'Kid Line' was dissolved at the end of the 1935-36 season when Primeau, though only 30 years old and with much of his career still be-fore him, decided to retire. He went into private business and spent his leisure hours coaching amateur hockey. He returned to the Leafs as coach in 1950-51, remaining for three years and leading the club to a Stanley Cup in his first season.

In the wake of Primeau's departure, Conacher and Jackson stayed with the Leafs for several years, performing well but not as expertly as with their friend and cohort. Conacher went to Detroit for a year in 1938-39 and then spent two seasons with the New York Americans before ending a 12-year career. Jackson joined Conacher on the Americans squad in 1939-40

Opposite: Charles 'Syl' Apps, the Hall of Fame center of the Toronto Maple Leafs, with the Stanley Cup, which the Leafs won in 1942.

Below: A Toronto newspaper cartoon celebrating Francis 'King' Clancy.

74

Right: Goalkeeper Walter 'Turk' Broda of the Maple Leafs, who

Below: Hall of Fame right wing Gordon Drillon of the Toronto Maple Leafs receives one of his many trophies.

and remained for two seasons. He moved to Boston in 1942-43 for the final three seasons of a 15-year career. The members of the 'Kid Line' were later inducted into the Hall of Fame — Conacher in 1961, Primeau in 1963 and Jackson in 1971.

On the defense side of the picture, King Clancy retired after the 1936-37 season. In his 16 years with the league, the battle-scarred veteran had taken to the ice in 593 regular-season games. He had scored 137 goals and tallied 143 assists, a noteworthy feat for a defenseman. He went into the Hall of Fame in 1958.

The aging George Hainsworth likewise departed Toronto in 1936-37, moving on to the Montréal Canadiens to play out the final season of his splendid 11-year career in the crease. In the 465 regular-season games he had played in those years, Hainsworth had amassed 29,415 minutes of ice time. He was named to the Hall of Fame in 1961.

While diminishing the team's strength in the mid-30s, the Primeau and Clancy retirements did not put the Leafs out of commission. Brought in at that time were a string of fine young players, among them three future Hall of Famers — center Charles (Syl) Apps, who would spend ten years with the club; wingman

Gordon (Gordie/Gord) Drillon, with six years in a Toronto uniform ahead of him and goalkeeper Walter (Turk) Broda, who, on replacing Hainsworth, would outdo his predecessor by playing for 16 years – all of them with the Leafs – and posting 629 regular-season games and 38,167 minutes of ice time.

Blessed always with fine talent, the Leafs were Stanley Cup contenders throughout the 1930s. With Dick Irvin in his first year as coach, they took the Cup at the close of the 1931-32 season. In the quarter-finals, they dropped Chicago, 6 goals to 2. Semi-final action saw them slip past the Montréal Maroons 4 goals to 3. In the championship round, they came up against a solid Ranger squad and walked away with a 3-games-to-0 victory.

Oddly, however, despite their strength, the Cup eluded the Leafs throughout the remainder of the decade. Though taking their division's first- or second-place spot for five of those eight years, they somehow managed always to come away losers in the Cup action, suffering six defeats in the championship round and one each in quarter- and semi-final play. Their next Cup was earned in 1941-42, with a 4-games-to-3 edging of Detroit. Handling the coaching duties that season was Hap Day, who had retired as a player in 1938 and had replaced Irvin in 1940. He was destined to write an unforgettable page in the Leafs' history book. By the time the 1940s had ended, Day would lead Toronto to five Cup championships.

The NHL's youthful years seemed to bring it in a full circle. The league had opened those years with six teams, had expanded to ten, and had, in the end, returned to six. But a team count does not tell the full story. On the positive side, the circuit by the 1940s had survived the Depression years, had built a number of attractive arenas – among them Montréal's Forum (opened in 1924), Detroit's Olympia (1927) and Toronto's Maple Leaf Gardens (1931) – and had firmly implanted itself in such other facilities as New York's Madison Square Garden and Chicago Stadium. Further, it had successfully established itself in the United States, a country that just a few years earlier had been generally unfamiliar with hockey.

Further, so far as the US was concerned, the NHL had tried to make the game more interesting to the fans south of the border by developing some American-bred playing talent. This was a movement that began with Black Hawks owner Frederic McLaughlin and then spread to several other clubs. While the Americans would always be outnumbered by the Canadians, a fair share would eventually build fine NHL careers for themselves. Listed in their ranks are the superb Frankie Brimsek (Hall of Fame, 1966) and fellow goaltenders Mike Karakas (eight years with the Black Hawks in the 1930s and 40s) and Pete LoPresti (five seasons with the Minnesota North Stars in the 1970s and one with the Edmonton Oilers in the 1980s). Others include center Pat LaFontaine of the Buffalo Sabres; defenseman Al Iafrate of the Washington Capitals; Joe Mullen, the NHL's all-time leading American-born point scorer; defenseman Phil Housley of the Winnipeg Jets; de-

fenseman Chris Chelios of the Chicago Black Hawks; defenseman Mathieu Schneider of the Montréal Canadiens; and coach Paul Holmgren of the Hartford Whalers, all of them in action as this book is being written.

Finally, the league had expanded its schedule through the years and had developed a string of new rules to make the game more interesting. It had gone from a 36- to a 44-game schedule in 1926-27; then to 48 games in 1931-32; and to 50 games in 1942-43. So far as game regulations were concerned, the delayed penalty rule was introduced in 1925-26; forward passing into defending and center zones was permitted beginning in 1927-28; two years later, forward passing inside all three zones was okayed (but not permitted across the blue lines); the penalty shot arrived on the scene in 1934-35, while 'icing the puck' was outlawed in 1937-38; the penalty shot was made one of the most exciting features of the game when, starting in 1938-39, the shooter could carry the puck right to the goal mouth if he so wished.

In all, despite the loss of the dropout units, the NHL had come a long way in its development. At hand now were the decades that would see the league grow to maturity and expand to its present roster of 26 teams playing in two conferences and four divisions.

Above: Hall of Fame goalie Frank Brimsek of the Boston Bruins.

CHAPTER FIVE

THIRD PERIOD

Decades to Maturity

Close to five decades have passed since the 1940s dawned with the world at war. Those five decades have proven to be a varied lot for the

Matthew (Mac) Colville and Alex Shibicky, goalie Jim Henry and defenseman Muzz Patrick.

some of them, such as the Rangers' fine rookie defenseman, Dudley (Red) Garrett, to die overseas.

One star after another departed. Gone was Boston's entire 'Kraut Line' (which, up against a burst of angry fan patriotism, had wisely changed its name to the 'Kitchener Line' at the outbreak of hostilities) – Milt Schmidt, Bobby Bauer, and Woody Dumart. Gone, too, was the fine young goaltender – Frankie Brimsek – whom the Bruins had brought in to replace the aging Tiny Thompson in 1938-39 and whose shutout abilities (26 by his departure in 1943) and agility in the crease had earned him the nickname, 'Mr. Zero.' Toronto lost its popular young center, Pete Langelle. Hardest hit of all, however, were the Rangers, sacrificing wings

best players of service age were gone. Left were amateurs and ex-professionals too old for the game and kids too young and green for league competition. In the main, the teams filled their rosters with youngsters who, while reasonably good amateurs, were below league standards.

But this it not to say that every last pick was an unhappy one. One exception was a Toronto find – Frank McCool, a 26-year-old goaltender who was so afflicted with a stomach ulcer that he was forced to down a quart of milk before every game. No matter his suffering, McCool served as a key performer in the Leaf's 1944-45 Stanley Cup win. He came through with three shutouts against Detroit in the championship round and one against the Canadiens in the semi-final series.

Another exception: Harry (Apple Cheeks) Lumley, who went into the crease for Detroit in 1943-44 and then performed dependably for five teams during the next 16 years. In 1980, he won a place for himself in the Hall of Fame.

Still another exception: Bill Durnan. He not only ranks as a fine wartime acquisition but also, in fact, a superb one. He became the Canadiens' goalie in 1943-44 and remained for seven years, performing splendidly the entire time. His prowess, actually, came as no surprise to the Montréal management. Durnan had long been recognized as an outstanding amateur and had been previously approached by a number of clubs, among them Toronto and Boston. But he enjoyed his amateur status, not only in hockey but in softball as well, and had never felt any desire to turn professional. However, recognizing what the war was doing to the NHL's playing personnel, he finally gave in to the appeals from Montréal.

So far as many a old-time fan is concerned, Durnan ranks among the finest goalkeepers ever to play the game, right up there with Hainsworth, Terry Sawchuk and a later great, Jacques Plante. In his first two seasons, he led the league in ice time, putting in 3000 minutes in each season. When Durnan retired at the end of 1949-50, he had amassed a impressive 22,945 regular-season minutes in the crease.

In six of his seven seasons, Durnan won the

Above: Bill Durnan, the Hall of Fame goalie for the Montréal Canadiens from 1943 to 1950.

Left: Jacques Plante, the Hall of Fame goalie, when he was with the Montréal Canadiens. He was the one who first used the face mask.

Above: Maurice 'Rocket' Richard of the Montréal Canadiens in a game with the Toronto Maple Leafs.

Far right: Richard waits to go into the game.

Dick Irvin. At first glimpse, Irvin liked the youngster's speed and accurate shooting, but wondered if he had the toughness necessary for professional play. Putting his concern to the test, Irvin assigned one of his roughest players — defenseman Murph (Hard Rock) Chamberlain — to go against Richard and behave in his customary intemperate fashion.

Chamberlain obliged by slamming Richard into the boards and knocking him to the ice. Irvin watched as Richard sprang back to his feet. Then watched as the newcomer, fists flying, charged into the defenseman. Then, with pleased fascination, watched as three teammates were finally needed to rescue Chamberlain. And then decided that Richard was going to be a Canadien.

Vezina Trophy, taking it four times in a row (see Chapter Seven for dates). And, again in six of those seven seasons, he led the league in goals against average. Today, he stands fourth on the list of goaltenders with the longest shutout streaks. In 1948-49 — playing, in turn against Chicago, Detroit, Boston — Durnan recorded four shutouts in a row over a stretch of 309 minutes and 21 seconds. Heading the list is Alex Connell of the Ottawa Senators, who came up with a consecutive six in 1927-28 over a span of 461 minutes, 29 seconds. (Note: Connell's feat was accomplished at a time when forward passing was not permitted in the attacking zone.) For his stamina and achievements, Durnan was inducted into the Hall of Fame in 1964.

Center Ted (Teeder/Terrible) Kennedy must also be mentioned as a splendid wartime acquisition, joining Toronto in 1942-43. Though a plodding type of skater, Kennedy made more than his fair share of goals and was named team captain following the 1948 season. In the first three seasons of his captaincy, the Leafs took two consecutive Stanley Cups. Beloved by the fans — who always greeted his positioning for a face-off with the yell C'mon, Teeder!' — Kennedy remained in the league for 14 years, retiring at the end of 1956-57 and going into the Hall of Fame in 1966.

As good as Durnan and Kennedy were, the best catch of the wartime era — and assuredly one of the best of any era — was a 21-year-old French Canadian firebrand named Joseph Maurice Richard. Hired by the Canadiens for the 1942-43 season, he proved to be a wing blessed with lightning-like speed and an amazingly hard and accurate backhand shot. Both quickly earned him the nickname 'The Rocket.'

Though he had a solid background in amateur hockey, Richard was an unknown quantity when he arrived for a tryout in the Canadien camp — at least, to sophomore coach

And a Canadien Richard was, becoming a Montréal legend as he played his way through 18 seasons, working 1,978 regular-season games and 133 in playoff action. At the core of the Richard legend lay several factors. First, there was his hot temper, memorably seen on the night when, on drawing a penalty for hitting Boston's Milt Schmidt with his stick, he broke the stick into pieces and hurled them at the referee. There was his dedication to the game, seen during a playoff meeting with the Bruins when, knocked momentarily unconscious by a blindside hit, he refused to be hospitalized and returned to the ice, topping off the evening with a goal. There was his stick handling ability, seen in the opposition's habit of assigning two men to hold him while a third snatched the puck away. There was his style, his habit of snaring the puck at the enemy's blue line, carrying it forward one-handed while fending off an opponent with the other, and streaking into position for one of his patented

backhand shots into the net. Above all else, there was his amazing scoring ability, so clearly seen throughout his career and especially evident in the second game of the 1943-44 semi-finals against Toronto when he tallied all of his team's 5 goals.

In six of his early seasons, Richard combined with fellow wing Toe Blake and center Elmer Lach to form the fearsome 'Punch Line'. Just how fearsome were they? In those six years — from 1942-43 through 1947-48 when Blake retired — they amassed 449 regular-season goals and 518 assists.

Of the three, Richard was the most proficient scorer — accounting for 187 of the line's combined total of 449. His total might have been higher had he not suffered a broken ankle just a few days into his rookie year, when he had recorded five goals and six assists. Out of commission for the rest of the season and with a history of injury in his amateur days, Richard worried that Irvin might not want him back. But Irvin did bring him back, and The Rocket repaid that faith by scoring 32 regular-season goals and 22 assists in 1943-44. Then, in 1944-45, he set a league record with 50 goals in a 50-game season.

In doing so, Richard wrote one of the great cliff-hanger yarns in NHL history. Throughout the season, he maintained an average of 1 goal per game. He put goal 49 on the board in the season's 48th game, a home stand against Chicago. He returned for game 49, again a session with Chicago, only to be held scoreless. The Canadiens then traveled down to Boston Gardens to play the seasonal closer against the Bruins. There, Richard slammed home goal 50, setting a mark that would not be equaled until 1980-81 when it was matched by the New York Islanders' Mike Bossy.

In the minds of many, Richard's achievement has overshadowed the record set earlier by the great Joe Malone — 44 goals in the 1917 season. But the two cannot really be compared. Malone brought in his 44 goals in a 20-game season.

By the time of his retirement in 1960, Richard had played in 978 regular-season games, scoring 544 goals and 421 assists, and in 133 playoff battles, where he tallied 82 goals and 44 assists — for a grand total of 1111 games, 626 goals and 465 assists. Along the way he led the league in scoring five times. Richard was named to the Hall of Fame in 1961. We'll see more of him in later pages.

Thanks to the likes of Richard, Kennedy and Durnan and to the public's need to escape the war's tensions for a few hours now and then, the league fared well at the gate during the war years. It was a gate that happily contradicted president Calder's fears. Unhappily, however, he did not live to see himself proved wrong. One of hockey's great pioneers and early executives, Calder died in 1943. The former manager of the New York Americans, Mervyn (Red) Dutton, was named to fill the presidency and served until 1946, retiring at that time to be replaced by Clarence S Campbell.

When the war ended, the stars in uniform began making their way back to the league, with most arriving in time for the 1945-46 season. Sadly, with the time away apparently

having taken the edge off their skills, a number never achieved their former greatness. Just as they had been hardest hit by the departures in 1942, the Rangers were now hardest hit by this new misfortune. Defenseman Muss Patrick played in 26 games that season and wing Alex Shibicky in 33, with both then retiring. Wing man Mac Colville put in 39 games with only seven goals and six assists, following with 14 games in 1946-47 without a goal or an assist before calling it quits. An exception was goaltender Jim Henry. He remained in the league for eight years, in that time serving not only the Rangers but also Chicago and Detroit. On his retirement, Henry had 405 regular-season games, 24,315 minutes of ice time, and 227 shutouts to his credit.

Boston's superb Frankie Brimsek returned to the crease and performed well, but certainly not as effectively as in pre-war days. Mister Zero was traded to Chicago in 1949-50 and retired a year later after a ten-year career of 514 regular-season games and 31,210 minutes on the ice.

The immediate post-war years saw the emergence of some fine new talent. Center Edgar Laprade came to the Rangers in 1945-46 and stayed for ten years and 500 games. Toronto picked up three top youngster in a two-year period — wing Howie Meeker and defensemen Jimmy Thomson and James (Gus) Mortson. Thomson and Mortson both enjoyed 13-year careers. The biggest surprise of the three was Meeker, a fine amateur who had been badly injured by an exploding grenade in the war and was thought by many fans to be done as a player. He fooled everyone by staying for eight years, in that time playing in 346 regular-season games.

Above: Frank Brimsek, the Boston Bruins goalie, stops a shot.

Opposite: 'Rocket' Richard poses for photographers after his 500th goal.

Opposite inset: The Richard Brothers — Henri 'the Pocket Rocket' (left) and Maurice 'Rocket' — both Hall of Famers.

Above: Leonard 'Red' Kelly of the Detroit Red Wings protects his goalie, Terry Sawchuk. Both players were elected to the Hall of Fame.

Detroit picked up two of the best post-war finds, one of them being center Leonard (Red) Kelly, who joined the Wings in 1947-48 at the start of what would be a 20-year career. He remained with the Wings until midway through his fourteenth season and then moved to Toronto for the remainder of his playing days. On his retirement at the end of 1966-67, he had 1316 regular-season and 164 playoff games under his belt. Kelly went into the Hall of Fame in 1969.

Detroit's other find was assuredly the Wings' greatest discovery and possibly the greatest discovery ever made in the game – an 18-year-old right wing named Gordon (Gordie) Howe. A skillful skater, an ambidextrous stick handler, an aggressive competitor and – above all else – possibly the most durable figure ever seen in any sport, he was to etch out a spectacular 32-year career on the ice (interrupted by two front-office years) before his retirement at age 52 in 1980.

Born at Floral, Saskatchewan, on 31 March 1928, Howe began playing hockey when he was six. At age 15, he captained his school team through an undefeated 11-game season that saw his outfit score 106 goals to the opposition's six. That same year, the NY Rangers brought him into camp for a tryout that, for two reasons, ended with his return to Floral: his own home-sickness and coach Lester Patrick's feeling that the boy was still too young and not sufficiently developed phsyically for professional competition. Two years later, Detroit signed him on and sent him to be seasoned in its farm system. The next season – 1946-47 – Howe was with the parent club, the youngest played to that date in the league's history.

What was to be an unforgettable career with the Wings started in mediocre fashion. In 58 games, the youngster managed but seven goals and 15 assists, not doing much better in the next two years. Much at fault for his poor production was a youthful impetuosity and fiery temper that saw him banished repeatedly to the penalty box. Of the many records Howe was to collect over the years, one was to be his first long-held first-place spot in the Wings' rankings for penalty minutes in a career: 1643. When he began to mature and control his temper, his goal and assist production went up.

But there came a moment in March 1950 when it looked as if Howe would not be given the chance to mature. During the Stanley Cup semifinal round against Toronto, he cut across the ice to intercept the puck-carrying Ted Kennedy. In the instant before the two men collided, Kennedy braked and, according to the Detroit squad, struck Howe in the face with his stick (later evidence indicated that Kennedy did not touch the youngster). Whatever actually happened, Howe went crashing into the sideboards and sustained a skull fracture. On his arrival at the hospital, the doctors thought he had so little chance of surviving that his parents were summoned from Saskatchewan. Howe not only lived through the ordeal but was back on the ice for the 1950-51 season and, as we'll see momentarily, on the threshold of his greatest years.

Coached by Hap Day and with such competitors as Syl Apps, goalie Turk Broda and then Ted Kennedy in the lineup, the Toronto Maple Leafs dominated the Stanley Cup scene in the 1940s, especially in the decade's latter half. They earned their first Cup of the decade in 1941-42, winning 4 games to 3 over Detroit. The Red Wings again served as their victim, this time 4 games to 3, in 1944-45. Then the

Left: Gordie Howe, the superstar for the Detroit Red Wings.

Below: Gordie Howe (left) comes in to assist the Red Wings goalie.

Leafs themselves took the Cup three years in a row – in 1946-47 over the Canadiens (4 games to 2); 1947-48 over Detroit (4 games to 0) and 1948-49 with Detroit once again on the short end of things by the same margin (4 games to 0). The Leafs became the first club in league history to claim the Cup in three consecutive years.

Their greatest victim, Detroit, joined the Leafs in Cup wins, as did Boston and the Canadiens. The Bruins opened the decade by walloping Detroit, 4 games to 0 in 1940-41. Montréal, under Dick Irvin, dropped Chicago in 1943-44, 4 games to 0 and then skated past Boston in 1945-46, 4 games to 1. As for Detroit, the Wings trounced Boston, 4 games to 0 in 1942-43 and then wrapped up the decade by slipping past the Rangers, 4 games to 3.

Three years before the decade ended, the NHL established what has become a league tradition – the annual All-Star game. The first game was played just before the start of the season. For information on the results of All-Star action through the years, see Chapter Seven.

THE 1950s

This was a ten-year stretch of excellent, at times magnificent, individual and team achievements.

Topping the list for individual accomplishments was Detroit's Gordie Howe. After a tentative two-season start and a skull fracture, he emerged as a scorer and assist-maker of awesome proportions. For the first four seasons of the decade, he ran away with the league's point production. By the time he was done, Howe had tallied 86 points (43 goals and 43 assists) in 1950-51; 86 (47 goals and 39 assists) in 1951-52; 95 (49 goals and 46 assists) in 1952-53 and 81 (33 goals and 48 assists) in 1953-54.

Howe missed the point leadership in 1954-55 and 1955-56, but reclaimed it the next year with a solid 89 (44 goals and 45 assists). His point production also gave him the league's top spot for goals and assists through the years – for goals: 1950-51, 1951-52, and 1952-53 and for sts: 1950-51, 1952-53, and 1953-54. He again took first-place honors for goals in 1956-57.

Dogging Howe's tracks was the Canadiens' hot-tempered and by-now-beloved Rocket Richard. The league's top spot for goal scoring went to him in 1953-54 and 1954-55, with respective tallies of 37 and 38.

The decade also saw some memorable players enter the league. Wing Frank (Big M) Mahovlich came to the Maple Leafs in 1956-57, proved durable and steady, and remained in the NHL for 22 years, going into the Hall of Fame in 1981. Earlier, the New York Rangers acquired goaltender Lorne (Gump) Worsley and center Camille Henry. Worsley played his rookie year in 1952-53, with Henry arriving a year later. Comically roly-poly but nevertheless as effective as they come, Worsley etched a 21-year career for himself, putting in 50,232 minutes of regular-season play in that time. Henry's career ran for 14 seasons. Worsley entered the Hall of Fame in 1980.

The Chicago Black Hawks, who spent most of the 1950s limping along in the bottom half of the league standings, picked up two gems near the end of the decade — 18-year-old left wing Bobby Hull in 1957-58 and, the next season, 19-year-old center Stan Mikita. Hull would remain a star for 23 years, Mikita, for 22. In 1959-60, Hull grabbed the league's point and goal championship — 81 points (39 goals and 42 assists), with those 39 tallies giving him the goal leadership — and went on to play his best years in the 1960s, as did his partner, the Czechoslovakian-born Mikita.

Left: Gordie Howe in a tense moment in a game with the Toronto Maple Leafs.

Below: The Toronto Maple Leafs score against goalie Lorne 'Gump' Worsley, who was elected to the Hall of Fame in 1980.

There is little doubt, however, that, for sheer numbers, the Canadiens reaped the greatest rookie crop of the decade. Among the newcomers were five future Hall of Famers.

That graceful and effortless performer, Jean Béliveau, played his rookie year in 1950-51 and became a club mainstay at center for 20 years, playing in 1125 regular-season games. In his fifth year, he took the league's goal and point top spots, scoring 47 tallies to win the former and joining them with 41 assists to give him a total of 88 for the latter berth. Hall of Fame: 1972.

Wing Bernie (Boom Boom) Geoffrion arrived along with Béliveau in 1950-51 to begin a 16-year career that would end with two seasons with the Rangers in the late 1960s. He became famous for introducing (along with the Rangers' Andy Bathgate and a few others) the slapshot. Performed with a golf-like swing of the stick, it was popularized in the 1960s by Chicago's Bobby Hull and altered the nature of the game. Bernie's version of the shot was executed with a hard backswing of two feet or so and then finished off with a hard forward slash that, so the fans swore, gave the puck the speed of a bullet. Hall of Fame: 1972.

Fellow wing Dickie Moore came on the scene a year after Geoffrion's arrival and stayed until 1964-65 when he moved to Toronto and then the St Louis Blues for his final two seasons. Moore took the league point championship in 1957-58 with 84 (36 goals and 48 assists) and then conjured up his best point production ever in 1958-59, leading the league with 96 (41 goals and 55 assists). In the playoffs that season, he scored 17 points (5 goals and 12 assists) to give himself a grand total of 113 points, an NHL record that stood until the end of the 1960s. Hall of Fame: 1974.

Left: Jacques Plante, the Montréal goalie, comes out of the net to make a save.

Opposite left: Canadien Hall of Famer Jean Béliveau.

Opposite right: Canadien Hall of Famer 'Boom Boom' Geoffrion after scoring his 270th goal.

Below: Henri 'Pocket Rocket' Richard of the Montréal Canadiens.

Goaltender Jacques Plante signed on in 1952-53. He spent ten years in Montréal's crease before moving on to play the second half of his career with the Rangers, St Louis, Boston, and the Edmonton Oilers. Blessed with lightning-like reflexes, he soon won the nickname 'Jake the Snake' for his ability to see shots coming so fast that the puck was almost invisible and then cut them off with his stick, skate or any part of the body that happened to be conveniently placed for a block. For five straight seasons – 1955-56 through 1959-60 – Plante won the Vezina Trophy and is the only man in the game ever to win the award that number of times consecutively. His streak was broken in 1960-61 by Toronto's Johnny Bower, but he returned to claim it the following year. To date, Plante and fellow Canadien Bill Durnan are the only goalies to win the trophy six times. Hall of Fame: 1978.

For many a Montréal fan, a 1955-56 arrival, despite his illustrious last name, seemed a dubious prospect – dubious because center Henri Richard, The Rocket's younger brother, looked pathetically on the small side at five feet six inches and 160 pounds. But he soon proved the skeptics wrong, showing himself to be fast, powerful and durable. He was so fast and powerful that, when he and The Rocket accidentally crashed into one another one night, he opened a cut in his brother that took 12 stitches to close. He himself required six stiches. As for durability, the younger Richard – nicknamed 'The Pocket Rocket' – appeared in 1256 regular-season games in a career that spanned 20 years. Hall of Fame: 1979.

The decade's individual performances were excellent, but were easily matched by those of the teams – or, to be more preicse, by those of the Red Wings and Canadiens. Granted, the Toronto Maple Leafs took the Stanley Cup in

Above: Gordie Howe (center), of the Detroit Red Wings, skates in to help his goalie, Terry Sawchuk, prevent a score by the Toronto Maple Leafs.

1950-51 with a 4-games-to-1 victory over the Canadiens, but from then on the decade belonged, in turn, to Detroit and Montréal.

Beginning in 1948-49, the Wings developed the habit of placing first in the league, a tradition that they maintained for seven years until they dropped into the second spot in 1955-56. Snapping at their heels for four of those seasons – 1951-52 through 1954-55 – were the Canadiens, who then forged into first place in 1955-56, only to be dislodged the very next year by – yes, Detroit.

Those same years saw the two units encounter each other repeatedly in Cup play. Their first meeting of the decade took place in the 1950-51 semi-finals, with the Canadiens winning and then advancing to the championship round, there to be humiliated at Toronto's hands. In the next five seasons, the pair battled it out four times:

1951-52: A solid Detroit win, 4 games to 0.
1953-54: A tight one, also a Detroit victory, 4 games to 3.
1954-55: Another tight one, with Detroit coming out on top, 4 games to 3.
1955-56: A one-sided affair in Montréal's favor, 4 games to 1.

There could have been a Detroit-Montréal encounter in 1952-53 but for one factor – Boston. Playing against a squad that was perhaps a bit over-confident, the third-place Bruins dropped the league-leading Wings in the semi-final round, only to lose the championship series to the Canadiens, 4 games to 1.

In the four Detroit-Montréal matchups, Detroit went home with the Cup three times. But there are fans and hockey historians,

especially in Montréal, who say that the Canadiens likely would have won the 1954-55 Cup and evened things up had it not been for an unfortunate – and genuinely riotous – incident near the season's end.

The trouble erupted in March 1955 when, with just four games left in the schedule, the Canadiens were leading the league. During an away game against Boston, Rocket Richard was high-sticked by defenseman Hal Laycoe. The contact opened Richard's scalp (eight stitches were needed to sew him back together) and threw him into a blind rang. Swinging hard, he broke his stick over Laycoe's back and then took on anyone in sight, including one official, Cliff Thompson, stunning him with a stick to the head. The result: league president Clarence Campbell suspended Richard for the rest of the season, plus the post-season action, costing The Rocket the point leadership for the year, and the Canadiens his services.

But the problem and all its ugliness did not end there. The Montréal fans, blindly certain that their beloved Rocket had been wronged and that fighting was basic to the game, were outranged at Campbell's decision. Further, they regarded the suspension as being ethnic in nature – an arrogant slap in the face for Canada's French-speaking people by a representative of the English-speaking elite. Thus, their mood was vicious when the team came home to the Forum for a meeting with the opponent who by now had become their arch enemy and who was closing in fast in the race for first place, Detroit – so vicious, in fact, that 200 policemen were placed on duty to keep the peace. It was a wise precaution because Campbell, in a show of authority and courage, decided to attend the game and, with his secretary, entered a virtual lion's den a few minutes after the opening face-off. A fan walked up to him and extended his hand in an apparent gesture of friendship, only to let fly with a punch when Campbell extended his own hand in return.

That did it. Instantly, a riot broke out in the stands, complete with flying eggs and refreshments, fistfights and a smoke bomb. Campbell and his secretary were quickly ushered to safety through a side door and, when the arena could no longer contain the melee, the fans poured into the streets and spread out for several blocks to overturn cars, topple garbage cans, loot stores and smash windows in shops and homes. The outburst, which did several

Left: Clarence Campbell on the ice of the Montréal Forum.

Below: The two Richards (fourth and fifth from left) follow the action on the ice.

million dollars worth of damage, lasted for hours and was finally calmed by the man who had caused it all in the first place. Richard went on the radio, said that he had been at fault in the Bruin fiasco, pleaded with the rioters to go home, and promised them a first-place next year.

The outcome of all the trouble: in a terse hand-written note to their front office, Campbell declared the game forfeited by the Canadiens; they fell to second place while Detroit surged into first; and, with Richard lost in the playoffs, they sacrificed (in the opinion of many a fan and historian) the Cup to the Wings.

Beginning in 1956-57, Detroit's fortunes turned sour for the remainder of the decade. Though placing first in the league that year, the Wings dropped the Cup semi-finals to Boston in 1957-58, they fell to third place and again lost the Cup semi-finals, this time to Montréal. For the rest of the decade, they placed in the bottom half of the standings and were not to play a first-place year until the mid-1960s.

And what of the Canadiens? Starting with their 1955-56 win over Detroit, they dominated Cup play for the rest of the decade. In great part, their success has been attributed to the Richard incident. Though a fine coach, Dick Irvin had been a source of worry to the Canadiens for several years because of the way he worked with his players. It was his style to needle them to greater effort, a style traditional among many coaches in all sports, but one that did not work well with the mercurial Montréal squad. Irvin was widely blamed for not keeping Richard soothed and thus contributing to the Boston fight that started all the trouble. In the wake of the riot, Irvin was dismissed and moved to the Black Hawks. The retired Canadien great, Toe Blake, took his place, remained for 13 years, and—riding his players with a tight yet disciplined rein—immediately led the team to five Cup victories:

1955-56: 4 games to 1 over Detroit
1956-57: 4 games to 1 over Boston
1957-58: 4 games to 2 over Boston
1958-59: 4 games to 1 over Toronto
1959-60: 4 games to 0 over Toronto

The Montréal Cup total for the decade: six Cups, five of them in a row, giving the team two records that have yet to be broken – most Cups in a decade and most consecutive Cups.

Below: Gordie Howe (#9) in a pileup at the goal mouth.

And so closed a ten-year period that had witnessed some of the league's most exciting moments on and off the ice and that, along the way, had produced two new rules, both intended (if that were possible) to make the game more exciting. In 1951, the league enlarged the goal cage from 3-by-7-feet to 4-by-8 feet and enlarged the face-off circle from a 10-foot to a 15-foot radius. In 1956, a player in the penalty box was permitted to return to the game when the opposing team scored a goal.

THE 1960s

Here was another decade to be marked by fine individual and team performances. But, as fine as such performances were, the decade's big hockey story was to take shape in 1966 and was to be known by a single name: expansion.

Individually, Gordie Howe, playing his fifteenth season as the decade opened, continued to be his usual superb and durable self, collecting no fewer than 70 points per season for the ten-year period (with one exception: 65 in 1966-67) and rising to 103 on one occasion – 1968-69. In 1962-63, he led the league with 86 points (38 goals and 48 assists), with his goal total giving him the goal championship for the year.

An equally great decade-long performance was recorded by the once-lowly Chicago Black Hawks. Perhaps because of the 'Muldoon curse' and more likely because of owner Frederic McLaughlin's 'revolving door' policy for coaches, the team had languished in the bottom half of the league's standings for 20 discouraging years after taking the 1937-38 Stanley Cup. Matters reached their lowest point in the mid-40s when McLaughlin died and the club was left rudderless, with a gate so bad that there was doubt the franchise could stay afloat.

Though Chicago's fortunes looked desperate to the public, matters were actually starting to

Above: Jean Béliveau (in white) fakes out the Maple Leaf goalie.

Left: Hall of Fame defenseman Pierre Pilote of the Chicago Black Hawks.

Right: Stan Mikita (right), the Hall of Fame center of the Chicago Black Hawks.

Below: Glenn Hall, the Hall of Fame goalie of the Chicago Black Hawks, falls on the ice to make a save.

improve inside the club. Two years after McLaughlin's death, a new ownership took over – Arthur Wirtz and his partner, the wealthy James D Norris (who, on failing in an attempt to buy the team back in the 30s, had purchased the Detroit Red Wings instead and whose family continued to hold a share in the Wings). Norris immediately repeated his Detroit experience. Pouring money into the Hawks, he stabilized a thoroughly discouraged club and began to rebuild it. The rebuilding was accelerated in the mid-1950s when he hired Tommy Ivan as his coach and general manager. Ivan had just coached Detroit to its sixth consecutive first-place finish and an impressive three Stanley Cups. He held the Hawks' coaching reins for little more than a season, but continued to serve as a club executive.

Ivan concentrated on strengthening Chicago's mediocre farm system, bringing to it three future Hall of Famers – defenseman Pierre Pilote, center Stan Mikita and a youngster named Bobby Hull, who would achieve big-league stardom when he was switched from the center spot to left wing. Pilote moved up to the parent club in 1955-56, Hull in 1957-58 and Mikita in 1958-59. Another superb addition and future Hall of Famer – Detroit's veteran goalkeeper Glenn Hall – joined in 1957-58. By 1960, the Hawks, now coached by Rudy Pilous, were not only fielding these men but also wing Kenny Wharram, a Chicago mainstay since 1951-52 and thought to be the fastest skater of the time; fellow wing Alvin (Ab) McDonald, in

the third season of what would be a 16-year career; and defenseman Elmer Vasko, who would spend 14 years with the NHL and two with the yet-to-be-born World Hockey Association. Chicago's glory days were at hand.

Of the group, Mikita and Hull proved to be the most memorable. Playing for a time at center in 'The Scooter Line' (with McDonald and Wharram on the wings), the Czechoslovakian-born Mikita emerged as one of the game's greatest battlers, usually besting opponents who towered above his 5-foot-9-inch frame and quickly earned from annoyed enemy fans in Montréal the nickname 'Le Petit Diable' (The Little Devil). In his first seven seasons, Mikita seemed to spend as much time in the penalty box as on the ice. In 1963-64, he led the league in penalty minutes, racking up 149. As a testament to his skill, however, he nevertheless took the league's point championship that same year, recording 89 (39 goals and a league-leading 50 assists).

Shocking the fans, Mikita completely changed his playing personality in 1965-66, transforming himself from a brawler to a highly controlled skater. According to hockey legend, the switch came about because of an encounter with his young daughter after she had watched him in action on television. She innocently wanted to know why everybody else got to play so much while her father spent most of his time cooling his heels and temper in the penalty box. Unable to answer, Mikita decided to behave differently in the future.

The new Mikita's production rose steadily as his penalty assessments declined. In 1966-67, he topped the league with 97 points (35 goals and a league-leading 62 assists) while putting in a mere 12 minutes of penalty time. He again sat at the top in points in 1967-68: 87 (40 goals and 47 assists), with 14 minutes of penalty time. Of equal importance, in those same two seasons, he was awarded the Hart Memorial Trophy as the NHL's Most Valuable Player, plus

the Lady Byng Trophy for sportsmanship and gentlemanly conduct. Mikita, who would play for 22 years, went into the Hall of Fame in 1983.

Mikita was an acknowledged superstar, but throughout his career he played second fiddle to Chicago's ranking commodity of the day — Bobby Hull. Hull served not only as the Hawks' basic mainstay but also as its principal draw and the darling of the Chicago fans through the 1960s and into the early 70s, right to that day when he signed for five years with the Winnipeg Jets of the new World Hockey Association for the then unheard-of bonus of $1 million. The adulation shown him, in the stands and in the press, was grounded in a number of factors — his blond good looks and flamboyant, powerful, and graceful skating style, all of which got him his nickname, 'The Golden Jet'; his consummate skill; his sheer courage and his scoring ability.

All of these characteristics made headlines and have since gone into hockey lore. For instance, in the matter of his power and skill, there was the 'shadow' strategy that the opposition developed in an effort to thwart him. All teams assigned a special man, usually the

Above: Black Hawk goalie Glenn Hall guards the net.

Far left: Superstar and Hall of Famer Bobby Hull of the Chicago Black Hawks.

opposing right wing, to cover Hull exclusively, 'shadowing' him wherever he went and trying to put a stop to his scoring shenanigans. Such stars-in-their-own-right as John Ferguson and Claude Provost of the Canadiens, Eddie Westfall of the Bruins, and Bob Nevin of the Rangers spent goodly portions of their careers chasing after Hull, giving him a bad time, and getting a battling bad time in return.

As for his courage, there was that night in the 1960s when, during a Cup playoff against Detroit, he took a stick across the face and landed in the hospital with a smashed nose. Ignoring the doctor's prognosis that he would not play again in the series, he walked out of his room and was in uniform for the next game, his face almost covered with a plaster dressing that made breathing next to impossible.

And his scoring abilities? That plaster-bandaged night, he produced a hat trick (originally three goals but then three goals without another score in between). In 1961-62, Hull led the league in goals and points, tallying 50

Below: Chicago Black Hawk left wing Bobby Hull.

scores for the goal championship, plus 34 assists for 84 points. He took the scoring lead again in 1963-64 with 43 tallies. Then, at mid-decade, The Golden Jet did what no man before him had done. He broke through a scoring barrier that had existed since the birth of the league.

Rocket Richard had arrived at that barrier in 1944-45 when he scored 50 goals in a season, doing so in 50 games. Hull and Montréal's Bernie Geoffrion had reached the barrier in 1961-62, tying Richard's mark but taking more than 50 games to get the job done. But, so far, no one had gotten beyond the 50-mark in a single year.

Then came the 1965-66 season. Though out of five games early in the season because of a knee injury, Hull recorded goal 50 in game 57. His efforts now to post the tie-and-record-breaking 51st goal became the premier sports story of the year, a story that hung fire while he went scoreless in games 58, 59 and 60. Game 61, a home stand against the Rangers, drew 21,000 spectators to Chicago Stadium — 4000 beyond the arena's listed seating capacity. They sat with breathless impatience while Hull was held at bay in the first and second periods. In the third period, after leading a power play that brought the Hawks up to the Ranger goal, Hull let fly with a wrist shot at the net. In the same split-second teammate Stan Mikita scooted across the goal mouth and tipped goalie Cesare Maniago's stick. Maniago recovered quickly, but not in time to stop the puck. It skidded home at 5:34 in the period for Hull's 51st goal.

Left: Bernie 'Boom Boom' Geoffrion (in white) scores a goal against the Toronto Maple Leafs.

Below: George 'Punch' Imlach of the Toronto Maple Leafs — a Hall of Famer.

But there was more to come. Hull broke his own record three times before the 70-game season ended, winding up with 54 goals. He went on to better his mark in 1968-69, driving home 58 goals in a 76-game season. Hull put in his best scoring year in 1974-75 when, playing with Winnipeg, he produced 77 goals.

On top of all else, Hull did much to alter the nature of the pro game. He did so by popularizing the slapshot that had been introduced by Montréal's Bernie Geoffrion and the Rangers' Andy Bathgate. Able to drive the puck at speeds in excess of 100 miles per hour with his vicious, golf-like swing, he prompted one player after another in the league to give it a try. Soon, with the puck now able to streak toward the goal from a greater distance and at a greater speed than was ever possible with the wrist shot, both defensive and offensive strategies began to change throughout the league and have remained unchanged ever since.

With the likes of Hull, Mikita, Pilote, Wharram and goalie Glenn Hall leading the pack, the Hawks won the Stanley Cup in 1960-61 — their first in twenty-three years — getting the job done by dropping the Canadiens in the semi-finals and the Detroit Red Wings in the championship round. They won both sessions by the same margin, 4 games to 2. For the rest of the decade, they consistently made their way to the Cup competition (except in 1968-69 when their sixth-place finish left them out of the playoffs) and just as consistently found the trophy beyond their reach. Twice they suffered losses in the championship round. Otherwise, they failed to get beyond the semi-finals.

The Toronto Maple Leafs, who had fallen on lean times in the wake of their 1950-51 Cup victory, returned to center ice in the competitions of the early 60s. Their success was due in part to coach George (Punch) Imlach, a man with a talented eye for identifying not only sharp newcomers but veterans with some excellent years still left in them. Coming to the Leafs in 1958-59, he led them to the playoffs for the next three years, losing twice in the championship round and once in the semi-finals. Then — with a lineup featuring such youngsters as center Dave Keon and wing Frank Mahovlich and such old pros as goalie Johnny Bower, wing Bob Pulford and defenseman Leonard (Red) Kelly, Bobby Baun and Carl Brewer — the Leafs took the Cup in:

> 1961-62: 4 games to 2 over Chicago
> 1962-63: 4 games to 1 over Detroit
> **1963-64:** 4 games to 3, again to Detroit

They went on to a pair of semi-final losses at Montréal's hands and then evened things by downing the Canadiens, 4 games to 2, in the 1966-67 championship round. Imlach remained at the Toronto helm until the end of 1968-69, in that time suffering two disastrous seasons. He was dismissed after taking four straight losses at Boston's hands in the Cup quarter-finals.

The Canadiens, of course, were not to be denied their share of the decade's Cup wins. Coached still by the fine Toe Blake, they claimed the Cup three times and moved to a fourth win under a new coach, Claude Ruel.

> 1964-65: 4 games to 3 over Chicago
> 1965-66: 4 games to 2 over Detroit
> 1967-68: 4 games to 0 over St Louis, an expansion team
> 1968-69: 4 games to 0 over St Louis again

The Boston Bruins, with a brilliant and aggressive young defenseman named Bobby Orr in the lineup, claimed the decade's final Cup in 1969-70. Once more, St Louis served as the punching bag, absorbing a 4-games-to-0 defeat.

By that time, the decade's single biggest hockey story had been told. It was a story that, as was said earlier, could be telescoped into a single word: expansion.

Starting back in 1927, NHL games had been broadcast on the radio. In the late 1940s, television began to aim its cameras at the ice, with the result that the game captured an increasingly large audience, with the situation being especially helped by the crowd-pleasing personality and on-ice talents of Bobby Hull. Television had likewise come to American pro football and baseball; there had been the same blossoming of interest and the two sports had replied to it by introducing a number of new teams. The NHL, however, tarried until 1966 before giving its own response. In that year, the league announced that its size would be doubled with the beginning of the 1967-68 season.

Six franchises were awarded in the next months. They went to four cities in the Midwest — St Louis, Philadelphia, Pittsburgh, and Bloomington, Minnesota (in the St Paul-Minneapolis area) — and to California's Los Angeles and Oakland. Each franchise carried a $2 million-dollar price tag, with the money to be divided among the old-line clubs. In return, they each agreed to supply the newcomers with 20 players apiece.

The distribution was accomplished through a draft of major- and farm-club personnel, held at Montréal in June, 1967. During its run of several days, the old clubs were allowed to protect the cream of their on-ice crop by sheltering 14 players (among them two goalies) from the new outfits. Prior to the draft, there were 120 players at the league's major level. At its end, that number had jumped to 240.

Realizing that 12 teams in a single circuit could prove confusing to the fans, the NHL reinstituted its divisional arrangement, splitting itself into East and West Divisions. Placed in the East Division were the old-line clubs. The West took all the newcomers. When play began that 1967-68 season, the West was manned by the following units:

CALIFORNIA SEALS (at Oakland)
LOS ANGELES KINGS
MINNESOTA NORTH STARS (at Bloomington)
PHILADELPHIA FLYERS
PITTSBURGH PENGUINS
ST LOUIS BLUES

Left: Defenseman Bobby Orr of the Boston Bruins, who was elected to the Hall of Fame in 1979.

Opposite: Toe Blake (left) of the Canadiens talks with his goalie, Jacques Plante.

Above: Bernie Parent, the Hall of Fame goalie for the Philadelphia Flyers, blocks a shot.

THE 1970s

Expansion continued to be a big story through the 1970s. It was a process that involved the establishment of two conferences and four divisions, the shifting of teams from one conference or division to another, and the movement of some teams to new cities. Altogether, for fans everywhere, it added up to a confusing page in the NHL's history. To avoid that same confusion, here, in brief year-by-year sketches, is what happened:

1970: Pleased with its expansion clubs and the fans they are drawing, the league grants two new franchises and brings its team total to 14. One franchise is awarded to Buffalo, with the other going to Vancouver. Buffalo's club is christened the Sabres, while the Vancouver operation

In great part, the expansion clubs were manned by as-yet untested prospects and veterans nearing the ends of their careers. Play in the West was not expected to be memorable, but it turned out to be better than anticipated, due to some veteran know-how on the one hand and a harvest of youthful exuberance on the other. Of the 144 games played against the East's old-liners, the West won 40 and tied 18, altogether a respectable record (league president Campbell had predicted just 30 wins). Further, contrary to the fear that – despite the growing interest in hockey – they would not fare well at the gate until firmly established, all but one drew good houses. Only the California Seals had to endure a struggle. In a bid to improve its fortunes through a stronger identity with its home city, the club changed its name to the Oakland Seals at mid-season, but never did do well and a decade later moved to Cleveland.

St Louis emerged as the strongest West team and advanced to the Cup finals for the first three years of the West's existence. There, as already reported, it served as little more than a punching bag for the East's representatives.

With new teams on its hands and reports of encouraging gate receipts, the league expanded its schedule twice in the late 1960s. It set a 74-game schedule for all clubs in 1967-68 and increased the number to 76 the following year.

chooses the name Canucks. Both clubs go into the East Division. At the same time, the league shifts an old-line outfit – the Chicago Black Hawks – to the West. The move is made to strengthen the competition coming out of the West.

1972: The league grows to 16 teams this year. Franchises are granted to the Atlanta Flames and the New York Islanders. Atlanta is assigned to the West Division. The Islanders are placed in the East.

1974: The award of two new franchises – to the Kansas City Scouts and the Washington Capitals – brings the NHL's strength to 18 clubs. More heavily manned than ever before in its history, the circuit abandons its divisional set-up and rearranges itself into two conferences – The Prince of Wales Conference and, in honor of the league

president, the Clarence Campbell Conference. Each conference is split into two divisions, with each named for a hockey great. They are:

PRINCE OF WALES CONFERENCE
NORRIS AND ADAMS DIVISIONS

CLARENCE CAMPBELL CONFERENCE
PATRICK AND SMYTHE DIVISIONS

The 18 teams are divided equally between the conferences. The seasonal schedule, which had been increased to 78 games in 1970, rises now to 80.

1976: This year sees two financially troubled clubs move to new cities. The Oakland Seals, continuing to suffer the fan indifference that has bothered them since

Below: Action in a game between the New York Islanders and the Montréal Canadiens.

their inception in 1976, transfer to the Midwest and become the Cleveland Barons. The Kansas City Scouts pack their bags and head for Denver, where they play as the Colorado Rockies.

1978: The circuit loses a team and drops in strength to 17 clubs. After struggling for two years in their new home, the Cleveland Barons merge with the Minnesota North Stars. The merger causes a slight realignment in the conferences. Originally assigned to the Campbell Conference, the North Stars are shifted to the Wales Conference.

1979: In this, its year of greatest growth since the 1967 expansion, the league balloons to 21 clubs, the number it continued to carry throughout the following decade. The four new teams come from the competing World Hockey Association, which, formed in 1972, has just gone out of business. The additions are: the Edmonton Oilers, the Québec Nordiques, the Hartford Whalers (formerly the New England Whalers), and the Winnipeg Jets. The Oilers and Jets go to the Campbell Conference. The Wales Conference receives the Nordiques and Whalers.

In the midst of its expansion and the logistical problems involved in settling the new teams within the circuit, the NHL was suddenly faced with a competing league. In 1972, the World Hockey Association came into being, founded by sports groups who wanted to cash in on the game's growing popularity but who didn't want to come up with the $6 million now being required for an NHL franchise. They went into the new circuit for about $300,000 apiece.

The Association, which would survive for a

Opposite: Wayne 'The Great' Gretzky, the all-star center for the Edmonton Oilers.

Below: Wayne Stephenson in goal for the Philadelphia Flyers.

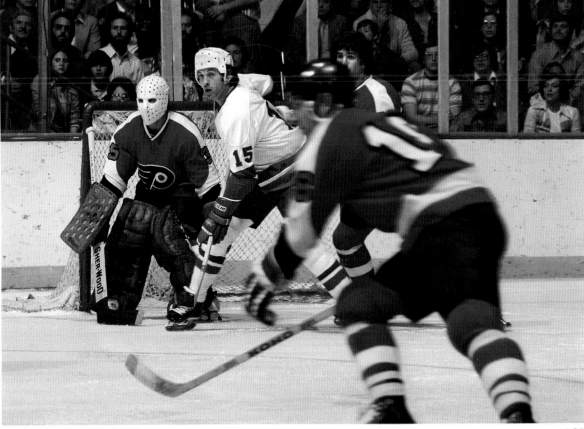

mere seven years, was to have a checkered career, with some of its clubs doing well at the gate while others — especially those located in smaller cities — floundered and were shifted from locale to locale in a desperate effort to keep them afloat. Before finally closing its doors, the circuit had put teams on the ice in more than 20 US and Canadian cities. Among the most successful of its outfits were the Alberta (later, Edmonton) Oilers, the Chicago Cougars, the Cleveland Crusaders, the Houston Aeros, the Los Angeles Sharks, the Minnesota Saints (at St Paul), the New England Whalers (playing at Boston Gardens) the New York Raiders (playing at Madison Square Garden), the Ottawa Nationals, the Québec Nordiques and the Winnipeg Jets.

Though the WHA owners may not have wanted to pay the NHL's franchise fee, they showed no fear when it came to parting with millions to obtain top personnel. Theirs was not a gesture of generosity but one of necessity. They realized full well that their only chance to attract good crowds right from the start lay in securing already established stars. They went after them with a vengeance that, in an era yet to become accustomed to spectacular sports pay checks did more than startle the NHL and the public.

For openers, they went to Bernie Parent, Toronto's rugged goaltender and a future two-time winner of the Vezina Trophy. A Miami franchise to be called the Screaming Eagles bought his services for $500,000 and then, finding that it would never be able to field a team, sent him to the Philadelphia Blazers. He remained with the club, suffering an injury while it suffered through a series of front-office and on-ice disasters, among the latter a string of nine straight losses. The next year, he rejoined the NHL, moving across town to rejoin one of his former employers — the Philadelphia Flyers — and win the two Vezina awards.

Acquired next was the Black Hawks' premier attraction, Bobby Hull. After prolonged negotiations, Hull signed a WHA contract worth, in total, $3.75 million. Of that sum, $2.75 million tied him down to a ten-year deal as player-coach. Hull received the remaining $1 million as a cash bonus, the largest bonus paid to that date in pro hockey.

Figured on an annual basis, the Boston Bruins' fine drawing card, center Derek Sanderson, got an even better deal: $2.75 million for five years — $530,000 per year as compared to an average of $375,000 annually for Hull's combined salary-bonus. Sanderson joined Parent on the Philadelphia Blazers for the 1972-73 season. When the team ran into its string of problems, Sanderson asked to be released and offered to return a part of his salary. The Blazers, themselves wanting out of the deal, gave him a million-dollar settlement. He was back home with the Bruins before the season ended.

Perhaps the New York Rangers were the hardest pressed of all by the WHA forays. Their top scorer, wing Vic Hadfield, was offered a $1-million contract, as was their superb defenseman, Brad Park. Handsome offers also went to center Jean Ratelle, wing Rod Gilbert and center Walt Tkaczuk. The Rangers, however, stepped in and stymied the raids by signing Hadfield and Park to five-year contracts worth about $1 million each. Ratelle and Gilbert signed for slightly less, and Tkaczuk accepted a

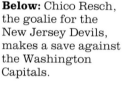

Below: Chico Resch, the goalie for the New Jersey Devils, makes a save against the Washington Capitals.

$100,000 offer.

Though the Rangers saved their own on-ice hides, they earned little but anger from their fellow NHL clubs. The league's player salaries had always been on the modest side – for example, Park had been earning around $12,000 – and had been kept there by a quiet agreement among the club owners. In the eyes of the owners, the Rangers had broken that agreement and had opened the way to an era of constantly increasing salaries.

The WHA raids were at their heaviest just before the circuit's 1972-73 opening, but they continued through the next years, causing a financial war that promised to bleed both leagues dry. In 1973, Detroit's indestructible Gordie Howe, now 45 years old and in the 23rd year of his amazing career, jumped to the WHA, going to the Houston Aeros. At the urging of the Red Wings' management, he had retired to a front office job with the club in 1971 and, now bored with it, readily accepted the new circuit's offer. Of all the records that he was to set, he collected one of his oddest at Houston: he played on the same team with his two sons, wing Mark and defenseman Marty. With Howe aboard, the Aeros took a first-place finish in his first season and then twice claimed the WHA's equivalent to

the Stanley Cup – the AVCO Trophy (donated by the Avco Financial Services Company).

Howe stayed with Houston until the start of the 1977-78 season, at which time he moved to the New England Whalers. He rejoined the NHL in 1979 when his club, renamed the Hartford Whalers, entered the league.

In 1977, the bidding war turned in a new direction. NHL President Clarence Campbell retired and was replaced by young John A Ziegler Jr, the first American to hold the post. Knowing what the war was doing to the two leagues, aware that the WHA was perennially on shaky financial ground and painfully aware that some of his own clubs were in deep trouble (notably, the former Oakland Seals who had moved to Cleveland and, on going broke there, were now merging with Minnesota), he set about developing plans to merge the two leagues. His plan never became a reality. The WHA went out of business in 1979, with its Edmonton, Hartford, Québec, and Winnipeg franchises being immediately absorbed into the NHL and expanding the league to 21 teams.

Before the NHL-WHA story closes, one last point must be mentioned. The two enemies found themselves on the same side of the fence and facing a common opponent – Soviet Russia – on five occasions during the 1970s. In 1972, arrangements were made to have Soviet teams visit the West periodically for a series of matches with squads composed of players from

Above: Gordie Howe (second from left, front row), after being elected to the Hall of Fame as a Red Wing, came out of retirement to play for the Houston Aeros and then the Hartford Whalers.

the NHL and WHA. The meetings, which are remembered as the International Series, took place in 1972, 1974, 1975-76, 1977-78 and 1979. The matches yielded the following results:

1972: Team Canada (manned by NHL personnel) met the Soviet National team for eight games, taking the series 4 games to

Right: The brilliant Bobby Hull left the Chicago Black Hawks to play for the Winnipeg Jets in the new World Hockey Association.

Opposite: The Edmonton Oilers, new to the NHL, square off against the Chicago Black Hawks.

Below: Gordie Howe and his two sons, Mark and Marty, played for the Houston Aeros of the World Hockey Association.

3, with 1 tie.

1974: Team Canada (this time consisting solely of WHA players) went against the Soviet National Team, losing the eight-game series 4 games to 1, with 3 ties.

1975-76: Playing one game each in what was called the 'Super Series,' eight NHL clubs (Boston, Buffalo, Chicago, Montreal, Philadelphia, Pittsburgh, and the New York Rangers and Islanders) faced a string of Soviet squads, coming away winners, 5 games to 2, with 1 tie.

1977-78: All-Star squads from the Soviet Union and Czechoslovakia met teams from the WHA in a string of matches that ran for more than three weeks. The WHA defeated the Soviet visitors 4 games to 3, with 1 tie, then overwhelmed the Czechs 6 games to 1, with 1 tie.

1979: A three-game meeting, called the Challenge Cup series, ended with a team of NHL performers defeating the Soviet Union, 2 games to 1.

Despite its many problems, the NHL produced some fine individual and team performances in the 1970s. Among the finest of the individual exploits in the first years of the decade were those of two Boston Bruins — defenseman Bobby Orr and center Phil Esposito. Both had joined the Bruins in the latter 1960s — Orr in 1966-67 as a rookie, and Esposito a year later after four seasons with the Black Hawks. Both emerged as full-fledged stars by 1969-70 and both played their best years in the early 1970s.

Cut in the mold of early greats Lester Patrick and Cyclone Taylor, Orr did not believe in limiting himself to a defensive role. He constantly

gathered in the puck near center ice, usually flicking it away from an opponent, and then moved it with lightning-like speed deep into enemy territory, arriving near the goal mouth for an attempted score or a sharply-hit pass to teammate Esposito, who customarily stationed out to the right of the net, snapped the puck home. Orr brought to his position an aggressive style that hadn't been seen in defenders for years, thrilling the fans and inspiring so many of his colleagues to follow suit that he opened the door to an era of hard-driving, attacking defensemen.

By the time the 1970s were at hand, his aggressiveness was making Orr's record look as if it belonged to a wing or center. From 1969-70 through 1971-72, he led the NHL in assists, posting respectively 87, 102, and 80. His 87 assists in 1969-70, along with 33 goals, gave him 120 points for the top spot in that department. In 1973-74, Orr again led in assist production, this time with 90. Then, in 1974-75, he led in both assists and points: 89 assists and, with 46 goals added, 135 points.

The opening of the door to a hard-driving and attacking defense was not Orr's only effect on pro hockey. He also exerted a lasting influence on the game's economics. Orr was the first player to employ an attorney – R Alan Eagleson of Toronto – to handle his contract negotiations. This strategy was to become common practice within a few years and would result in steadily increasing player pay. In time, Eagleson headed the founding of the NHL Players Association.

And in time, Eagleson and Orr became enmeshed in prolonged Bruin negotiations that

ended with Orr leaving Boston and signing with the Black Hawks in 1976-77. He worked with the Hawks for two seasons and then retired, the victim of long-damaged knees. The winner of five league trophies – Hart, Ross, Norris, Calder, and Smythe – over the years (see Chapter Seven for dates), Orr was inducted into the Hall of Fame in 1979, the year of his retirement.

His playing partner, the slower-moving and deliberate Esposito, came to the Bruins after a low-scoring four seasons with Chicago. On arrival, he showed immediate improvement and led the league in assists that 1967-68 season, recording 49. The next year, he upped his assists to a solid 77 and again led the league. Along with 49 goals, those 77 assists also gave him the season's point leadership, 126.

Then, with Orr, Esposito blossomed with the coming of the 1970s. It hardly seems a coincidence that his best scoring was done in the same seasons that Orr was taking the league's assist honors. For six straight years – 1969-70 through 1974-75 – Esposito led the league in goals. His record: 43, 76, 66, 55, 68 and 61. In five of those six years, he took the point leadership.

Esposito, regardless of his skills and accomplishments, was traded to the New York Rangers in 1975-76 when he was in his 13th year of NHL play. He went as part of a swap for Brad Park, Jean Ratelle and wing Joe Zanussi. He skated with the Rangers for five years before retiring in 1981 with a record of 1282 regular season games, 717 goals and 873 assists to his credit.

But, splendid as they were, Orr and Esposito were not the only ones to make hockey history in the 1970s. They were joined by many another. For example:

Marcel Dionne, the Los Angeles Kings' great center, began a string of 50-goals-or-more seasons in 1978-79 that lasted through 1982-83 and reached a career total of 1000 points in fewer games than any player before him.

Chicago's durable goalie Tony Esposito (Phil's brother) led the league in ice time for the three seasons from 1974-75 through 1976-77, putting in more than 4000 minutes of playing time in each. Starting in 1978-79, he again played three league-leading seasons, posting respectively 3780, 4140 and 3935 minutes in the crease.

Wing Al Hill of the Philadelphia Flyers set a league record when, going against the St Louis Blues on 17 February 1977, he recorded the most points made by a player in his first game – 5 (2 goals and 3 assists).

At the turn of the decade, what was assuredly the NHL's greatest playing career to that time came to a close. After rejoining the league in 1979 with his Hartford Whalers, Gordie Howe played a season and then, 52 years old and a grandfather, retired. Ended was a playing career of 32 years – almost exactly half the lifetime of the league itself. And ended was a career that had set an enviable number of all-time NHL records, chief among them:

Below: Bobby Orr brings the puck up for the Boston Bruins.

Left: Hall of Fame center Phil Esposito when he was with the Boston Bruins.

MOST SEASONS: 26 (plus 6 in the WHA)
MOST GAMES: 1767 (plus 419 in the WHA)
MOST GOALS: 801 (plus 174 in the WHA)
MOST 20-OR-MORE-GOAL SEASONS: 22 (plus 5 in the WHA)

Additionally, Howe held (and still does) the record for most appearances on the NHL's All-Star list, 21 in all, with 12 on the first team and nine on the second unit. On six occasions between 1951-52 and 1962-63, he received the Hart Trophy as the league's Most Valuable Player. The Art Ross Trophy for the league's leading point maker went to him six times in those same years (for dates of these awards and his All-Star years, see Chapter Seven). Howe holds the distinction of being named to the Hall of Fame before his playing career actually ended. He was inducted into the Hall in 1972, during the time he was holding a front office job with Detroit and the year before he moved to the WHA's Houston.

On the level of team accomplishments in the 1970s, the Canadiens were their usual splendid selves in Cup play. Under their new coach, Scotty Bowman — and manned by such impeccable talents as goaltender Ken Dryden, center Jacques Lamaire, wing Guy Lafleur and defensemen Guy Lapointe and Serge Savard — they downed Chicago, 4 games to 3, in 1970-71 and again in 1972-73, this time by a margin of 4 games to 2. Then, under Bowman's direction, they moved on to four straight Cup victories: Over the Flyers in 4 games, 1975-76; over Boston in 4 games, 1976-77; over Boston 4 games to 2, 1977-78; and over the Rangers, 4 games to 1, 1978-79.

Boston — with Orr, Esposito and the fine vet-

Above: Goalie Tony Esposito (Phil's brother) in action for the Chicago Black Hawks against the New York Islanders.

Right: Marcel Dionne of the Los Angeles Kings being checked by Bryan Trottier of the New York Islanders.

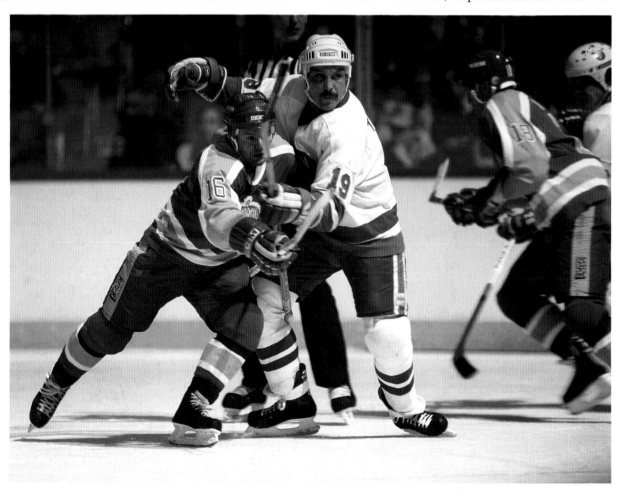

eran wing, John Bucyk (Hall of Fame, 1981) leading the way – took the Cup honors in 1971-72, defeating the New York Rangers 4 games to 2. The three Bruins scored a total of 27 goals from the opening round action through the championship games. Each accounted for 9 tallies.

In 1973-74 and 1974-75, the Cup belonged to coach Fred Shero's rough-and-tumble Philadelphia Flyers, whose bruising style of play saw them quickly dubbed 'The Broad Street Bullies' and earned them a record 1750 minutes of penalty time in 1973-74. Led by center Bobby Clarke, goaltender Bernie Parent and the brawling wingman, Dave Schultz (and taking inspiration from a pre-game appearance by singer Kate Smith, their 'good luck charm,' whose recording of 'God Bless America' always launched their home games), the Flyers first battled it out with Boston. On winning 4 games to 2, they returned the following year to meet Buffalo. The result was the same: a 4-games-to-2 victory. For their efforts, the Flyers became not only the first expansion club to win the Cup but also the first to claim it in consecutive years.

1980 TO THE PRESENT

For the first time since the NHL's first expansion in 1967-68, the league remained a cohesive unit through an entire decade, with 21 member teams. Although the number of clubs remained consistent, there were two franchise movements. The Atlanta Flames moved to Calgary, Alberta, on 24 June 1980 and became the Calgary Flames. On 30 June 1982, the Colorado Rockies were transferred to East Rutherford, New Jersey, and became the New Jersey Devils.

Late in 1989, the NHL announced plans for another expansion, with teams to begin play in the 1991-92 season.

Two dynasties won 8 out of the 10 Stanley Cups presented in the 1980s. The NY Islanders opened the decade with four consecutive Cup victories, while the Edmonton Oilers won four Cups in five years, missing out in 1986 when the Montréal Canadiens won their record 23rd Stanley Cup. In 1989, Edmonton's provincial rivals, the Calgary Flames, won their first championship in franchise history.

Left: Defenseman Denis Potvin of the New York Islanders.

Below: Scotty Bowman, the coach of the Montréal Canadiens, watches the action on the ice.

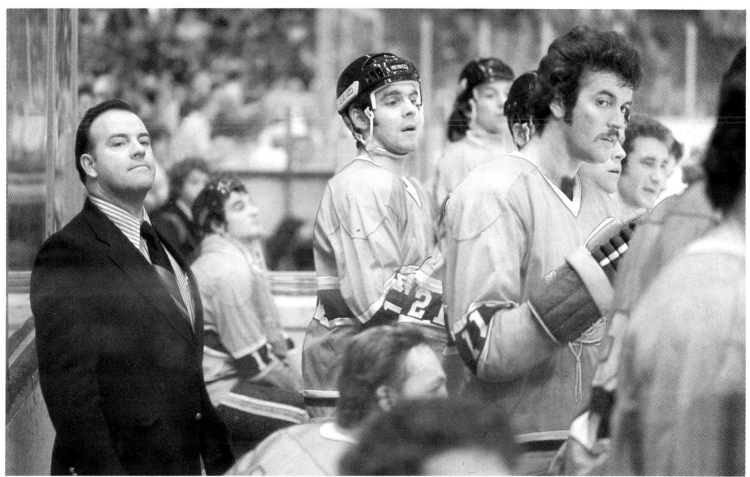

Right: Denis Potvin
of the New York
Islanders hoists the
Stanley Cup over his
head.

In 1981, a major conference realignment was undertaken, in great part to equalize the competition throughout the league; the revision saw a conference exchange of divisions that placed the Norris Division in the Campbell Conference, and the Patrick Division in the Wales Conference. By the start of the 1982-83 season, the league was organized as follows:

CLARENCE CAMPBELL CONFERENCE
SMYTHE DIVISION
CALGARY FLAMES

EDMONTON OILERS
LOS ANGELES KINGS
VANCOUVER CANUCKS
WINNIPEG JETS

NORRIS DIVISION
CHICAGO BLACK HAWKS
DETROIT RED WINGS
MINNESOTA NORTH STARS
ST LOUIS BLUES
TORONTO MAPLE LEAFS

PRINCE OF WALES CONFERENCE
ADAMS DIVISION
BOSTON BRUINS
BUFFALO SABRES
HARTFORD WHALERS
MONTRÉAL CANADIENS
QUÉBEC NORDIQUES

PATRICK DIVISION
NEW JERSEY DEVILS
NEW YORK ISLANDERS
NEW YORK RANGERS
PHILADELPHIA FLYERS
PITTSBURGH PENGUINS
WASHINGTON CAPITALS

The NHL turns another corner in 1993-94, with divisional realignment offering more geographical rivalries and two new teams beginning play in the new campaign. The Mighty

Above: Center Bobby Clarke of the Philadelphia Flyers is involved in a brawl with the New York Rangers.

Left: Bryan Trottier of the New York Islanders playing against the Minnesota North Stars.

Ducks of Anaheim, owned by the Disney Corporation, and the Florida Panthers, owned by Wayne Huizenga of the Blockbuster Video chain, give the league solid new ownership in the South and on the West Coast. The Minnesota North Stars made a move to Dallas, Texas, giving the league exposure in other new regions.

The NHL would also rename the four divisions and two conferences in 1993-94. The Norris, Smythe, Adams and Patrick divisions, in existence since 1974-75, would henceforth be known as the Central, Pacific, Northeast and Atlantic divisions. The 26 teams in the NHL were realigned this way:

WESTERN CONFERENCE
PACIFIC DIVISION
ANAHEIM MIGHTY DUCKS
CALGARY FLAMES
EDMONTON OILERS
LOS ANGELES KINGS
SAN JOSE SHARKS
VANCOUVER CANUCKS

CENTRAL DIVISION
CHICAGO BLACK HAWKS
DALLAS STARS

DETROIT RED WINGS
ST LOUIS BLUES
TORONTO MAPLE LEAFS
WINNIPEG JETS

EASTERN CONFERENCE
NORTHEAST DIVISION
BOSTON BRUINS
BUFFALO SABRES
HARTFORD WHALERS
MONTRÉAL CANADIENS
OTTAWA SENATORS
PITTSBURGH PENGUINS
QUEBEC NORDIQUES

ATLANTIC DIVISION
FLORIDA PANTHERS
NEW JERSEY DEVILS
NY ISLANDERS
NY RANGERS
PHILADELPHIA FLYERS
TAMPA BAY LIGHTNING
WASHINGTON CAPITALS

One of the first NHL expansion teams, the New York Islanders, appeared on the Cup scene at the close of the 1970s and, proceeding to dominate the action into the early 1980s, outdid

Below: Fast action in a Québec Nordique game.

Left: Mike Bossy of the New York Islanders in the center slot against the Winnipeg Jets.

Below: Wayne Gretzky of the Edmonton Oilers beats New Jersey Devils' Chico Resch for a goal.

Philadelphia's 1970s performance by taking the prize home four times in a row:

1979-80: Over Philadelphia, 4 games to 2
1980-81: Over Minnesota, 4 games to 1
1981-82: Over Vancouver, 4 games to 0
1982-83: Over Edmonton, 4 games to 0

The Islanders, coached by Al Arbour, brought an excellent array of young veterans to the Cup playoffs, among them goaltender Billy Smith, defenseman Denis Potvin and an attack unit built of Clark (Jethro) Gillies, Robert (Butch) Goring, Bryan (Trots) Trottier and Mike (The Hatchet Man) Bossy. Of the entire unit, Bossy was the figure destined to make the biggest headlines. He led the league in goals, with 69, in 1978-79, and followed suit in 1980-81 with 68. In that latter season, he tied the record set by Rocket Richard, scoring 50 goals in 50 games. Like Richard, he wrote a cliffhanger story in tying down his final tallies. Two were needed in

game 50, a meeting with the Québec Nordiques, and both were scored within four minutes of the

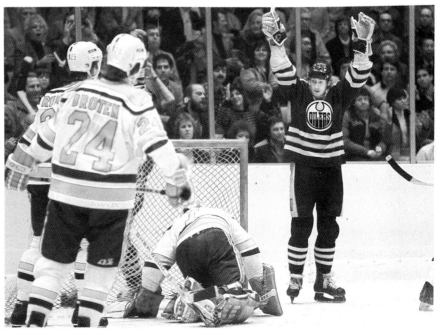

final buzzer. The 50-goals-in-50-games mark was almost tied that season by Charlie Simmer of Los Angeles. He scored 49.)

Still another expansion unit – the Edmonton Oilers – moved to the front in Cup action at the 1980s' midway mark. After taking a drubbing at Islander hands the year before, the Oilers knocked off their arch-enemies, 4 games to 1 (scoring one shutout along the way) in 1983-84. They returned to the Cup playoffs in 1984-85 to emerge as champions with a 4-games-to-1 victory over the Philadelphia Flyers. In 1986-87 they were on top again, over the Flyers 4 games to 3, and they followed it up with a Cup victory over the Bruins in four games in 1987-88. The Oilers closed out the decade with a 4-1 Cup victory over the Bruins in 1989-90.

Like the Islanders, the Glen Sather-coached Edmonton squad featured a string of fine young veterans, among them defensemen Kevin Lowe and Paul (Coff) Coffey, thought to be the fastest skater in the league, and, on offense, Wayne Gretzky, Jari Kurri, Glenn Anderson, Mark Messier and rugged Dave Semenko. None of these players is still with the Oilers – and one of them has become one of the great icons of the sport. Now with the Los Angeles Kings, Wayne Gretzky is steadily fashioning for himself one of the NHL's most notable careers.

A brilliant amateur, Gretzky turned professional in 1978 when, at age 17, he was put under contract by the WHA's Indianapolis Racers. Beset by more financial problems than usual that year, the Racers passed him on to the Edmonton Oilers during the season and then watched him – despite widespread fears that his six-foot straw-like frame would never withstand the rigors of pro play – develop into a star of such magnitude that his appearances almost invariably guaranteed capacity houses. Soon dubbed 'The Great,' the youngster played his first NHL game at age 18 and in 1980-81 led the league in assists and points – tallying 109 in the former category and 164 in the latter. He did even better in 1981-82, leading all across the board with 92 goals, 120 assists and 212 points.

Gretzky's 92 goals in 1981-82 currently ranks as an all-time record in the scoring department. Topping that was another 1981-82 achievement: the surpassing of the Richard and Bossy records of 50 goals in 50 games. Gretzky outdid them by coming up with his 50 tallies in 39 games, the fastest half-hundred goals in NHL history. By game 50's final buzzer, he had clocked 61 goals. In 1983-84, he returned with another 61 goals in 50 games.

In addition to his most-goals and most-points (215 in 1985-86) feats, Gretzky holds a string of other all-time league records at the time of this book's writing. They include:

MOST ASSISTS, ONE SEASON: 163 (1985-86)
MOST GOALS, ONE SEASON, including playoffs: 100 (1983-84)
MOST ASSISTS, ONE SEASON, including playoffs: 174 (1985-86)
MOST POINTS, ONE SEASON, including playoffs: 255 (1984-85)

To date, Gretzky has won the Hart Trophy as the season's Most Valuable Player nine times. The Art Ross Trophy for the season's point-scoring leadership has gone to him nine times. He has received the Lady Byng Trophy three times, and, as the Most Valuable Player in the Stanley Cup playoffs, the Conn Smythe Trophy two times. For his records and the dates of his various honors, see Chapters Seven and Eight.

The 1987-88 hockey season got off to rousing start when the finest players from the world's leading hockey nations met for the fourth Canada Cup tournament. Canada, led by the unbeatable duo of Wayne Gretzky and the Pittsburgh Penguins' Mario Lemieux, defended their title with a best-of-three victory over the Soviet Union, each match decided by identical 6-5 scores.

The emergence of Lemieux as a worthy successor to Wayne Gretzky's title as the world's greatest hockey player was to play itself out for much of the season. That changing of the guard at the top of the scoring ladder was completed during the 1987-88 NHL campaign, when for the first time since the 1978-79 season, a player compiled more points than Wayne Gretzky. That player was the Magnificent Mario Lemieux, who victimized opposing goaltenders for 70 goals and 98 assists. Lemieux, who had been touted as the heir apparent to the Gretzky throne since he entered the league in 1984, finally ascended to the top of the leader board by becoming only the second player in league history to compile more than 160 points in a season.

Although Lemieux's magic won him numerous personal accolades, including the Pearson, Hart and Art Ross trophies, his performance couldn't carry the Penguins into the playoffs. Despite finishing over .500 (36-35-9) for the first time since 1979, Pittsburgh finished in the basement of the Patrick Division, the NHL's toughest allotment. Only seven points separated the six teams in the division, with the New York Islanders leading the way with 88 points, the lowest total for a Patrick Division winner since the league realigned in 1975.

The New Jersey Devils, who had sat on the sidelines every spring since the team arrived in the Garden State in 1982, went undefeated in their final eight games — including an overtime victory on the last night of the schedule — to move into the postseason for the first time. The Devils, buoyed by the goaltending of Sean Burke and the timely scoring of Kirk Muller, Pat Verbeek and John MacLean, took the Boston Bruins to the seventh game of the conference finals before bowing out of postseason play.

The Montréal Canadiens finished atop the Adams Division for the first time since 1981-82 with 103 points, thanks to the league's finest defensive squad and an opportunistic offense. Stéphane Richer chipped in with 50 goals for the Habs, the first Canadien to reach that vaunted mark since Guy Lafleur in 1979. A youthful Boston squad, with 11 rookies pulling on the Bruins' jersey during the regular season, came in second to Montréal with 94 points. Buffalo and Hartford grabbed the final two playoff spots. The Sabres rebounded from a dismal 1987 campaign with a 21-point improvement under coach Ted Sator. The Whalers, division winners in 1987, dropped to fourth place, prompting a slow rebuilding process that continues to this day.

Wayne Gretzky suffered through an injury-plagued season, missing 16 games with eye and knee troubles and losing the scoring title to Lemieux. Edmonton went a respectable 7-5-4 in

Gretzky's absence, prompting suggestions that the Oilers may have missed the offensive wizardry of Paul Coffey more than they missed the Great One. Coffey, who was embroiled in a contract dispute with Oilers' owner Peter Pocklington, refused to report to the team. 'Peter Puck,' as the Oilers' boss was often called in the Edmonton media, and club manager/coach Glen Sather let Coffey boil on the sidelines for half the season before dispatching him to Pittsburgh for a quartet of players. It was a sign of the times in Edmonton, and before the next season began, the Oilers' richest resource would be tapped into a new market.

The Calgary Flames, bolstered by the 100-point contributions of Hakan Loob and Mike Bullard, plus the emergence of rookie Joe Nieuwendyk and defenseman Gary Suter, captured the Smythe regular-season crown with 105 points. The Flames also made a deal that seemed to ensure Stanley Cup success, sending talented marksman Brett Hull and grinder Steve Bozek to St Louis for top-notch blueliner Rob Ramage and goaltender Rick Wamsley.

Winnipeg and Los Angeles finished third and fourth respectively. The Jets featured a pair of 40-goal scorers in Dale Hawerchuk and Paul MacLean, but they suffered defensively, allowing 310 goals over the 80-game schedule. The Kings, who had sent marquee player Marcel Dionne to the New York Rangers at the trading deadline in 1987, saw their average attendance plummet to the 11,000 mark for the fourth straight year. The Kings' majority owner Jerry Buss then unloaded the club on Bruce McNall, a collector of rare coins, who promised LA hockey fans that the Kings would soon live up to their stately name.

The Norris Division, dubbed the 'Snore-is' Division by many of its critics, featured only one team with a .500 record. The Detroit Red Wings, piloted by Jacques Demers, aka 'The Great Motivator,' improved by 15 points to climb to the top of the Norris with a 41-28-11 mark. Guided by the multi-talented Steve Yzerman, the rugged Bob Probert and the flashy Petr Klima, the Wings' performance won Demers his second consecutive Jack Adams Award as the league's top coach. St Louis, Chicago and Toronto grabbed the final three playoff berths, although the Leafs, with 52 points, would have finished last by a wide margin in any other division. The Leafs and Black Hawks combined for a major trade in the preseason, with Toronto sending team captain Rick Vaive, marksman Steve Thomas and defender Bob McGill to the Windy City for Ed Olczyk and Al Secord. The deal worked well for both sides: Olczyk led the Leafs in scoring and Vaive topped the Hawks in goals.

A well-rested Wayne Gretzky was all the Edmonton Oilers required in the postseason. Gretzky, who was planning to be married in the summer, approached the playoffs with restored determination and optimism, and the well-oiled Edmonton machine responded by mowing through their opposition in the playoffs. Gaining momentum with every game, the Oilers had little trouble reaching the Stanley Cup finals, downing the Winnipeg Jets in five games, dousing the Calgary Flames in four and then clipping the Detroit Red Wings in five matches.

The Boston Bruins, after a rough six-game series with the Sabres, met the Montréal Canadiens in the Adams Division finals. The Habs captured the opening tilt of the series, but dropped the next four to the determined Bostonians, who were seeking their first Stanley Cup finals berth in a decade. That search was fulfilled after an emotionally-draining seven-game series victory over the New Jersey Devils in the conference championship.

The Boston-New Jersey series featured one of the most embarrassing episodes in NHL history, when three amateurs were forced to officiate Game Four of the series — an incident known as 'Yellow Sunday.' Following Game Three, a 6-1 victory for Boston, Devils coach Jim Schonfeld attacked referee Don Koharski both verbally and physically, earning a one-game suspension from the league. The Devils, however, got a restraining order from a New Jersey judge that enabled Schonfeld to take his place behind the bench. In a display of solidarity, the referee and linesmen slated to work the match refused to take to the ice if Schonfeld was allowed to coach. Three amateur officials, who were part of the off-ice officiating team, were asked to substitute for the 'striking' NHL officials. After a lengthy delay, complicated further because NHL president John Ziegler could not be located, the three amateurs finally took to the ice, wearing yellow jerseys for the first period until striped sweaters could be procured. Although the game was played without incident, it was a severe black eye for the NHL.

Unfortunately, there were more problems in the Stanley Cup finals, but these were caused more by divine intervention than by human error. The Boston Bruins met the Oilers in the 1987-88 finals, where the Oilers captured the first three games, scoring the winning goal in the third period of each game. Edmonton's

Below: Boston's Craig Janney, seen here slipping under a check by Edmonton's Craig Muni, compiled 16 points for the Bruins in the 1988 playoffs.

ers and executives together on the ice and had a group picture taken, starting a tradition that continues to this day. Ironically, that image is the final portrait of the Great One wearing the Edmonton Oiler colors.

The hockey world, and indeed the entire sporting community, was shocked three months later, when on 8 August 1988 Oilers' owner Peter Pocklington and GM Glen Sather announced they had traded Wayne Gretzky, Mike Krushelnyski and Marty McSorley to the Los Angeles Kings for Jimmy Carson, Martin Gélinas, three first-round draft choices and $15 million in cash. Hockey fans across Canada were infuriated, blaming everyone from the greedy Peter Puck to Gretzky's new bride, actress Janet Jones, for this betrayal of trust. Gretzky was more than a hockey player to Canadians, he was a national symbol of how Canadians viewed themselves: polite, patient and patriotic. The entire affair had more innuendo and whispers of conspiracy than a John Le Carre novel. Both sides spent weeks blaming each other, but the fact remained that Wayne Gretzky was now an LA King, and the hockey map would never be the same.

The addition of the world's greatest hockey player certainly boosted the fortunes of the Los Angeles Kings. The classy Great Western Forum became a celebrities hangout as the brightest stars of Hollywood clustered in the stands to glimpse Tinseltown's newest commodity. With full houses roaring their approval, the Kings climbed 23 points to second place, finishing with the third most wins in the league. Los Angeles placed three scorers in the top 10: Gretzky, line mate Bernie Nicholls – who became the fourth player to score 70 goals in a season – and Luc Robitaille, who was quickly evolving into the league's best left winger. The trade to LA also forced Gretzky to establish hockey history with a different team. Entering the 1988-89 season, Gretzky was only 14 points

Left: Wayne Gretzky poses with his new LA Kings jersey after the 'trade of the century' in August 1988.

defense completely smothered the Bruins' forwards, holding the Bruins to less than 10 shots in all but one period throughout the entire series. In Game Four, with the score tied 3-3, a power failure at Boston Garden forced the postponement of the game. It was the first Stanley Cup game to be suspended since 1951.

Edmonton quickly put the Bruins on the sidelines when action resumed in Edmonton, with an easy 6-3 victory. Following the victory skate around the ice surface, Wayne Gretzky, who was selected as the Conn Smythe Trophy winner after compiling a record 13 points in the finals, gathered all the players, coaches, train-

Below: The Edmonton Oilers' players, coaches and training staff gather on the ice to celebrate their Stanley Cup win in 1988.

Above: After only one season in the City of Angels, Wayne Gretzky was selected to become the ninth captain in franchise history.

253 goals and compiled 74 points.

The Patrick Division, a free-for-all in 1988, was a two-team race in 1989. with Washington and Pittsburgh battling for top spot most of the season. Mario Lemieux asserted himself as the game's top performer, collecting 85 goals and 199 points, the third-highest total in NHL history. The Magnificent Mario led the loop in goals, assists, powerplay goals, short-handed goals and first goals. Paul Coffey, obtained midway through the 1988 schedule, was a standout along the blueline for the Pens, leading all NHL rearguards with 113 points. Rob Brown, the Canadian Junior Player of the Year in 1987, also chipped in with 118 points, despite missing 12 games. However, their offensive wizardry couldn't camouflage a porous defense that allowed 349 goals, the second highest in the league. Even the addition of Tom Barrasso, who came over from Buffalo in November, couldn't repair the defensive deficiencies that dropped the Pens to second, five points behind the Capitals.

In a surprising move that gleaned the attention of the entire sporting world, former Canadiens superstar and Hall-of-Famer Guy Lafleur announced that he was planning a comeback. Most hockey scribes scoffed at the suggestion, but the NY Rangers and GM Phil Esposito did not. Espo knew the professionalism of Lafleur would be a boost to his team and he quickly signed up the 37 year old. Not only did Lafleur make the team, but he also displayed the form that had made him one of the league's foremost entertainers, compiling 45 points in limited action.

Despite the presence of Lafleur and two outstanding rookies in Brian Leetch and Tony Granato, the Rangers resembled their baseball cousins, the Yankees, more than a contending hockey club. Phil Esposito canned coach Michel Bergeron in the last week of the season, after the team had struggled through most of the campaign, and picked up the coaching reigns himself. Espo's maneuver backfired, however, as the Broadway Blues lost every game they played with Esposito behind the bench, leading to their quick dismissal from the playoffs and Espo's quick departure from the Rangers organization.

In Washington, the Capitals made a bold attempt to reverse their postseason fortunes by trading their all-time leading scorer, Mike Gartner, and defenseman Larry Murphy to Minnesota for Dino Ciccarelli and Bob Rouse. The additions helped the Caps capture the Patrick Division flag, but it was the same old story in the playoffs, with the Capitals suffering a quick one-round knockout at the hands of the underdog Philadelphia Flyers.

The Montréal Canadiens registered their finest season since 1977-78, compiling 115 points, though they did not have a marksman among in the league's top 25 scorers. The Habs, with new coach Pat Burns implementing a system that stressed overall defense, easily captured the Adams Division crown. Russ Courtnall, stolen from the Leafs in November, Patrick Roy and Norris Trophy winner Chris Chelios were the Canadiens' leaders. The remaining three playoff spots were closely contested, with

away from surpassing Gordie Howe as the league's all-time scoring leader. On 15 October, in a game against the Oilers, Gretzky recorded career point number 1851 to drop Mr Hockey into second place on the NHL's all-time points leader board. For good measure, Gretzky later added the winner in overtime as Peter Pocklington, Bruce McNall and former champ Gordie Howe looked on.

Unfortunately for the Kings, the Calgary Flames, the best team in the NHL with 117 points, also resided in the Smythe Division, and all signs indicated that the road to the Stanley Cup would have to go through this prairie town. The Flames were red hot all season long, with Joe Mullen and Joe Nieuwendyk each reaching the magical 50-goal plateau.

The Gretzkyless Oilers dropped to third place, although Jimmy Carson, a key ingredient in the deal, reached the 100-point mark for the rebuilding champions. The Vancouver Canucks tightened up the reigns along the blueline and this improved system carried the squad into the playoffs. The Canucks, with young Trevor Linden shining on offense, and goaltender Kirk McLean and rearguard Paul Reinhart anchoring the defense, allowed only

only nine points separating Boston, Buffalo and Hartford.

Detroit captured their second consecutive Norris crown, although they finished with a less-than-impressive .500 record at 34-34-12. St Louis, Minnesota and Chicago grabbed the final three postseason slots.

For the first time in many years, the playoff race appeared to be wide open. All eyes were focused on the Smythe Division, where the Gretzky-led Kings were up against his former teammates, the Oilers, in the first round. The Kings prevailed in seven exciting matches, eliminating the defending champions from the postseason. Los Angeles ran out of miracles against the Calgary Flames, who had been blessed with a few miracles in their opening round series with Vancouver. The Flames, who finished 43 points ahead of the Canucks, needed an overtime goal in the seventh game by Joel Otto for the right to face the Kings. That was the last close shave the Flames would have until the finals. They easily turned Gretzky's Kings into paupers in four straight before grounding the Black Hawks in five quick matches.

The Montréal Canadiens had an easier road through the playoffs, harpooning the Whalers in four, blasting the Bruins in five and downing the Flyers in five. The Habs-Flyers series, a chippy affair throughout, turned particularly nasty when Flyers goaltender Ron Hextall skated 50 feet out of his cage to attack Canadiens rearguard Chris Chelios in the waning moments of the last game. Although Chelios escaped unscathed, Hextall drew a lengthy suspension that took effect at the start of the following season.

The Montréal-Calgary final was a rematch of the 1986 series, but this time the Flames' firepower overpowered the defensive-minded Habs and they slipped past Montréal in six close games. The decisive sixth match was played at the Montréal Forum and marked the first time

Left: Lanny McDonald, who scored exactly 500 goals in his NHL career, hung up his blades after the Flames won the Cup in 1989.

that the Canadiens lost the Cup on home ice. The championship finals also signified the end of Lanny McDonald's distinguished career. The mustached star, who collected both his 500th goal and 1000th point during the season, scored a key goal in the final game that gave the Flames a lead they would never surrender. Al MacInnis, the first defenseman to lead in postseason scoring, was anointed as the Conn Smythe Trophy winner.

Left: Montréal defender Craig Ludwig challenges Calgary sophomore Joe Nieuwendyk during the 1989 Stanley Cup finals.

The postseason silverware parade was headed by Wayne Gretzky, who regained the Hart Trophy as the league's MVP. Patrick Roy became the first 'triple crown' goaltender, capturing the Vezina, Jennings and Trico goaltending awards. Brian Leetch took home the Calder as the league's best freshman, while Joe Mullen captured the Lady Byng.

The 1989-90 campaign was one of the most exciting in recent memory, with an average of only 16 points separating first from fourth in the league's four divisions. Only the Boston Bruins were able to reach triple figures in points, the first time since the NHL aligned into four divisions that only one team had at least 100 points. The 1989-90 campaign also marked the arrival of a number of outstanding Soviet players, who were granted permission by their sports federation to leave the Russian leagues and join teams in the NHL for the first time. The Soviet's most explosive offensive unit, the KLM Line, migrated to the NHL, with Sergei Makarov joining the Flames while Vladimir Krutov and Igor Larionov signed with the Vancouver Canucks. Other prominent Soviet stars such as Alexei Kasatonov and Viacheslav Fetisov (New Jersey) and Helmut Baldaris (Minnesota) also made their presence felt in North America.

The Bruins, with former player Mike Milbury debuting behind the bench, combined an airtight defense with an opportunistic offense to lead the Adams Division, and all of hockey, with 101 points. Behind the blueline, the goaltending tandem of Andy Moog and Réjean Lemelin and perennial all-star Ray Bourque combined to allow only 232 goals, one of the lowest totals in Bruins history. The Boston attack was bolstered by Cam Neely's 55 goals, while newly acquired veterans Dave Poulin and Dave Christian provided inspiration and leadership.

A number of injuries hampered the Montréal Canadiens for much of the season, the most damaging being a pair of setbacks to all-star goaltender Patrick Roy. Yet, the Montréal system was so well-defined that the team still led the league in goals against, with Rick Wamsley supplying steady goaltending in Roy's absence. The Habs still managed 93 points, good for a third place finish in the Adams.

Pierre Turgeon and Dave Andreychuk each hit the 40-goal plateau to lead the Buffalo Sabres into second place with 98 points. Rick Dudley, a fiery competitor on and off the ice, replaced Ted Sator behind the bench and guided the Sabres to their best finish since 1984. Hartford grabbed the fourth playoff spot with 85 points, a full 54 points better than the sinking Québec Nordiques, who finished last in the NHL with 31 points. Although they were the league's worst team, the Nordiques were a good draw on the road, with young superstar Joe Sakic and Hall-of-Famer Guy Lafleur – who signed as a free agent with Québec after a one-year stay with the Rangers – delighting audiences around the NHL globe.

The Norris Division showed signs of improvement with three teams finishing at or above the .500 mark. The Toronto Maple Leafs compiled 80 points, their highest total in a decade. Featuring one of the league's most potent offensive attacks, the Leafs fired a team record 337 pucks behind enemy goaltenders during the campaign. Led by Gary Leeman, Ed Olczyk, Vincent Damphousse and Al 'Wild Thing' Iafrate, the Leafs excited the Gardens' faithful at Church and Carleton for most of the season.

There was delight in Detroit and outraged shock in St Louis when the Red Wings acquired Bernie Federko, the Blues' all-time leading scorer, in a preseason deal. Federko, the first player in league history to register 10 consecutive seasons with at least 50 assists, had played his entire career in St Louis and it was evident his heart was not in Motown. The Wings, who gave up Adam Oates and Paul MacLean for Federko and Tony McKegney, slumped to last place, missing the playoffs and ending the coaching career of Jacques Demers. Federko, who finished the campaign with 57 points, his lowest total since his sophomore season, retired shortly after the completion of the schedule.

The Blues, however, flourished, climbing to second place in the Norris. Oates, one of the game's finest playmaking centers, was a natural on-ice companion for Brett Hull, who led the league in goals that season with 72.

Below: Patrick Roy, who in 1986 became the youngest player ever to win the Conn Smythe Trophy, has emerged as the NHL's finest goaltender.

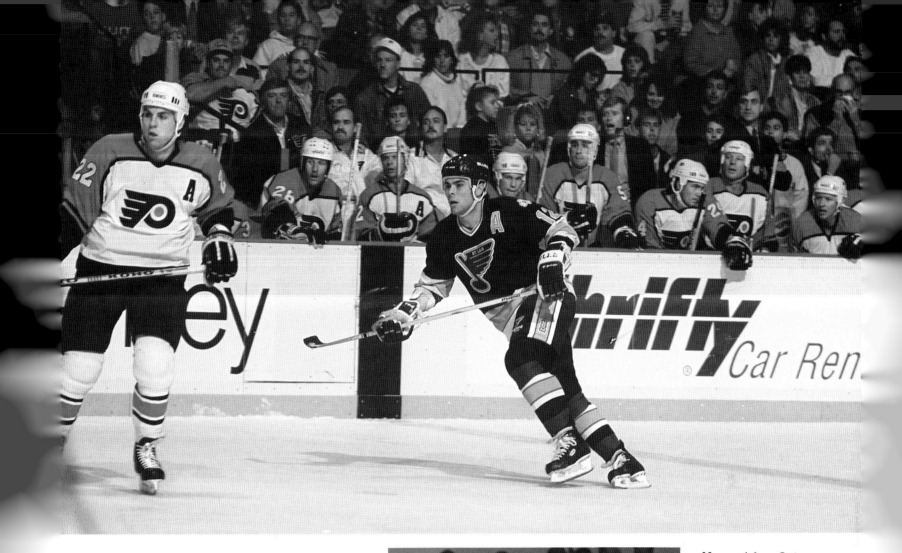

Oates drew 79 assists and collected 102 points while MacLean added 34 goals and a team-leading plus/minus mark of plus 23.

In Chicago, the Black Hawks improved by 22 points to ascend the Norris throne. Mike Keenan, who replaced Bob Murdoch as coach in 1988, guided the Hawks to their best finish in seven years. Steve Thomas with 40 goals and Steve Larmer with 90 points were the key factors in the Hawks' attack.

Mario Lemieux was unseated as the NHL's leading scorer during the 1989-90 season, after a back injury limited him to only 59 games. Despite the setback, Lemieux still managed to collect 123 points, although his Pittsburgh teammates couldn't rally without their fallen star. The Pens went winless in their last eight games to finish one point behind the NY Islanders, earning only a berth on the postseason sidelines. The battle for top spot in the Patrick Division was a three-horse race between the Rangers, Devils and Capitals. Despite a late-season swoon, the NY Rangers captured first place with new coach Roger Neilson at the reins. The Broadway Blues, bolstered by the late-season additions of Bernie Nicholls from Los Angeles and Mike Gartner from Minnesota and the superb late-season netminding of rookie Mike Richter, finished atop the standings for the first time since 1942.

Bryan Murray's eight-year reign as the coach of the Washington Capitals came to an ironic conclusion when he was fired and replaced by his brother Terry. The Caps finished below .500 for the first time since 1982, although their 78 points clinched third place in the tight Patrick Division.

Above: Adam Oates has collected at least 50 assists in every season since 1988-89.

Left: In 1988-89, Mario Lemieux joined Wayne Gretzky as the only players since Gordie Howe in 1952-53 to lead the league in goals, assists and points in the same season.

Above: Mark Messier's tireless dedication and resourceful leadership skills vaulted the Edmonton Oilers back into the Stanley Cup winner's circle in 1990.

Most of the attention during the 1989-90 season was focused on the Smythe Division, where Wayne Gretzky returned to the top of the scoring ladder with 147 points. Gretzky was closely pursued by former teammate Mark Messier, who finished in the runner-up position with 129 points, a career high. Messier's gritty performance in leading the Oilers to second place in the Smythe earned him the Hart Trophy as the league's MVP. King Gretzky's troops fell to fourth place, 10 points in arrears of third-place Winnipeg and 24 points behind the defending Cup holders, the Calgary Flames, who took the Smythe's regular-season crown with 99 points. The Flames, with Nieuwendyk, Doug Gilmour and MacInnis all recording at least 90 points apiece, were augmented by Soviet star Sergei Makarov, who was chosen as the NHL's best rookie following an 86-point performance as a freshman.

In the playoffs the Flames were burned by the LA Kings, giving the giant-killing Kings their second straight upset over a defending Cup champion. The Edmonton Oilers rebounded from a three games to one deficit to defeat the Winnipeg Jets before sweeping Gretzky's Kings from the postseason. The Oilers, led by their newly formed 'Kid Line' of Mark Lamb, Joe Murphy and Adam Graves, confidently moved into their sixth Stanley Cup finals by outlasting a determined Chicago team in six games. Once again, their opponents were the Boston Bruins, who had easily downed Montréal and Washington after a tough seven-game battle with Hartford in the opening round.

The first game of the finals was an epic battle that needed three periods of overtime to decide. Petr Klima, in one of his rare shifts in the extra session, slipped a slapshot between Andy Moog's legs after 55 minutes of overtime to give the Oilers a 3-2 win in the opening contest and a series lead they would never relinquish. Edmonton wrapped up the set in five games, outscoring Boston 20-6 and proving to the hockey world, and to themselves, that there was life after Wayne Gretzky. Bill Ranford, who brilliantly replaced injured incumbent Grant Fuhr in the Oilers' cage, was selected as the Conn Smythe Trophy winner.

There were a number of interesting off-season developments in the NHL prior to the 1990-91 season. Mike Keenan added the general manager's portfolio to his coaching duties in Chicago, and he quickly shook up the Hawks' roster. Keenan unloaded one of the Hawks' most popular players, Denis Savard, to Montréal, in return for former Norris Trophy winner Chris Chelios. It was a move that would solidify the Chicago blueline and elevate the team into the upper echelon of the NHL's elite. In another major roster move, the Winnipeg Jets sent Dale Hawerchuk, their all-time leading scorer, to Buffalo for all-star defenseman Phil Housely.

There were a number of changes in the coaching fraternity as well. Bob Johnson returned to the NHL with the Pittsburgh Penguins, one of the league's most talented, though underachieving, teams. Only four other new bench pilots were slated to start the season: Doug Riserbrough (Calgary), Bryan Murray (Detroit), Bob Gainey (Minnesota) and Dave Chambers (Québec), although that number would dramatically rise by the season's end.

The media backlash over the selection of Sergei Makarov, an 11-year veteran of the Red Army Moscow team, as the Calder Trophy winner forced the league to adapt new rules on the awarding of the annual freshman prize. Because of the influx of players from Europe, it was determined that a player must be under the age of 26 to qualify as the league's best newcomer.

One of the most alarming stories of the 1990-91 season was the erosion of the Toronto Maple Leafs franchise. Once one of the league's most respected organizations, the Leafs became the laughing stock of the NHL during the 1990-91 campaign. Although the team had seen only limited success on the ice over the past 24 years, the death of owner Harold Ballard left the team in complete disarray. Doug Carpenter was fired after a disastrous 1-9-1 start and GM Floyd Smith, in a desperate search for answers, traded away 15 players, including Al Iafrate, Ed Olczyk, Mark Osborne and John Kordic. Floyd's follies landed the Leafs in last place in the Norris and the team missed the playoffs for the fifth time in 10 years.

Despite the Leafs' misadventures, the Norris proved to be the league's most productive division, with the Chicago Black Hawks and St Louis Blues battling all season long for the NHL's top regular-season honors. The Hawks, with 49 wins and 106 points, won the President's Trophy, thanks in large part to the herculean efforts of rookie goaltender Ed Belfour. Belfour led all NHL goaltenders in games played, wins, minutes played and goals against to capture the Calder, Vezina, Jennings and Trico goaltending awards. The youth of Jeremy Roenick, the leadership of Steve Larmer and the defensive skills of Selke Award-winning forward Dirk Graham all combined to make the Hawks the league's finest all-around squad.

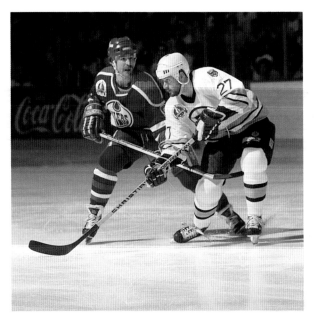

Left: Edmonton's Glenn Anderson checks Boston's Dave Christian, one of five members from Team USA's gold medal-winning team at the 1980 Olympics still active in the NHL.

Below: Chicago's Eddie Belfour captured six individual awards in 1990-91.

The St Louis Blues, powered by super sniper Brett Hull and the magic of playmaker Adam Oates, finished with 105 points, the second-best finish in franchise history. Hull scored 86 goals, the highest total in league history by a player not named Gretzky, while Oates added 90 assists and 115 points. Another secret to the Blues' success was the makeup of their defense, which resembled the great Montréal Canadiens' units of the 1970s.

Detroit and Minnesota, both with under .500 records, clinched the final two playoff posts. The North Stars, despite their .475 winning percentage, were playing inspired hockey for first-year coach Bob Gainey. Detroit, with long-time Washington pivot Bryan Murray holding down both the coach and general manager positions, had a promising cast of rookies, including Sergei Fedorov, Paul Ysebaert and Keith Primeau.

One of the major surprises of the 1990-91 season was the play of the Pittsburgh Penguins, who captured the Patrick Division regular-season title despite having Mario Lemieux in the lineup for only 26 games. The Penguins' GM Craig Patrick, in his first full season at the helm of the team, supplied coach Bob Johnson with a rich assortment of talented veterans such as Larry Murphy, Grant Jennings, Peter Taglianetti, Ulf Samuelsson, Scott Young and Gordie Roberts to help such maturing youngsters as Jaromir Jagr, Mark Recchi, Kevin Stevens and Paul Stanton. Perhaps his finest maneuver was acquiring Ron Francis from the Hartford Whalers. Francis, the Whalers' all-time leading scorer, was an outstanding individual, both on and off the ice. Add to this mix such Stanley Cup

veterans as Joe Mullen, Bryan Trottier and Paul Coffey and it was evident the Penguins were ready for a serious shot at Lord Stanley's vaunted mug.

The Patrick Division was once again the loop's toughest aggregation, with only 12 points dividing the first five teams. The Rangers, Capitals and Devils won the 80-game lottery to decide the remaining three playoff berths.

With Mario Lemieux on the shelf most of the season, Wayne Gretzky returned to the top of the scoring ladder again, collecting 163 points to lead all NHL scorers. Gretzky, who led the league in assists for the 12th consecutive season, became the first player to reach the 2000-point mark, in a game against the Winnipeg Jets on 26 October 1990. Gretzky's Kings played up to his level by finishing in first place for the first time in franchise history, winning the Smythe crown with 102 points. Calgary, Edmonton and Vancouver finished 2-3-4 in the Smythe although Vancouver, with Pat Quinn holding the reins as general manager, seemed poised for a rebirth of fortune. Quinn made a blockbuster deal with St Louis at the trading deadline that breathed new life into the franchise, obtaining Geoff Courtnall, Cliff Ronning, Sergio Momesso and Robert Dirk for Garth Butcher and Dan Quinn. Calgary received an outstanding season from 5'6" Theoren Fleury, who became the smallest player in NHL history to score 50 goals in a season. Another key contributor for Calgary was rearguard Al MacInnis, who became the fourth defenseman to record 100 points in a season. Edmonton, without Jari Kurri, who played in Italy, and Mark Messier, who missed 27 games due to injury, recorded their fewest wins since 1981.

The Boston Bruins retained their Adams family crown by using their rich farm system to supply talent through most of the season. The Bruins, with 11 rookies spending time with the team, made only one transaction during the season, receiving Petri Skriko from Vancouver in January. Ray Bourque and Cam Neely were solid as usual while Ken Hodge, Jr and training camp walk-on Jeff Lazaro were the best of the freshman crop.

Montréal, Buffalo and Hartford completed the playoff picture in the Adams. Montréal's tight defensive structure, Buffalo's free-wheeling offense and Hartford's ability to stay ahead of the lowly Québec Nordiques were the key elements in the Adams equation. Québec finished in the league's basement for the second consecutive season, giving them first shot at Eric Lindros, the most heralded junior prospect since Mario Lemieux. Although Lindros was already on record as saying he would not play

for the Nordiques, Québec boss Marcel Aubut was adamant that the team would choose Lindros at the annual draft in June.

In one of the wildest postseasons in recent memory, two teams that missed the playoffs in 1990 made their way to the Stanley Cup finals in 1991, a championship series first. Pittsburgh, with a healthy Mario Lemieux leading the way, squeezed past New Jersey, Washington and Boston to reach the finals for the first time in franchise history. While it seemed just a matter

Below: In only his second-ever playoff appearance, Mario Lemieux led the Penguins to the Stanley Cup championship with 44 points in 23 games.

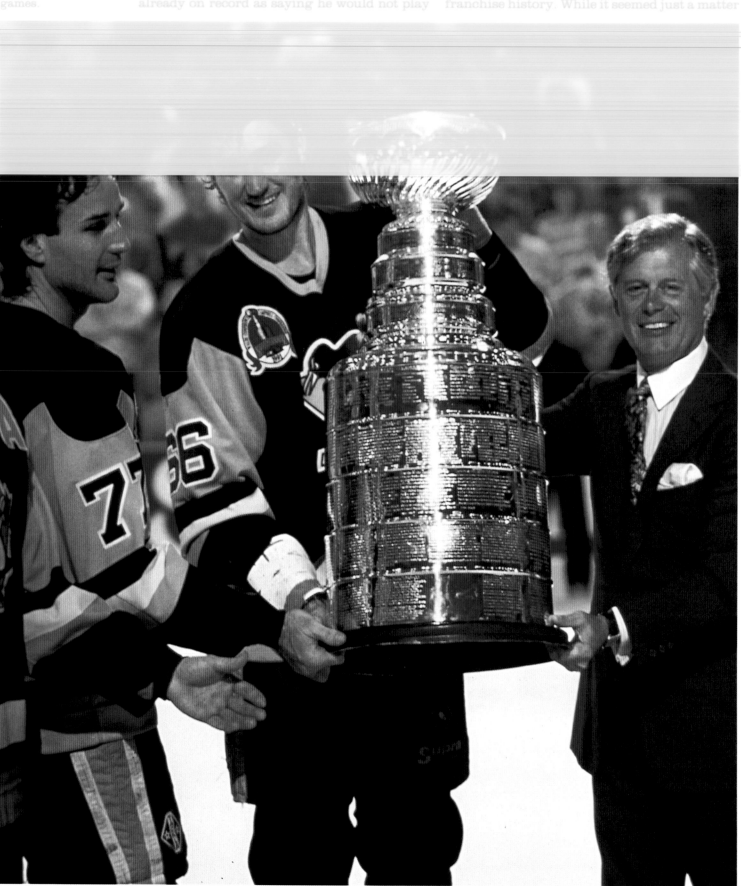

of time before the Penguins' prolific lineup played to its potential, Pittsburgh's opponent in the finals was a complete surprise. The Minnesota North Stars, who finished the regular season with a 27-39-14 mark, downed Chicago, St Louis and Edmonton to earn a place in the Stanley Cup finals. It marked the first time that two post-1967 expansion teams had met in the finals, and the first time since 1936 that two teams who had never won the Cup found themselves in the greatest show on ice.

In the finals, the sheer strength of the Penguins' lineup slowly outworked the overachieving North Stars, putting a Stanley Cup banner in the Penguins' igloo after six games. Lemieux, who led all scorers with 44 points, the second highest total in postseason history, won the Conn Smythe Trophy. Other winners in the NHL's silverware parade were Brett Hull, who took home the Hart Trophy; Wayne Gretzky, who paired Lady Byng with his Art Ross; and Ray Bourque, who captured his fourth Norris Trophy as the league's best defenseman.

It was an oddly calm off-season in the trade market, with no major transactions of note being completed. There was, however, L'Affair Lindros to keep the scribes busy throughout the summer. As expected, the Québec Nordiques made Eric Lindros their first selection in the 1991 Entry Draft and, as promised, Lindros refused to appear at the Québec table or don the Nordiques' jersey, starting a standoff that continued all summer. After Lindros refused a $50 million, 10-year contract to suit up with the Nordiques, Québec president Marcel Aubut issued his ultimatum: sign or sit. NHL rules gave Aubut the rights to Lindros for two years, and Aubut informed the hockey public that he would retain those rights until Lindros changed his mind, effectively keeping the future superstar off NHL ponds.

Lindros did get to perform his magic in some NHL arenas, although it was in the uniform of Team Canada, not the Québec Nordiques. Canada and the United States played host to the fifth Canada Cup Tournament during the summer and fall of 1991, and Lindros became the first non-professional to make the Canadian team. He performed very well, collecting five points in eight games, as Canada went undefeated in winning their fourth Canada Cup. The series was noteworthy for another reason. In Game One of the championship round, Team USA defenseman Gary Suter checked Wayne Gretzky into the boards, causing the NHL's all-time leading scorer to drop to the ice in pain. It marked the start of recurring back troubles that would hamper the Great One for seasons to come.

For the first time since 1979, the NHL welcomed a new member to its family for the 1991-92 season: the San Jose Sharks. The Sharks were granted a franchise in the Smythe Division, and their pond was stocked with players from the existing 21 teams and a cross-pollination pool with the Minnesota North Stars, whose former owners George and Gordon Gund were the new bosses of the California franchise.

The revolving door in the NHL coaches' offices continued to turn, with new pivots arriving in Boston (Rick Bowness), Edmonton (Ted Green), Hartford (Jim Roberts) and Winnipeg (John Paddock). The Toronto Maple Leafs appeared to be well on the way to righting their sinking ship by hiring Cliff Fletcher, former mastermind of the Atlanta/Calgary Flames, as their president and general manager.

The 1991-92 season marked the 75th anniversary of the NHL, and during the season there were a number of celebrations and special occasions. On the opening night of the schedule, the original six teams played each other, with the Toronto-Montréal match gathering the most media attention. Each of the original six squads wore special historic uniforms that represented the early history of the team.

For the second time in three years, only one NHL team climbed above the 100-point mark during the 1991-92 season. The NY Rangers, who received a major boost when they acquired Mark Messier from the Edmonton Oilers in early October, won their first President's Trophy as the league's best regular-season club by amassing 105 points. With Messier providing the inspiration and Norris Trophy-winning rearguard Brian Leetch contributing the spark, the Rangers recorded their best season in franchise history. Rookies Tony Amonte and Doug Weight made key contributions, as did noted marksman Mike Gartner, who became the first player in league history to record his 500th goal, 500th assist, 1000th point and 1000th game in the same season.

Above: Mike Gartner began his career with the Cincinnati Stingers of the WHA in 1978-79, the only season of his professional career that he didn't score at least 30 goals.

The Detroit Red Wings were the class of the Norris Division, winning 43 games to outdistance second-place Chicago by 11 points. Once again, Steve Yzerman was the Wings' most valuable commodity, while rookies Nicklas Lidstrom, Ray Sheppard and Vladimir Konstantinov easily adapted to life in the NHL. The Black Hawks dropped to second place, despite the efforts of Jeremy Roenick, who became just the second Black Hawk to score 50 goals in a season.

The Toronto Maple Leafs pulled two major trades during the season, the first coming just before the season began when GM Cliff Fletcher acquired Glen Anderson, Grant Fuhr and Craig Berube from Edmonton. When the Leafs continued to struggle, Fletcher struck oil again, this time in Calgary. The Leafs new hockey boss swung the biggest trade in NHL history when he obtained Doug Gilmour, Ric Nattress, Rick Wamsley, Jamie Macoun and Kent Manderville for Gary Leeman, Alexander Godynyuk, Craig Berube, Jeff Reese and Michel Petit. Armed with a new contract and playing in his home province, Doug Gilmour once again played with the reckless abandon that made him one of the league's finest two-way performers. Although the Leafs missed the postseason train, the franchise appeared to be back on the tracks.

Brett Hull once again led all NHL snipers with 70 goals, but it was a disappointing season in Missouri. Much of the blame was draped on the shoulders of St Louis GM Ron Caron. Caron, who disrupted team chemistry in 1991 by dealing four character players at the trade deadline, decided to sign free agent Brendan Shanahan off the roster of the New Jersey Devils in the off-season. Shanahan didn't come cheap, as Caron was ordered to compensate the Devils with de-

Above: Doug Gilmour, who scored the Cup-winning goal for Calgary in 1986, was the protagonist in a ten-player trade between Toronto and Calgary, the biggest deal in league history.

The defending champion Pittsburgh Penguins received a major blow to their aspirations to repeat when coach Bob Johnson was forced to resign because of a brain tumor. Although Johnson vowed to return, he succumbed to his illness on 26 November 1991. His replacement, Scotty Bowman, was the winningest coach in NHL history and a masterful tactician who had piloted the St Louis Blues, Montréal Canadiens and Buffalo Sabres. Bowman, who joined the Penguins staff as the Director of Player Development in 1991, remained on the sidelines in the beginning, allowing assistant coaches Rick Kehoe and Rick Paterson to run the team practices. Slowly, Bowman gained the confidence of the Penguins, and although the team struggled to a 39-32-9 finish, they were playing controlled, confident hockey by the season's end.

Once again, Pittsburgh GM Craig Patrick retooled the Pittsburgh machine as the season progressed, unloading Paul Coffey in a three-way deal with LA and Philadelphia that landed the Penguins Rick Tocchet, Kjell Samuellson and Ken Wregget.

Washington and New Jersey nailed down the remaining playoff posts. The Capitals received clutch scoring from their defense to clinch second place, while the Devils, using a patient though somewhat plodding approach, finished fourth.

Right: Although Steve Yzerman failed to score 50 goals in 1991-92 for the first time in four seasons, he still collected 103 points to lead the Red Wings in scoring.

fenseman Scott Stevens, one of the finest back-liners in the game. Although Shanahan was a gifted offensive performer, many critics felt the loss of Stevens would leave St Louis singing the blues. Caron also raised the ire of the fans when he traded popular Adam Oates, the feeder who filled Brett Hull's goal-scoring appetite, to Boston for Craig Janney. This turnaround on the roster was one of the reasons the Blues slipped to third place, 15 points behind the front running Black Hawks. Minnesota, back on *terra firma* after their Stanley Cup run a year earlier, remained in fourth place.

A dramatic turnaround was experienced in Vancouver, where the Canucks forged to the top of the Smythe mountain. The four players the Canucks received from St Louis at the conclusion of the 1991 season — Ronning, Courtnall, Momesso and Dirk — all contributed efforts that were second to none during the 1991-92 campaign. Ronning finished second in team scoring, Courtnall's 12 powerplay goals was second best on the team, Momesso's plus-22 was the second best mark in the club, while Dirk was a solid second-line defender. Pavel Bure, nick-named the 'Russian Rocket,' won the Calder Trophy as the league's best rookie, while Trevor Linden, Greg Adams and goaltender Kirk McLean all played supporting roles in the Canucks' 96-point season.

For the first time since 1973, the Flames failed to make the playoffs, falling to fifth place after a season of unrest and inner turmoil. GM Doug Risebrough fired himself as coach, but replacement Guy Charron couldn't relight the Flames' fuse. The 10-player deal with the Leafs, while turning around the fortunes of the Toronto team, seemed to extinguish all hopes the Flames had of attaining a playoff berth.

The LA Kings, Edmonton Oilers and Winni-

Above: The 'Russian Rocket,' Pavel Bure (center), is one of the new breed of Russian-trained players starring in the internationally flavored NHL.

peg Jets all finished with above .500 records, while the expansion San Jose Sharks finished with a respectable 39 points in their freshman campaign. Though hardly fearsome, the Sharks' attack had some bite, with Pat Falloon, Kelly Kisio and Doug Wilson all helping the new franchise establish a healthy fan base and an exciting on-ice product.

The status quo remained in the Adams Division. Québec once again missed the playoffs despite a gifted roster of young talent. Joe Sakic, Mats Sundin, Owen Nolan, Valery Kamensky and Stéphane Fiset were all expected to be stars in the NHL, but it would take some time for those luminaries to mature. With the Eric Lindros affair hanging over the team, it was a difficult year for Nordique fans.

The Montréal Canadiens claimed first place for the second time in four seasons, thanks to the determined play of Kirk Muller, who was brought in from New Jersey for Stéphane Richer, and a return to form by Patrick Roy, who captured his third Vezina Trophy as the league's best goaltender.

Once again, the Bruins inserted a fistful of rookies into the lineup, with Joe Juneau and Glen Murray displaying the most promise. The Bruins were without their offensive leader, Cam Neely, for most of the year. Neely, who suffered a serious thigh injury during the 1991

Left: Although he was hampered by injuries in his first two NHL seasons, Valery Kamensky is one of the most talented young players in the league.

playoffs, made a courageous nine-game return, only to be shelved once again by a knee injury. Neely's woes mirrored the Bruins' troubles, as they once again fell victim to the Pittsburgh Penguins' juggernaut in the playoffs.

There was cause for optimism in Buffalo when the Sabres acquired superstar Pat LaFontaine from the NY Islanders for Pierre Turgeon. Although he suffered a broken jaw soon after joining the team, LaFontaine still managed to compile 93 points in 57 games. Dale Hawerchuk led the team in scoring, marking the 11th straight season he had led his team in point production. However, Buffalo's lack of playoff caliber goaltending cost them again, as they failed to advance beyond the opening round for the seventh consecutive year.

There were other problems in the Adams family as well. Hartford's dwindling attendance and poor on-ice performance gave rise to the rumor that the team would be forced to relocate. The Hartford brass were optimistic, and with young talent such as Zarley Zalapski, Geoff Sanderson, Pat Verbeek and Terry Yake, there was hope the Whalers could remain afloat.

Towards the end of the 1991-92 season, with only a handful of games left on the schedule, the NHL fell victim to the labor troubles that had befallen both major league baseball and the NFL. By starting the season without a collective bargaining agreement, the NHL governors were gambling they could reach a compromise with the players during the course of the campaign. However, on 1 April 1992, the NHL Players Association proved they weren't April fools by calling the first league-wide strike in NHL history. NHL president John Ziegler and

Players Association chief Bob Goodenow negotiated for 10 days before a new agreement was signed. Although the playoffs would be delayed, they would be played, a possibility that seemed remote when the strike began. Although the league's integrity was saved, John Ziegler's job was not. Shortly after the conclusion of the playoffs, Ziegler was asked to resign, ending his 15-year tenure as NHL president. He was replaced, on an interim basis, by Gil Stein, one of the NHL's vice presidents and the league's general council.

The Penguins, revitalized by the 10-day pause, stormed through the playoffs, although they needed a dramatic comeback in their opening series, rebounding from a three games to one deficit to defeat the Washington Capitals in seven games. Against the NY Rangers in the division finals, Mario Lemieux suffered a broken bone in his hand when slashed by Rangers forward Adam Graves. Although no major penalty was called on the play, Graves was suspended for the duration of the playoffs. The severity of Lemieux's injury was questioned, for he quickly returned to lead the Penguins past the Rangers and Bruins and into their second straight Stanley Cup finals.

The Penguins' adversaries in their Stanley Cup march were the Chicago Black Hawks, who entered the finals riding a postseason record 11-game winning streak. The Hawks jumped into a 4-1 lead in the series lid-lifter, only to see the Penguins fight back to win the match 5-4. The Penguins, on an eight-game unbeaten streak of their own, proceeded to win the remaining three games and win their second consecutive Stanley Cup championship. The Penguins' mar-

Below right: Chicago's Dirk Graham could slow down Pittsburgh's Troy Loney, but he was unable to stop the Pittsburgh Penguins' express, which steamrolled to their second straight Stanley Cup title with a four-game sweep over the Black Hawks in the 1992 finals.

Below: Pat LaFontaine had the finest season of his career in 1992-93, collecting a team record 95 assists and 148 points.

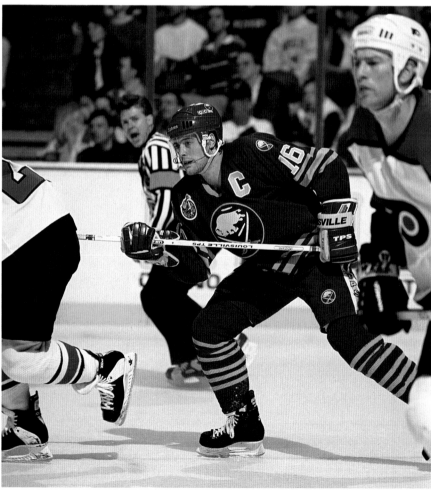

gin of victory in the four-game sweep was five goals.

Mario Lemieux, who once again led all playoff scorers with 34 points, became the second player to win back-to-back Conn Smythe trophies, joining Bernie Parent on that post-season honor roll.

It was a summer of change for the NHL in 1992, starting with the office of the president. It was decided that a commissioner would be chosen to replace John Ziegler, though whether this new title also meant new powers remained to be seen. Eventually, National Basketball Association Vice President Gary Bettman was hired for the newly formed position on the strength of his expertise in labor management.

There were also two new teams joining the NHL family in 1993: the Ottawa Senators, re-surrected after almost 60 years, and the Tampa Bay Lightning, the league's first foray into Florida. The Lightning, with Phil Esposito in the boardroom and Terry Crisp behind the bench, were in the news early and often. Esposito signed Manon Rheaume, a female goal-tender who helped lead Canada to the Women's World Championship in 1992. She got her first start in an exhibition game on 23 September 1992, against St Louis, allowing two goals in one period of work. She was eventually assigned to the Lightning's International Hockey League farm team in Atlanta.

L'Affair Lindros, which dragged on throughout the 1991-92 season, took another interesting – and embarrassing – turn when the Québec Nordiques finally traded the budding superstar. Unfortunately, they traded him to two different teams. After supposedly sealing a

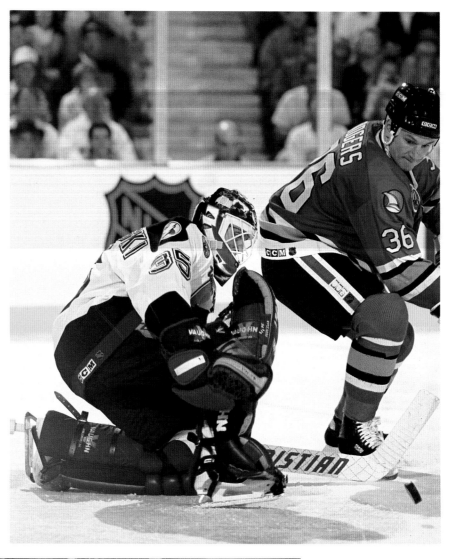

Above: Tampa Bay's Pat Jablonski stops San Jose's Jeff Odgers in a battle of two of the NHL's newest expansion teams. Tampa Bay's 53 points in 1992-93 was one of the finest finishes by a first year club.

Left: A trio of Buffalo Sabres surround Ottawa's Sylvain Turgeon, who led the expansion Senators with 25 goals.

Above: The Flyers signed Eric Lindros to a $20 million contract, the richest deal ever awarded to a NHL rookie.

Below: The 'Finnish Flash,' Winnipeg Jets' rookie Teemu Selanne tied for the league lead with 76 goals in 1992-93.

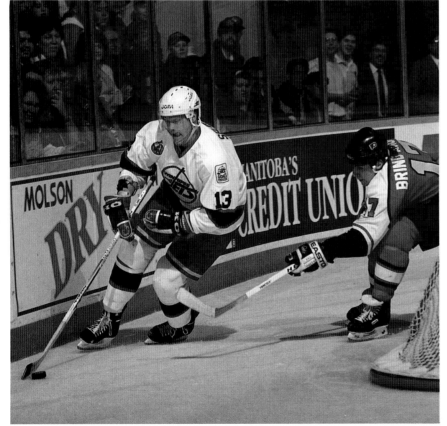

Huffman, Mike Ricci, two first round draft selections and a considerable amount of cash, estimated to be in the area of $15 million. All of this for a player who had yet to skate in an NHL game.

The most surprising coaching change came in Toronto, where the Leafs hired Pat Burns, former pivot of the Montréal Canadiens and one of the NHL's great coaches. In other coaching merry-go-round action, Boston brought in Brian Sutter, who had been dropped by St Louis; Calgary landed esteemed Canadian Olympic strategist Dave King; Mike Keenan stepped aside in Chicago so protegee Darryl Sutter could take over; Los Angeles stole Barry Melrose – coach of the AHL champion Adirondack club – from under the noses of the parent Red Wings; Montréal gave the 'Great Motivator', Jacques Demers, the job he had been waiting for his whole coaching life; New Jersey appointed 'Miracle on Ice' mentor Herb Brooks as their new coach; and St Louis replaced Brian Sutter with long-time employee Bob Plager. Ottawa chose former Boston coach Rick Bowness as their first head coach, while Tampa Bay went with Terry Crisp, who piloted the Flames to the Cup in 1989.

With the introduction of two new teams, the league expanded the schedule to 84 games, including a series of 'neutral site' games in cities around North America that didn't have NHL franchises. Midway through the year, the league announced that it was expanding again in 1993-94, adding the Florida Panthers in Miami and the Mighty Ducks of Anaheim.

In many ways, the 1992-93 season was one of contrasts: spectacular achievement matched with outrageously poor performance, and emotional highs mixed with bitter lows. It was a year in which the Russian imports finally played to their potential, and a year in which two teams struggled not to match the Washington Capitals' record for ineptitude established in 1975. It was also a year which saw the game of hockey come very close to losing its two greatest stars.

For the first time since 1967, every playoff participant finished the season with above .500 records. Fourteen players scored at least 50 goals and 21 skaters reached the 100-point plateau, both NHL records. Each division had its own incredible story to tell in this, one of the most intriguing seasons in NHL history. Before the schedule began, it was announced that Wayne Gretzky was suffering from a serious back injury that would keep him on the sidelines for a considerable amount of time. Luckily for hockey fans everywhere, Gretzky returned to the Kings before the All-Star break. In his absence, the Kings played consistent hockey, although they ironically struggled when the Great One finally returned to the lineup. With a young crop of defensemen and a revitalized Gretzky, the Kings finished in third place with a 39-35-10 record.

After two years of negotiations, the Winnipeg Jets were finally able to sign Finnish superstar Teemu Selanne. Although Selanne was expected to be a fine NHL prospect, no one imagined that he would be one of the game's dominant performers in his first year. Selanne

deal with the Philadelphia Flyers, the Nordiques invited the NY Rangers to the table and encouraged the Broadway Blues to up the ante. The Rangers met the Flyers' bid and raised it, and the Nordiques assured them they had landed Lindros. The Flyers immediately protested, forcing the league to hire an independent arbitrator to solve the problem. He determined that the Nordiques and Flyers had a deal and the marriage was finally consummated, sending Lindros to Philadelphia for Ron Hextall, Peter Forsberg, Steve Duchesne, Kerry

crushed every existing rookie record by collecting 76 goals, 132 points, 24 powerplay goals and 387 shots on goal. The Jets, nicknamed 'Team United Nations' because of the wide variety of nationalities on their roster, slipped into fourth place in the Smythe with a 40-37-7 record.

The Vancouver Canucks, bolstered by a 60-goal contribution from Pavel Bure, retained their Smythe Division crown by compiling 101 points, four points ahead of the revitalized Calgary Flames. The Flames, with Dave King calling the shots, rebounded from their worst season in two decades to finish second. The Edmonton Oilers continued to trade away most of the talent that won them five Stanley Cups. Of the team that captured the championship in 1990, Bill Ranford, Craig MacTavish, Craig Simpson and Petr Klima were the only major names that escaped GM Glen Sather's house-cleaning. The incessant roster shuffling, combined with owner Peter Pocklington's constant threat to move the franchise unless city officials renegotiated the club's lease at Northlands Coliseum, kept the team off balance all season. As a result, the Oilers missed the playoffs for the first time in franchise history.

Only one season after capturing the President's Trophy, the NY Rangers had a dismal season, falling quickly from the penthouse to the outhouse. Injuries to Mark Messier, Brian Leetch and James Patrick complicated matters, but the Rangers' greatest problem was a lack of focus. Clubhouse squabbling between Messier and coach Roger Neilson sent Neilson to the unemployment line and the NY Rangers to the sidelines when the playoffs began. The lone bright spot for the Rangers was the play of Mike Gartner, one of the game's most consistent performers. Gartner became the first player in league history to record 14 consecutive 30-goal seasons, finishing the campaign with a team-leading 45 goals.

Mario Lemieux was healthy as the 1992-93 season started, which was good news for the league but bad news for opposing goaltenders. Lemieux was on pace to easily eclipse the 200-point mark when a routine checkup in early January disclosed he was suffering from Hodgkins Disease, a serious, though treatable, form of cancer. The Penguins and the entire sporting community were shocked, but Lemieux remained calm and confident. After six weeks on the sidelines receiving radiation therapy, Lemieux miraculously returned to action. The Penguins lost their first game with their captain back, then rolled off an incredible NHL record 17-game winning streak. Pittsburgh, with Lemieux, Kevin Stevens, Rick Tocchet and Ron Francis all reaching the 100-point mark, won their first President's Trophy as the NHL's top regular-season club. The unsung hero in the Pittsburgh camp was goaltender Tom Barrasso, who won a league-leading 43 games and finished among the leaders in all four major goaltending statistical categories for the defending Cup champions.

The Washington Capitals, who set an NHL record by having three different defensemen (Hatcher, Iafrate and Cote) score at least 20 goals, finished second, while the NY Islanders,

with clever Al Arbour still calling the shots behind the bench, climbed into third. Eric Lindros, the much-heralded rookie, missed 23 games with injuries, but still finished the campaign with a respectable 41 goals and 75 points. The Flyers, with rookie goaltender Tommy Soderstrom registering five shutouts and forward Mark Reechi establishing a team record with 123 points, won their final eight games to finish only four points behind the fourth place New Jersey Devils.

Once again, the Norris Division was one of the league's strongest, thanks to the revitalization of the Toronto Maple Leafs franchise. With MVP candidate Doug Gilmour setting club records for points and assists and rookie netminder Felix Potvin leading the league in goals-against average, the Leafs climbed back into the playoffs with a club-record 99 points and a franchise-high 44 victories. The strong play of Potvin enabled GM Cliff Fletcher to play his most valuable trump card, dealing Grant Fuhr to Buffalo for sniper Dave Andreychuk, who contributed 17 goals in his first 17 games as a Leaf.

The Chicago Black Hawks finished atop the Norris, although their road to the top was not a smooth one. Early in the season, Mike Keenan suddenly resigned as the Hawks' general

Above: Mario Lemieux's courageous battle with Hodgkin's Disease and his sensational comeback were the sports stories of the year in 1992-93.

Above: Andrei Kovalenko led all Québec rookies in scoring with 27 goals and 41 assists in 1992-93.

Above right: Québec rearguard Alexei Gusarov registered a plus/minus rating of plus-18 in 1992-93, after finishing the 1991-92 campaign with a mark of minus-9.

Right: The Sabres' Alexander Mogilny thrilled fans throughout the league with his speed, finesse and scoring prowess in 1992-93.

manager, prompting team president Bob Pulford to return to the GM's chair of the defending Campbell Conference champions. The Hawks refused to bend under the ensuing controversy and clawed their way to the top, thanks in large part to Chris Chelios and Ed Belfour, who both returned to the form they displayed in 1990-91. Detroit, with Steve Yzerman and Sergei Fedorov exhibiting All-Star moves, finished second. St Louis snuck into the last playoff spot after a calamitous second half by the Minnesota North Stars. The Stars, Cup finalists just two seasons previously, played the season under a cloud of uncertainty after team owner Norman Green expressed his desire to relocate the team. The puzzle was completed when Green announced that the team was moving to Dallas, Texas, for the 1993-94 season, bringing to an end the teams' 26-year stay in the Land of Lakes.

Another surprising story was being written in Québec, where the Nordiques set an NHL record by improving by 55 points to finish the season with 104 points. Bolstered by the addition of five first-line players from the Flyers and the maturing of some of their own young talent, the Nordiques pushed for the division title most of the campaign. Mats Sundin and Joe Sakic each reached the 100-point plateau, while Ron Hextall solidified the last line of defense.

The Buffalo Sabres, one of the league's most potent offensive units, finished fourth. Pat LaFontaine, who led the scoring race during much of Lemieux's absence, completed the season with a team record 148 points. Alexander Mogilny finally realized his potential, tying for the league lead in goals with 76. Montréal, with Jacques Demers calling the shots behind the bench, finished third with 102 points. Vincent Damphousse, obtained from the Oilers at the start of the season, became the first player to lead three different teams in scoring in three

consecutive seasons, topping all point-getters on the Maple Leafs in 1991 and the Oilers in 1992.

Boston, who started the season going 13-3-2, finished even stronger, winning 18 of their final 21 games to win the Adams Division title. Joe Juneau, with 121 points and 90 assists as a

rookie, and Adam Oates, were the catalysts for the Beantowners' balanced attack. In Hartford, the team's woes on the ice and at the box office continued but there was cause for hope. Geoff Sanderson developed into a front-line forward, while Terry Yake, Patrick Poulin and Michel Nylander were Hartford's stars of the future. It wasn't enough to earn a playoff berth, however, as the Whalers settled into fifth place.

Even the struggle for the NHL basement took on a special significance because of the rookie teams joining the league. The battle was expected to be a three-horse race between the league's newest members, Ottawa and Tampa Bay and the sophomore San Jose Sharks. However, the Tampa Bay franchise, using shrewd free-agent signings and astute draft selections, enjoyed an outstanding rookie season. The same could not be said for the Ottawa Senators or San Jose. The Sharks had very little bite, setting an NHL record for the fewest ties in a season (2) and only narrowly escaping the basement, thanks to having 11 wins to Ottawa's 10.

In the playoffs, Wayne Gretzky delivered on his promise to lead the Kings into the promised land. Although the Kings lost in five games to the Montréal Canadiens in the Stanley Cup finals, the club captured the attention of the California fans with its dedicated drive and determination. Wayne Gretzky compiled 40 points, the third highest total of his postseason career, in leading the Kings to their first Campbell Conference title.

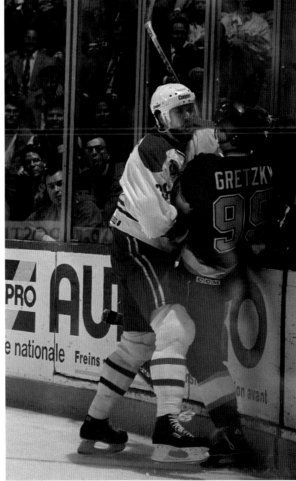

Above: A triumphant group of Montréal Canadiens hoists the Stanley Cup for the 24th time in franchise history.

Left: The Montréal Canadiens defense, led by Eric Desjardins, kept constant pressure on Wayne Gretzky and the Kings throughout the 1993 Stanley Cup finals.

CHAPTER SIX

TO THE
PLAYOFFS

The Stanley Cup

The year was 1893. Hockey fever was stretching from coast to coast in Canada, helped along by the nation's expansion into its westward reaches, where the harsh winters on the plains made for superb playing conditions. To hockey enthusiasts, it seemed that teams were being born everywhere and that more and more fans were venturing out into the cold to watch them go at each other.

But something was missing. Popular though the game was, it was still a formless enterprise that had yet to become a truly respectable sport. Three enthusiasts — Ottawa newspaper publisher P D Ross, government official Lord Kilcoursie, and the young son of Canada's governor general — thought that they had an answer to the problem. What was needed was a handsome and distinguished prize for each year's best team. The prize would serve a double purpose. It would give hockey greater esteem and, in turn, increase the game's growing popularity.

To get the most prestigious award they could lay their hands on, the three turned to the young man's father, the governor-general, and asked him to donate a perpetual trophy to the game. Frederick Arthur, Lord Stanley of Preston, agreed to the request. Though not himself particularly interested in hockey, he paid 10 guineas (the equivalent of $48.67 at the time) for a silver-plated nickel bowl lined with gold. Mounted on an ebony base, it stood one foot high and measured 22 inches across the mouth. It was immediately named in Stanley's honor and, in time, far exceeded the dreams of its originators. It caught the eye of the public, endowed hockey with an instant respectability because of the connection with the Stanley name, and became the most sought-after prize in the game, first at the amateur level and then, when play-for-pay finally took precedence, at the professional level. Further, presented continually since 1893 (with one exception: in

Page 141: The Stanley Cup.

Right: An Edmonton Oiler drinks from the Stanley Cup.

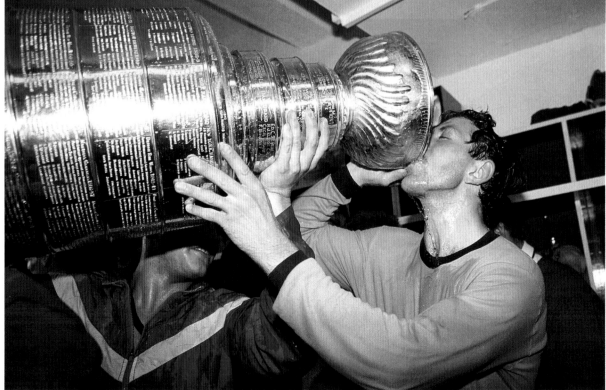

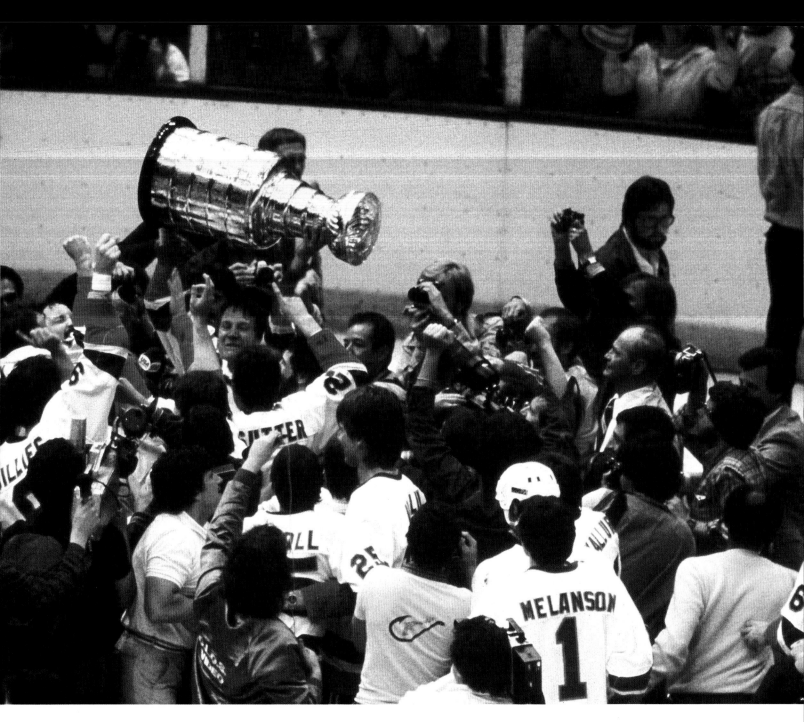

1918-19, when the championship series between the Canadiens and the Seattle Metropolitans was canceled midway through because of the widespread flu epidemic that claimed the life of Montréal's Bad Joe Hall), the Cup has come to rank not only as hockey's most distinguished award but also as one of the most distinguished in all sports.

It is also an award whose history is punctuated with odd incidents. For one, Lord Stanley never saw a Cup competition. He went home to England after his brother's death to become the new Earl of Derby ten months before the first championship match was held. For another, the Cup was once lost by a group of alcoholically happy winners who took it out for a ride in their car. For still another, it was once stolen — but, fortunately, for only a few minutes. The theft occurred at the start of the 1961 playoffs when the Chicago Black Hawks, as was their privilege after taking the preceding year's championship, had the Cup on display at their stadium. A Canadien fan picked the thing off its mounting and came close to strolling out of the stadium before being collared by the police. When questioned as to why he had taken the trophy, he replied that he was simply returning it to its rightful home in Montréal.

In addition to such misadventures, the original Cup was dropped on a number of occasions and suffered a series of dents and scars. Such accidents often occurred in the moments after the final game of the championship round when, on receiving the trophy, the victors held it high and skated around the rink. In 1968, a replica was built and the original was consigned to the Hockey Hall of Fame. Since then, the replica has been presented to the championship squad and is the one that is escorted wildly over the ice to the frenzied joy of the team's ecstatic fans.

The Cup's effect on the game's respectability and fan interest was immediate. An already-popular sport was given a boost that could be readily seen in the crowd that showed up at Montréal's Victoria Rink to watch the first championship meeting. As of that year, the gate was the largest ever attracted to a hockey game. The Montréal Amateur Athletic Association defeated an Ottawa squad and became the first team to have its name inscribed on the Cup.

In the next years, though professional teams were fast taking shape and earning an increas-

Above: The New York Islanders parade on the ice with the Stanley Cup after their 1983 championship.

143

ing share of fan attention, the Cup was awarded exclusively to amateur outfits. The fact is that the Cup seems to have spurred the formation of many new amateur outfits. They all wanted a shot at this most prestigious of honors. Even the smallest of towns in the most remote areas could not avoid being bitten by the desire for lasting hockey fame.

Perhaps the team that represented the most distant of outposts took shape at Dawson City, the center of the Klondike's gold rush. Calling themselves the Dawson City Klondikers, the players won a spot in the 1905 Cup competition and headed for Ottawa, some 3300 miles to the east. Theirs was a journey that, beginning on 19 December 1904, can only be described as heroic, even for hardy and venturesome gold rush types.

The first leg carried them by dogsled to Skagway. Pushing their way through temperatures that dropped to 20 degrees below zero Fahrenheit, the players arrived in Skagway with their fair share of frostbitten and frozen hands and feet. There, they boarded a scow that pitched its way southward to Seattle, where they connected with a train for Vancouver. From Vancouver they traveled by rail to Ottawa, ending their journey 21 days after departing Dawson City and one day before they were to skate against the Ottawa Silver Seven, a powerhouse club that had taken the Stanley Cup two years in a row – in 1903 and 1904.

The Klondikers-Silver Seven match triggered much public interest, mainly because of the distance that the visitors had traveled. But the game itself failed to match its hoopla. The Silver Seven took the first game 9-2 and then proceeded to wallop the Dawson City team 23-2 in the second match. Ottawa's Frank McGee scored 14 goals in the second game, establishing a single-game scoring record that remains unchallenged today.

The next years, marking the emergence of the professional game, saw the Cup pass out of amateur hands and into the keeping of the pros. In the east, the Ontario Hockey League, the Eastern Canada Hockey Association (which soon changed its name to the Canadian Hockey Association), and the National Hockey Association all were formed, while the Patricks' Pacific Coast Hockey Association took shape in the far west. The Cup was eventually placed in the charge of the National Hockey Association, and top teams from these leagues now vied to claim it in an annual elimination tournament.

Until the 1916-17 season, all the competitors were Canadian outfits. It was then that the Cup battles saw their first US participant, the PCHA's Seattle Metropolitans. As you'll recall from Chapter Two, the American encroachment into what had hitherto been an exclusively Canadian enterprise triggered a burst of outrage among fans north of the border and among the eastern teams, who had no love for the upstart Pacific Coast operation to begin with. The fuss ballooned to such proportions that the Metropolitans, on reaching the finals, announced that they would not play unless the

Opposite: Bryan Trottier of the New York Islanders holds the Stanley Cup aloft in celebration.

Below: The traditional handshake between winners and losers – Islanders and Rangers.

NHA assured them that the Cup would be allowed to leave Canada should they win. The NHA grudgingly gave the requisite promise. The Metropolitans – managed by Pete Muldoon (later the author of Chicago's infamous 'Muldoon Curse') and captained by Bobby Rowe – went against the Montreal Canadiens and became not only first US team seen in Cup competition but also the first US team to take the prize home.

The National Hockey League was formed in 1917 and entered Stanley Cup play with its fellow leagues. A short nine years later, in 1926, with the rival leagues now having gone out of business, the NHL took charge of the trophy and has been responsible for conducting the annual Stanley Cup playoffs ever since.

THE CUP PLAYOFF SYSTEM
Often confusing the fans – and at times annoying them – the Stanley Cup playoff system has long been a complicated affair involving many

teams. As a case in point, of the 21 clubs in the NHL today, no fewer than 16 compete in the playoffs.

The system's complexity can be traced back to the PCHA's Patrick brothers. Obviously believing in the concept of 'the more the merrier,' they introduced the multi-team concept to the playoffs on the grounds that the Cup competition was likely to bore the fans (and, of course, jeopardize gate receipts) if only the very top units participated. There's no denying that the

brothers had a point, especially if one team, as has periodically been the case in the years since, took off during the season and left everyone else far behind.

Further, the Patricks felt it only fair to have the playoffs welcome teams as far back in the standings as fourth place. They argued that a perfectly solid unit should not be excluded from championship action because of a poor seasonal performance that had been caused not by ineptitude but by player injuries. It deserved a shot at the Cup.

The multi-team concept was introduced in the 1917-18 Cup playoffs and has since become a tradition, but one that has been altered many times in its detail as hockey executives have sought to devise the best playoff format possible. For example, when the NHL took charge of the Cup and the playoffs in 1927, the league consisted of ten teams split between two divisions — the Canadian and American. Three teams from each division were permitted to enter the playoffs — for a total of six out of the ten. The playoffs themselves were staged in three rounds: the quarter-finals, the semi-finals and the championship series. In the quarter- and semi-final rounds, the teams competed in two-game sets, causing the league to incorporate an odd little scoring wrinkle to decide the winners. To avoid the stalemates that a win apiece could bring, the winners were the squads with the highest number of goals scored. The championship round was a best three-games-out-of-five event.

Another system was tried in the 1928-29 playoffs, with the quarter-finals being decided by the goals scored, while the semi-final and championship rounds were settled on a best-two-games-of-three basis. Though varied in its detail from time to time, this system remained in effect until the mid-1930s. The total-goal system was dropped in 1936 and all playoff games have been decided by wins ever since.

Above: The Montréal Canadiens celebrate one of their many Cup victories of the 1970s.

Far left: Philadelphia fans show their delight at a Flyers' goal.

Above: Mike Bossy (right) is congratulated by Barber of the Flyers after the New York Islanders eliminated Philadelphia.

In 1992-93, 16 of the NHL's 24 teams participated in the Cup competition, with the play-offs being divided into four steps: the division semi-finals, the division finals, the conference championships and the Cup championship itself.

To begin, each division within a conference (the Adams and Patrick in the Prince of Wales Conference, and the Norris and Smythe in the Clarence Campbell Conference) sends four of its teams against each other in the divisional semi-finals, meaning a total of eight per conference and a league total of 16. The schedule calls for the division's first- and fourth-place clubs to meet in a best-of-seven series, while the second- and third-place teams stage a best-of-seven series of their own.

The division finals are played in a best-of-seven series, after which the two winners in each division — in 1992-93, the Islanders and Montréal in the Wales Conference and the Kings and Toronto in the Campbell Conference — go against each other for their respective conference championships. Again, the teams meet in a best-of-seven series, with the victors moving on to the Cup championship itself. The championship tourney is another best-of-seven event. The 1992-93 play saw Montréal take the Cup by defeating the Kings, 4 games to 1.

From 1942-43 through 1967-68 (when the divisions had been abandoned because the NHL was down to six clubs), there was no quarter-final round. Now played first was a semi-final round that pitted the league's first- and third-place teams against each other while the second- and fourth-place squads did battle. The winners then went to the championship series. Both the semi-final and championship rounds were decided on a best-of-seven-games basis.

The league's expansion in 1967-68 immediately brought its club total to 12, with the number advancing to 21 by 1992-93. A number of variations were attempted on the playoff system until the present one was established in the early 1980s.

CUP ACTION

Through the long years since its introduction, the Stanley Cup competition has provided fans with memorable individual and team play on the one hand, and an assortment of odd and comic moments on the other. Here, choosing highlights from each category, are what the decades of action have produced.

Using the 1992-93 playoffs as an illustration, here is exactly how the division semi-finals are organized.

WALES CONFERENCE	CAMPBELL CONFERENCE
ADAMS DIVISION:	**NORRIS DIVISION:**
BOSTON BRUINS (1ST PLACE) VS BUFFALO SABRES (4TH)	CHICAGO BLACK HAWKS (1ST PLACE) VS ST LOUIS BLUES (4TH)
QUÉBEC NORDIQUES (2ND) VS MONTRÉAL CANADIENS (3RD)	DETROIT RED WINGS (2ND) VS TORONTO MAPLE LEAFS (3RD)
PATRICK DIVISION:	**SMYTHE DIVISION:**
PITTSBURGH PENGUINS (1ST) VS NEW JERSEY DEVILS (4TH)	VANCOUVER CANUCKS (1ST) VS WINNIPEG JETS (4TH)
WASHINGTON CAPITALS (2ND) VS NEW YORK ISLANDERS (3RD)	CALGARY FLAMES (2ND) VS LOS ANGELES KINGS (3RD)

The semi-finals winners advance to the division finals.
The teams that appeared in the 1992-93 division finals were:

WALES CONFERENCE	CAMPBELL CONFERENCE
ADAMS DIVISION:	**NORRIS DIVISION:**
MONTRÉAL VS BUFFALO	TORONTO VS ST LOUIS
PATRICK DIVISION:	**SMYTHE DIVISION:**
PITTSBURGH VS NEW YORK ISLANDERS	LOS ANGELES VS VANCOUVER

1917-18

An oddity marked the Cup competition in this, the NHL's first year of operation. The games in the championship series were split between two different sets of rules, with three being played under what were called 'eastern rules' while two were governed by 'western rules.'

The reason for the split: vying for the Cup were the Toronto Arenas of the NHL, and the Vancouver Cougars of the Pacific Coast Hockey Association. The NHL used the rules earlier established by the NHA — six-man squads (with the old-time rover position having been dropped) and the prohibition against passing ahead of the center line. The PCHA, however, continued to employ the rover and so fielded seven-man teams. The Pacific league also permitted forward passing.

In an attempt to even things out, the circuits agreed to divide the games between the rules on a three-two basis. Predictably, Vancouver won the two 'western-rule' meetings, but saw the Cup to go Toronto for three victories under the 'eastern-rule' set up.

1919-20

The championship round played this season has often been called the strangest in Cup history. Pitting the NHL's Ottawa Senators against the PCHA's Seattle Metropolitans, the series opened in Ottawa during an unseasonably warm March that proceeded to melt the arena's natural ice. Much to the amusement — and, sometimes, the impatience — of the fans, the players were constantly frustrated by having the puck disappear in gray slush when it went flashing into the soft spots that, in increasing number, were marring the playing surface.

The teams put up with the problems for three days and then shifted the series to Toronto's Mutual Arena, which boasted an artificial ice surface. The series, which was played under the eastern-western rules split, went to Ottawa, 3 games to 2.

1927-28

When this season's Cup action is mentioned, one man invariably comes to mind — Lester Patrick. Now truly deserving his nickname, The Silver Fox, Patrick was a rapidly graying 44 years of age. Having sold his PCHA, he had signed on as coach for the infant New York Rangers the previous year, going on to do his job so well that he had taken them to an American Division first place in their maiden season and now, on their sophomore outing, had brought his players all the way to the Cup's championship round here to face the Montréal Maroons.

The first game proved disastrous for the Rangers, with the Maroons shutting them out, 2-0. In the first minute of the second period of the second game, things looked even worse when New York's fine goaltender, Lorne Chabot,

Below: The Philadelphia Flyers scuffle with the New York Rangers.

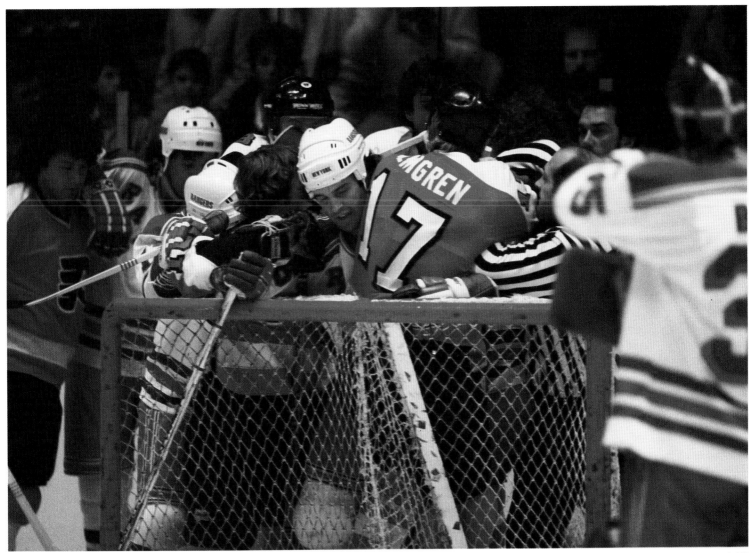

149

Above: Lester Patrick filling in for injured goalie Lorne Chabot in the 1928 Stanley Cup's second game between the New York Rangers and the Montréal Maroons.

took a flying puck in the eye, headed for the hospital and was declared out of action for the rest of the series.

Chabot's loss stopped the game for several minutes because, in common with the league's other clubs, the Rangers did not carry a back-up goaltender. Patrick knew that two fine retired goalies were in the stands and he asked the Maroons' manager, Eddie Gerard, for permission to use one. Gerard, protecting his own team against the strong Ranger contingent and thus in no mood to be generous, turned Patrick down and, so the reports of the day went, laughingly told The Silver Fox to suit up and play the position himself.

It was a challenge that the coach accepted, though he was middle-aged, had ended his own playing days two seasons earlier and had work-

ed as a goalie only once in his life. He grimly climbed into equipment that didn't fit and, with the crowd roaring encouragement, skated out to take his place in front of the cage. Once there, he gave a clumsy, heroic and effective demonstration in net tending, spending most of his time on his hands and knees as he fended off shots and held the Maroons scoreless for two periods.

In the third period, his Rangers drove in a tally to take a 1-0 lead. Seeing that the sweat-coated Patrick was fast approaching exhaustion, they fought valiantly to protect him, with the crowd now hoarse as it cheered his blocks whenever the puck managed to come near him. For most of the period, it seemed as if their encouragement and the Ranger talent might give Patrick a win for the night. But, in the closing seconds, he moved too late as the puck came knifing toward him. Into the net it skittered to tie the game, 1-1, and send the action into overtime.

His face was drawn and pale – and the eyes of everyone in the stadium were on him as Patrick struggled through seven minutes of overtime. Then, wrapping things up for the night, his splendid Frank Boucher broke the tie with a game-winning tally. Broken, too, in that moment was the tension that had prevailed for more than 60 minutes. The cheering in the grandstands, accompanied by programs and hats sailing into the air and out onto the rink, was described in the press as deafening – and the behavior of the Rangers as delirious when they crowded triumphantly around their exhausted coach.

Ever since, whenever sports writers and hockey historians have remembered Patrick's feat, they have, quite rightfully, written that his clumsy but nevertheless effective goaltending that long-ago night gave the Cup playoffs some of their most gallant moments.

With a replacement goalkeeper, the Rangers went on to cap Patrick's efforts by winning the Cup, 3 games to 2.

1932-33

This season produced the longest game in Cup history – the fifth and deciding semi-finals match between Toronto and Boston. For three regulation periods, the Bruins and the Red Wings fought each other to a scoreless standstill, and then proceeded to hammer at each other for five overtime frames, at the end of which not a tally had been put on the scoreboard. A full 160 minutes had been played without the puck once entering the net.

By now, the time was well past one o'clock in the morning and the players, not to mention the fans, were fast approaching exhaustion. A consultation was held in the stands with league president Frank Calder as to how to settle the whole matter. Calder came out against halting the game and continuing it later, a tactic that would have delayed the start of the championship round. He suggested instead that things might be quickly wrapped up if the teams simply removed their goalies from the ice. It was an idea that no one in the stadium liked. Nor was another brainstorm greeted happily – that the match go to the team that won a coin toss.

And so the two clubs skated out for a sixth overtime period. Four minutes and 46 seconds later – at ten minutes to two in the morning – Toronto's Ken Doraty gathered in a pass from teammate Andy Blair and flicked it into the net for a win. The Maple Leafs, undoubtedly still recovering from the long battle, faced the New York Rangers a mere eighteen hours later in the championship round. The New Yorkers took the Cup home after a 3-games-to-1 victory.

1949-50

It has long been a tradition for the Cup champions, holding their prize high overhead, to circle the ice triumphantly in the moments following their victory. This year saw a happy wrinkle added to that tradition. A player who

Above: The tools of the trade.

had not participated in the championship round was brought down to the ice from the stands and handed the Cup so that he could spend a moment displaying it to the crowd.

Young Gordie Howe, playing in his third season, had just put in his best year to date, scoring 35 goals and 33 assists in regular-season action and leading the Detroit Red Wings to the playoffs. But disaster had struck in game one of the semi-final round against Toronto. During the action, Howe and the Leafs' Ted Kennedy had come close to a collision, with Kennedy braking at the last moment and Gordie somehow flying onto the boards and sustaining a fractured nose and cheekbone, a cut eyeball and, worst of all, a skull fracture. The Wings accused Kennedy of high-sticking their star – jamming his stick in Howe's face. Later evidence indicated that

Right: A young
Gordie Howe in the
hospital – 1950.

Below: Gordie Howe.

Kennedy was innocent and had not made contact with the youngster.

No matter what had actually happened, Howe was rushed to hospital, where he underwent three hours of surgery and was declared so close to death that his parents were summoned to his bedside from their home in Floral, Saskatchewan. Miraculously, however, Howe began to recover while, simultaneously, his angry teammates went on to win the semi-final round, along the way so attacking and battering Kennedy that his coach was forced to remove him from the ice repeatedly in an effort to save him from lasting harm.

From the semi-finals, the Red Wings moved against the New York Rangers in the championship round, a string of see-saw battles that saw the clubs deadlocked at the end of six games. Revealing the physical toughness that would enable him to carve out a 26-season career, Howe was in the stands for the seventh and deciding match. New York took the advantage in the first period with two goals and added another in the second frame. For their part, the Wings evened things up before that period ended. From there on, until 8:21 of the second overtime, the score remained tied. Then, 15 feet out from the goal cage, wing Pete Babando grabbed a pass from his center, George Gee, and backhanded the puck home to give Detroit the win and the Cup.

As the Cup was being presented to the Wings, the crowd chanted 'We want Howe!' His teammates beckoned him to the ice. The young man came slowly out of the stands, accepted the Cup and stood quietly with it as a mounting and roaring accolade engulfed him.

1950-51

This season's championship round – played by Toronto and the Canadiens – ranks as an all-time oddity. For the first and only time in league history, every game in the round went into overtime, with Toronto finally winning the Cup, 4 games to 1. Only once before had two teams come close to so many extra sessions – in 1939-40 when Toronto and the New York

Rangers had decided four of their six championship games in overtime.

1964-65

For those who like their hockey rough, game six in the championship round between the Canadiens and the Chicago Black Hawks is possibly the most memorable in Cup play.

The trouble actually started at the end of game four when Chicago's Stan Mikita tapped Montréal's Jean Béliveau on the head with his stick. The hit was intended to be a playful one, but Béliveau didn't see it that way. He whirled on Mikita and would have attacked him had not his teammates pulled him away. Though avoiding a battle that night, the Canadiens were more than ready for one in game five.

And they got it — in the person of Chicago wing Eric Nesterenko, who decided that his opposite number, John Ferguson, could do with a few whacks of his stick. Ferguson disagreed, pulling off his glove and letting fly with a punch that floored Nesterenko. With that, the scene was set for the brawling game six.

From the very first face-off, there were flying fists. Mikita and Canadien defenseman Terry Harper staged the best of the lot, a battle that sent them rolling across the ice. Before all was said and done in the first period, the referee handed out 56 minutes worth of penalties to 14 players, a league record.

The game ended in a 2-1 win for Chicago. Montréal, however, went on to blank the

Hawks, 4-0, in the seventh and deciding game, taking the Cup by a 4-games-to-3 margin.

1973-74

The competition this year went down in league history for one reason alone — it marked the first time that an expansion club won the Cup. The club: the rough-and-tumble 'Broad Street Bullies,' the Philadelphia Flyers.

In business since 1967, the Flyers were to hockey in the early 1970s what the New York Mets had once been to baseball — a laugh. But, under head coach Fred Shero and with a mighty assist from offensive coach Mike Nykoluk, they had developed into a deliberately rough-playing powerhouse by the 1973-74 season. Led by fleet center Bobby Clarke (not himself a rough performer but a finesse player), goalie Bernie Parent and such hard-nosed stalwarts as defenseman Andre (Moose) Dupont and wings Dave (The Hammer) Schultz, Bob (Hound) Kelly and Don (Big Bird) Saleski, the Philadelphians placed first in their division and, on arriving at the playoffs, knocked off Atlanta, 4 games to 0, in the quarter-finals, and then pushed aside the New York Rangers, 4 games to 3, in the semifinals.

The championship round pitted them against the Boston Bruins with their perennially awesome combination of Bobby Orr and Phil Esposito. In the first two games, each team took a win by the same score, 3-2. Philadelphia then forged ahead in games three and four, winning 4-1 and 4-2. But the Bruins handed them a 5-1 shellacking in game five, only to let game six — and, with it, the Cup — escape by a slim 1-0 margin.

To prove that they had won on the basis of talent and not by fluke, the Flyers returned to the championship round the next year and became not only the first expansion unit to win the Cup but also the first to take it in successive years. They did so by downing the Buffalo Sabres, 4 games to 2.

Above: Stan Mikita of the Chicago Black Hawks.

Left: Bobby Orr of the Boston Bruins.

153

Above: The Edmonton Oilers beat the Chicago Black Hawks in the 1985 Stanley Cup semifinals.

1984-85

The competition this year belonged to Edmonton and will long be cherished by Oiler fans as the one that saw their team set one playoff record after another. Superb on both offense and defense and at the net, the Oilers swept through the preliminary rounds – defeating Los Angeles, Winnipeg, and Chicago – and then knocked out the injury-riddled Philadelphia Flyers in the championship series, 4 games to 1, to claim their second successive Cup.

Over the route, the club played 18 games. In the process, its personnel tied or broke no fewer than 25 playoff records. To name a representative few:

Wing Jari Kurri scored 19 playoff goals, tying the number tallied by Philadelphia's Reggie Leach in 1976, with his last one coming in the fifth and final game of the championship round.

Kurri also set a new record for the most 3-or-more-goal games in a playoff series. He posted one 4-goal outing and three 3-goal matches. The previous record had been held by teammate Mark Messier, with three 3-goal games in the 1982-83 competition.

Center Wayne Gretzky broke his own record for playoff point scoring, posting 47 (17 goals and 30 assists). His previous record was set in the 1982-83 competition, when he collected 38 (12 goals and 26 assists over a 16-game stretch).

Paul Coffey broke a defenseman's scoring record that had been shared for years by Boston's Bobby Orr and Brad Park. He tallied 12 goals over the 18-game route. Both Orr and Park had been tied at nine, with Orr setting the record in 1969-70, and Park matching it in 1977-78.

Coffey then went on to claim another defenseman's record, one that had belonged to Orr since the 1971-72 competition. In his 18 games, Coffey recorded 25 assists. Orr had posted 19 in 15 playoff games.

Finally, Coffey's 12 goals and 25 assists combined to give him a record point production of 37-12 points better than the 25 (8 goals and 17 assists) amassed by the New York Islanders' Denis Potvin in 1980-81.

As countless fans saw it, the 1984-85 competition established as fact a strong suspicion that they had harbored since the dawn of the 1980s: that Edmonton – with the likes of Gretzky, Kurri, Coffey, wing Mark Messier and goalkeeper Grant Fuhr aboard – was destined to be the super-power of the decade. They may be right. But, with the fortunes of hockey, especially the dangers of injury and the sudden loss of personal skills being what they are, only time will tell.

1990-91

The NHL crowned a new champion in 1991, passing the Stanley Cup scepter to the game's finest individual talent, Mario Lemieux and his Pittsburgh Penguins' teammates.

The 1991 playoffs were full of surprises, with all five teams that collected over 100 points in the regular season being eliminated by a lesser opponent. In the Campbell Conference, the Min-

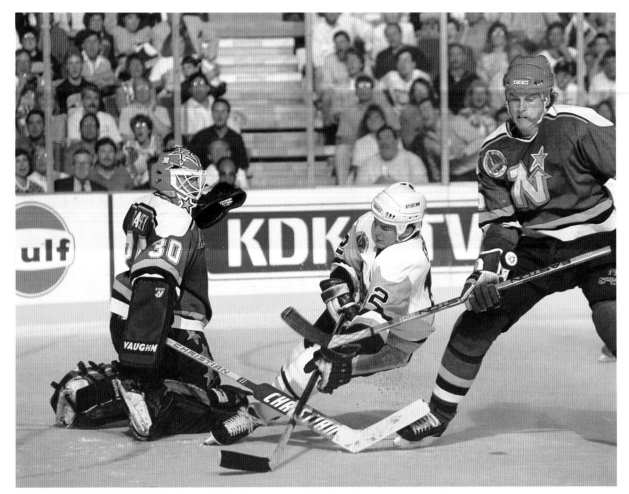

Left: Stanley Cup finalists against the Pittsburgh Penguins in 1991, the Minnesota North Stars begin play in 1993-94 as the Dallas Stars.

Below: The Pittsburgh Penguins, who finished out of the playoffs in eight of the previous nine seasons, captured their first Stanley Cup in 1991, with the offensive talents of Mario Lemieux leading the way.

nesota North Stars, owners of a 27-39-14 regular-season mark, defeated Chicago, St Louis and Edmonton to make the finals for the first time since 1981. Pittsburgh, led by the magnificent Lemieux and rookie sensation Jaromir Jagr, held back New Jersey, Washington and Boston to make their initial appearance in the finals.

For the first time since 1934, two teams that had never won the Stanley Cup were meeting in the finals. Coached by former Montréal Canadiens' captain Bob Gainey and guided by wily veterans Brian Bellows, Brian Propp and Bobby Smith, the North Stars managed to win a pair of games, but they were no match for the Penguins' firepower. Mario Lemieux collected 44 points, the second-highest playoff total ever, to win the Conn Smythe Trophy and lead the Penguins to a six-game victory. Mark Recchi, Kevin Stevens, Larry Murphy and goaltender Tom Barrasso were brilliant in supporting roles as Pittsburgh became the first team since the 1980 NY Islanders to win the Cup in their first appearance in the championship finals. The Penguins' 8-0 victory in the decisive game marked Bob Johnson's last game as an NHL coach. He died later that year of a brain tumor.

1992-93

On its 100th birthday, the Stanley Cup returned to hockey's most fabled shrine, the Montréal Forum, in the city where it was first presented in 1893. The Montréal Canadiens won 16 of their last 18 playoff games — ten of those victories coming in overtime — to capture their 24th Stanley Cup title. Led by the offensive contributions of Paul Dipietro, Kirk Muller and

John LeClair, the motivational coaching of Jacques Demers and the goaltending of Conn Smythe Trophy winner Patrick Roy, the Canadiens retained their royal designation as 'Les Glorieux.'

It was a postseason that featured upsets, unlikely heroes and 28 overtime games. Even the defending champion Pittsburgh Penguins fell victim to the underdog, losing a seventh-game overtime decision to the NY Islanders.

The Conference finals featured the Toronto Maple Leafs, led by the versatile Doug Gilmour, losing a tough seven-game series to the Los Angeles Kings, who won the Campbell Conference crown for the first time. The NY Islanders

YEAR	CHAMPION	COACH	RESULTS (GAMES)	LOSER
1917-18	Toronto Arenas	Dick Carroll	3-2	Vancouver
1918-19			*	
1919-20	Ottawa Senators	Pete Green	3-2	Seattle
1920-21	Ottawa Senators	Pete Green	3-2	Vancouver
1921-22	Toronto St. Pats	Eddie Powers	3-2	Vancouver
1922-23	Ottawa Senators	Pete Green	3-2	Edmonton
1923-24	Mont. Canadiens	Leo Dandurand	2-0	Calgary
1924-25	Victoria Cougars	Lester Patrick	3-1	Mont. Canadiens
1925-26	Mont. Canadiens	Eddie Gerard	3-1	Victoria
1926-27	Ottawa Senators	Dave Gill	2-0 (2 ties)	Boston
1927-28	NY Rangers	Lester Patrick	3-2	Mont. Maroons
1928-29	Boston Bruins	Cy Denneny	2-0	NY Rangers
1929-30	Mont. Canadiens	Cecil Hart	2-0	Boston
1930-31	Mont. Canadiens	Cecil Hart	3-2	Chicago
1931-32	Tor. Maple Leafs	Dick Irvin	3-0	NY Rangers
1932-33	NY Rangers	Lester Patrick	3-1	Toronto
1933-34	Chi. Black Hawks	Tommy Gorman	3-1	Detroit
1934-35	Mont. Maroons	Tommy Gorman	3-0	Toronto
1935-36	Det. Red Wings	Jack Adams	3-1	Toronto
1936-37	Det. Red Wings	Jack Adams	3-2	NY Rangers
1937-38	Chi. Black Hawks	Bill Stewart	3-1	Toronto
1938-39	Boston Bruins	Art Ross	4-1	Toronto
1939-40	NY Rangers	Frank Boucher	4-2	Toronto
1940-41	Boston Bruins	Cooney Weiland	4-0	Detroit
1941-42	Tor. Maple Leafs	Hap Day	4-3	Detroit
1942-43	Det. Red Wings	Jack Adams	4-0	Boston
1943-44	Mont. Canadiens	Dick Irvin	4-0	Chicago
1944-45	Tor. Maple Leafs	Hap Day	4-3	Detroit
1945-46	Mont. Canadiens	Dick Irvin	4-1	Boston
1946-47	Tor. Maple Leafs	Hap Day	4-2	Mont. Canadiens
1947-48	Tor. Maple Leafs	Hap Day	4-0	Detroit
1948-49	Tor. Maple Leafs	Hap Day	4-0	Detroit
1949-50	Det. Red Wings	Tommy Ivan	4-3	NY Rangers
1950-51	Tor. Maple Leafs	Joe Primeau	4-1	Mont. Canadiens
1951-52	Det. Red Wings	Tommy Ivan	4-0	Mont. Canadiens
1952-53	Mont. Canadiens	Dick Irvin	4-1	Boston
1953-54	Det. Red Wings	Tommy Ivan	4-3	Mont. Canadiens
1954-55	Det. Red Wings	Jimmy Skinner	4-3	Mont. Canadiens

*No decision

Below: LA's Pat Conacher (#15) and Montréal's Stephan Lebeau (#47) face off during action in Game One of the 1993 Stanley Cup finals.

YEAR	CHAMPION	COACH	RESULTS (GAMES)	LOSER
1955-56	Mont. Canadiens	Toe Blake	4-1	Detroit
1956-57	Mont. Canadiens	Toe Blake	4-1	Boston
1957-58	Mont. Canadiens	Toe Blake	4-2	Boston
1958-59	Mont. Canadiens	Toe Blake	4-1	Toronto
1959-60	Mont. Canadiens	Toe Blake	4-0	Toronto
1960-61	Chi. Black Hawks	Rudy Pilous	4-2	Detroit
1961-62	Tor. Maple Leafs	Punch Imlach	4-2	Chicago
1962-63	Tor. Maple Leafs	Punch Imlach	4-1	Detroit
1963-64	Tor. Maple Leafs	Punch Imlach	4-3	Detroit
1964-65	Mont. Canadiens	Toe Blake	4-3	Chicago
1965-66	Mont. Canadiens	Toe Blake	4-2	Detroit
1966-67	Tor. Maple Leafs	Punch Imlach	4-2	Montréal
1967-68	Mont. Canadiens	Toe Blake	4-0	St Louis
1968-69	Mont. Canadiens	Claude Ruel	4-0	St Louis
1969-70	Boston Bruins	Harry Sinden	4-0	St Louis
1970-71	Mont. Canadiens	Al MacNeil	4-3	Chicago
1971-72	Boston Bruins	Tom Johnson	4-2	NY Rangers
1972-73	Mont. Canadiens	Scotty Bowman	4-2	Chicago
1973-74	Phil. Flyers	Fred Shero	4-2	Boston
1974-75	Phil. Flyers	Fred Shero	4-2	Buffalo
1975-76	Mont. Canadiens	Scotty Bowman	4-0	Philadelphia
1976-77	Mont. Canadiens	Scotty Bowman	4-0	Boston
1977-78	Mont. Canadiens	Scotty Bowman	4-2	Boston
1978-79	Mont. Canadiens	Scotty Bowman	4-1	NY Rangers
1979-80	NY Islanders	Al Arbour	4-2	Philadelphia
1980-81	NY Islanders	Al Arbour	4-1	Minnesota
1981-82	NY Islanders	Al Arbour	4-0	Vancouver
1982-83	NY Islanders	Al Arbour	4-0	Edmonton
1983-84	Edmon. Oilers	Glen Sather	4-1	NY Islanders
1984-85	Edmon. Oilers	Glen Sather	4-1	Philadelphia
1985-86	Mont Canadiens	Jean Perron	4-1	Calgary
1986-87	Edmon. Oilers	Glen Sather	4-3	Philadelphia
1987-88	Edmon. Oilers	Glen Sather	4-0	Boston
1988-89	Calgary Flames	Terry Crisp	4-2	Montréal
1989-90	Edmon. Oilers	John Muckler	4-1	Boston
1990-91	Pitts. Penguins	Bob Johnson	4-2	Minnesota
1991-92	Pitts. Penguins	Scotty Bowman	4-0	Chicago
1992-93	Mont. Canadiens	Jacques Demers	4-1	Los Angeles

couldn't maintain the pace they established in the first two rounds and dropped a five-game set to the Canadiens.

In the finals, the LA Kings appeared poised to deliver the Cup to Hollywood, but a careless error derailed their victory train. Already up one game after a 4-1 victory in the opening match, and leading 2-1 with 90 seconds remaining in Game Two, the Kings' Marty McSorley was caught using an illegal stick, resulting in a two-minute penalty. The Canadiens, with goaltender Roy on the bench for an extra attacker, scored on the ensuing powerplay and eventually won the game in overtime. The Kings never recovered, despite the efforts of Wayne Gretzky, and dropped the next three games — two of them in overtime – as Montréal won their first Cup since 1986.

STANLEY CUP CHAMPIONS

While there has not been space in this chapter to report on every Cup competition, no hockey history can be considered complete without a listing of the teams that have participated in the championship round. They are listed above, beginning with 1917, the year in which the National Hockey League was formed.

PRE-NHL STANLEY CUP WINNERS

1892-93	Montréal Amateur Athletic Association
1893-94	Montréal Amateur Athletic Association
1894-95	Montréal Victorias
1895-96	Winnipeg Victorias (Feb)/Montréal Victorias (Dec)
1896-97	Montréal Victorias
1897-98	Montréal Victorias
1898-99	Montréal Shamrocks
1899	Montréal Shamrocks
1900-01	Winnipeg Victorias
1901-02	Montréal Amateur Athletic Association
1902-03	Ottawa Silver Seven
1903-04	Ottawa Silver Seven
1904-05	Ottawa Silver Seven
1905-06	Montréal Wanderers
1906-07	Kenora Thistles (Jan)/Montréal Wanderers (March)
1907-08	Montréal Wanderers
1908-09	Ottawa Senators
1909-10	Montréal Wanderers
1910-11	Ottawa Senators
1911-12	Québec Bulldogs
1912-13	Québec Bulldogs
1913-14	Toronto Blueshirts
1914-15	Vancouver Millionaires
1915-16	Montréal Canadiens
1916-17	Seattle Metropolitans

CHAPTER SEVEN

RECOGNITIONS WON

In common with the other professional sports groups, the National Hockey League annually recognizes its finest talent with a series of individual awards. Also in common with its fellow organizations, the NHL maintains an annual All-Star list and operates a Hall of Fame. The Hall has two branches, one in Canada and one in the United States.

This chapter lists the pro game's awards and their recipients over the years. We'll begin with the individual awards, listing them in alphabetical order, move to the All-Star results, and finally to the two Halls of Fame.

INDIVIDUAL AWARDS
ART ROSS TROPHY
The Art Ross Trophy was first awarded in 1947. Since it honors the player who leads the league in points (computed on goals and assists) scored during regular season, it was made retroactive so that all points leaders in the history of the

Far right: Center Bobby Clarke of the Philadelphia Flyers.

Page 158: A gallant save.

Below: Right wing Guy Lafleur of the Montréal Canadiens.

league could be recognized. The Trophy was presented to the NHL by the colorful Arthur Howie Ross, for many years the Boston Bruins' manager-coach.

Because just one man can be named for the trophy, a three-step system has been long used to break the scoring ties that inevitably occur on occasion. Should two or more players tie for first place, the award goes to the man who scored the most goals. Should there still be a deadlock, the winner is the man who saw action in the fewest games. And, should a tie then still persist, the matter is settled by naming the man who scored his first goal at the earliest point in the season.

Several cash awards are made in conjunction with the trophy. The overall winner receives $10,000, with $6000 and $4000 going to the runners-up.

Above: Center Wayne Gretzky skating for the Oilers.

1917-18	Joe Malone, Montréal Canadiens	1955-56	Jean Beliveau, Montréal Canadiens
1918-19	Newsy Lalonde, Montréal Canadiens	1956-57	Gordie Howe, Detroit
1919-20	Joe Malone, Québec	1957-58	Dickie Moore, Montréal Canadiens
1920-21	Newsy Lalonde, Montréal Canadiens	1958-59	Dickie Moore, Montréal Canadiens
1921-22	Punch Broadbent, Ottawa	1959-60	Bobby Hull, Chicago
1922-23	Babe Dye, Toronto	1960-61	Bernie Geoffrion, Montréal Canadiens
1923-24	Cy Denneny, Ottawa	1961-62	Bobby Hull, Chicago
1924-25	Babe Dye, Toronto	1962-63	Gordie Howe, Detroit
1925-26	Nels Stewart, Montréal Maroons	1963-64	Stan Mikita, Chicago
1926-27	Bill Cook, New York Rangers	1964-65	Stan Mikita, Chicago
1927-28	Howie Morenz, Montréal Canadiens	1965-66	Bobby Hull, Chicago
1928-29	Ace Bailey, Toronto	1966-67	Stan Mikita, Chicago
1929-30	Cooney Weiland, Boston	1967-68	Stan Mikita, Chicago
1930-31	Howie Morenz, Montréal Canadiens	1968-69	Phil Esposito, Boston
1931-32	Busher Jackson, Toronto	1969-70	Bobby Orr, Boston
1932-33	Bill Cook, New York Rangers	1970-71	Phil Esposito, Boston
1933-34	Charlie Conacher, Toronto	1971-72	Phil Esposito, Boston
1934-35	Charlie Conacher, Toronto	1972-73	Phil Esposito, Boston
1935-36	Sweeney Schriner, New York Americans	1973-74	Phil Esposito, Boston
1936-37	Sweeney Schriner, New York Americans	1974-75	Bobby Orr, Boston
1937-38	Gord Drillon, Toronto	1975-76	Guy Lafleur, Montréal Canadiens
1938-39	Toe Blake, Montréal Canadiens	1976-77	Guy Lafleur, Montréal Canadiens
1939-40	Milt Schmidt, Boston	1977-78	Guy Lafleur, Montréal Canadiens
1940-41	Bill Cowley, Boston	1978-79	Bryan Trottier, New York Islanders
1941-42	Bryan Hextall, New York Rangers	1979-80	Marcel Dionne, Los Angeles
1942-43	Doug Bentley, Chicago	1980-81	Wayne Gretzky, Edmonton
1943-44	Herbert Cain, Montréal Canadiens	1981-82	Wayne Gretzky, Edmonton
1944-45	Elmer Lach, Montréal Canadiens	1982-83	Wayne Gretzky, Edmonton
1945-46	Max Bentley, Chicago	1983-84	Wayne Gretzky, Edmonton
1946-47	Max Bentley, Chicago	1984-85	Wayne Gretzky, Edmonton
1947-48	Elmer Lach, Montréal Canadiens	1985-86	Wayne Gretzky, Edmonton
1948-49	Roy Conacher, Chicago	1986-87	Wayne Gretzky, Edmonton
1949-50	Ted Lindsay, Detroit	1987-88	Mario Lemieux, Pittsburgh
1950-51	Gordie Howe, Detroit	1988-89	Mario Lemieux, Pittsburgh
1951-52	Gordie Howe, Detroit	1989-90	Wayne Gretzky, Los Angeles
1952-53	Gordie Howe, Detroit	1990-91	Wayne Gretzky, Los Angeles
1953-54	Gordie Howe, Detroit	1991-92	Mario Lemieux, Pittsburgh
1954-55	Bernie Geoffrion, Montréal Canadiens	1992-93	Mario Lemieux, Pittsburgh

BILL MASTERTON MEMORIAL TROPHY

The award, which is undoubtedly the most touching of all NHL honors, took shape in the days following the tragic death of Minnesota forward Bill Masterton due to injuries sustained in a 1968 game. Masterton, though never a star player, was highly respected for his sportsmanship, hard work, perseverance and dedication to the game. The Professional Hockey Writer's Association (then called the National Hockey League Writer's Association) donated the trophy to commemorate those qualities. Named is the player judged to represent them best during the season's play. Additionally, the Association awards a $2500 grant to the Bill Masterton Scholarship Fund.

1967-68	Claude Provost, Montréal Canadiens
1968-69	Ted Hampson, Oakland
1969-70	Pit Martin, Chicago
1970-71	Jean Ratelle, New York Rangers
1971-72	Bobby Clarke, Philadelphia
1972-73	Lowell MacDonald, Pittsburgh
1973-74	Henri Richard, Montréal Canadiens
1974-75	Don Luce, Buffalo
1975-76	Rod Gilbert, New York Rangers
1976-77	Ed Westfall, New York Islanders
1977-78	Butch Goring, Los Angeles
1978-79	Serge Savard, Montréal Canadiens
1979-80	Al MacAdam, Minnesota
1980-81	Blake Dunlop, St Louis
1981-82	Chico Resch, Colorado
1982-83	Lanny McDonald, Calgary
1983-84	Brad Park, Detroit
1984-85	Anders Hedberg, New York Rangers
1985-86	Charlie Simmer, Boston
1986-87	Doug Jarvis, Hartford
1987-88	Bob Bourne, Los Angeles
1988-89	Tim Kerr, Philadelphia
1989-90	Gord Kluzak, Boston
1990-91	Dave Taylor, Los Angeles
1991-92	Mark Fitzpatrick, New York Islanders
1992-93	Mario Lemieux, Pittsburgh

CALDER MEMORIAL TROPHY

The trophy is named for Frank Calder, the league president from its inception in 1917 until his death in 1943. During the 1936-37 season, Calder decided to recognize each season's most outstanding rookie with the trophy. It was originally called the Frank Calder Award, with the name being changed to the Calder Memorial Trophy soon after his death.

Each season's outstanding rookie is chosen by a vote of the Professional Hockey Writers' Association. The restrictions imposed on eligibility call for a player not to have participated in more than 25 games during the preceding season, nor in six or more games in each of any two preceding seasons in any major professional league.

The winner receives $10,000, runners-up $6000 and $4000.

1932-33	Carl Voss, Detroit
1933-34	Russ Blinco, Montréal Canadiens
1934-35	Sweeney Schriner, New York Americans
1935-36	Mike Karakas, Chicago
1936-37	Syl Apps, Toronto
1937-38	Cully Dahlstrom, Chicago
1938-39	Frankie Brimsek, Boston
1939-40	Kilby MacDonald, New York Rangers
1940-41	John Quilty, Montréal Canadiens
1941-42	Grant Warwick, New York Rangers
1942-43	Gaye Stewart, Toronto
1943-44	Gus Bodnar, Toronto
1944-45	Frank McCool, Toronto
1945-46	Edgar Laprade, New York Rangers
1946-47	Howie Meeker, Toronto
1947-48	Jim McFadden, Detroit
1948-49	Penny Lund, New York Rangers
1949-50	Jack Gelineau, Boston
1950-51	Terry Sawchuk, Detroit
1951-52	Bernie Geoffrion, Montréal Canadiens
1952-53	Gump Worsley, New York Rangers
1953-54	Camille Henry, New York Rangers
1954-55	Ed Litzenberger, Chicago
1955-56	Glen Hall, Detroit
1956-57	Larry Regan, Boston
1957-58	Frank Mahovlich, Toronto
1958-59	Ralph Backstrom, Montréal Canadiens
1959-60	Billy Hay, Chicago
1960-61	Dave Keon, Toronto
1961-62	Bobby Rousseau, Montréal Canadiens
1962-63	Kent Douglas, Toronto
1963-64	Jacques Laperrière, Montréal Canadiens
1964-65	Roger Crozier, Detroit
1965-66	Brit Selby, Toronto
1966-67	Bobby Orr, Boston
1967-68	Derek Sanderson, Boston
1968-69	Danny Grant, Minnesota
1969-70	Tony Esposito, Chicago
1970-71	Gil Perreault, Buffalo
1971-72	Ken Dryden, Montréal Canadiens
1972-73	Steve Vickers, New York Rangers
1973-74	Denis Potvin, New York Islanders
1974-75	Eric Vail, Atlanta
1975-76	Bryan Trottier, New York Islanders
1976-77	Willi Plett, Atlanta
1977-78	Mike Bossy, New York Islanders
1978-79	Bobby Smith, Minnesota
1979-80	Ray Bourque, Boston
1980-81	Peter Stastny, Québec
1981-82	Dale Hawerchuk, Winnipeg
1982-83	Steve Larmer, Chicago

Right: Defenseman Jacques Laperriére of the Montréal Canadiens – winner of the Calder Memorial Trophy in 1964.

1983-84	Tom Barrasso, Buffalo
1984-85	Mario Lemieux, Pittsburgh
1985-86	Gary Suter, Calgary
1986-87	Luc Robitaille, Los Angeles
1987-88	Joe Nieuwendyk, Calgary
1988-89	Brian Leetch, New York Rangers
1989-90	Sergei Makarov, Calgary
1990-91	Ed Belfour, Chicago
1991-92	Pavel Bure, Vancouver
1992-93	Teemu Selanne, Winnipeg

CONN SMYTHE TROPHY

The trophy, which was presented to the NHL by the Maple Leaf Gardens in 1964, recognizes the most valuable player in the Stanley Cup finals. Named for the major force behind the building of the Gardens and the Toronto Maple Leafs, the honor carries a $10,000 cash award. The winner is chosen by the Professional Hockey Writers' Association.

1964-65	Jean Beliveau, Montréal Canadiens
1965-66	Roger Crozier, Detroit
1966-67	Dave Keon, Toronto
1967-68	Glenn Hall, St Louis
1968-69	Serge Savard, Montréal Canadiens
1969-70	Bobby Orr, Boston
1970-71	Ken Dryden, Montréal Canadiens
1971-72	Bobby Orr, Boston
1972-73	Yvan Cournoyer, Montréal Canadiens
1973-74	Bernie Parent, Philadelphia
1974-75	Bernie Parent, Philadelphia
1975-76	Reggie Leach, Philadelphia
1976-77	Guy Lafleur, Montréal Canadiens
1977-78	Larry Robinson, Montréal Canadiens
1978-79	Bob Gainey, Montréal Canadiens
1979-80	Bryan Trottier, New York Islanders
1980-81	Butch Goring, New York Islanders
1981-82	Mike Bossy, New York Islanders
1982-83	Bill Smith, New York Islanders
1983-84	Mark Messier, Edmonton
1984-85	Wayne Gretzky, Edmonton
1985-86	Patrick Roy, Montréal Canadiens
1986-87	Ron Hextall, Philadelphia
1987-88	Wayne Gretzky, Edmonton
1988-89	Al MacInnis, Calgary
1989-90	Bill Ranford, Edmonton
1990-91	Mario Lemieux, Pittsburgh
1991-92	Mario Lemieux, Pittsburgh
1992-93	Patrick Roy, Montréal Canadiens

EMERY EDGE TROPHY
ALKA-SELTZER PLUS AWARD

The Emery Edge Trophy was presented by the league in collaboration with Emery Worldwide to the player with the season's highest plus-minus rating. The overall winner additionally received $2000, with each team leader being awarded $500 to be donated to his favorite charity. The Alka-Seltzer Plus Award replaces it, contributing $5000 on behalf of the winner to the charity of his choice and $1000 on behalf of each individual team winner.

1982-83	Charlie Huddy, Edmonton
1983-84	Wayne Gretzky, Edmonton
1984-85	Wayne Gretzky, Edmonton
1985-86	Mark Howe, Philadelphia
1986-87	Wayne Gretzky, Edmonton
1991-92	Paul Ysebaert, Detroit
1992-93	Mario Lemieux, Pittsburgh

Left: Conn Smythe was captain of the University of Toronto team.

Below: Wayne Gretzky.

163

Above: Center Bobby Clarke of the Philadelphia Flyers.

FRANK J SELKE TROPHY

Named for the man who spent more than 60 years in hockey as a coach, manager and executive, the award is presented by the NHL's Board of Governors and honors the best defensive forward of the year. The recipient is selected by the Professional Hockey Writers' Association and receives a cash award of $10,000. The runners-up are awarded $6000 and $4000. The Trophy has been presented since 1977.

1977-78	Bob Gainey, Montréal Canadiens
1978-79	Bob Gainey, Montréal Canadiens
1979-80	Bob Gainey, Montréal Canadiens
1981-82	Steve Kaspar, Boston
1982-83	Bobby Clarke, Philadelphia
1983-84	Doug Jarvis, Washington
1984-85	Craig Ramsey, Buffalo
1985-86	Troy Murray, Chicago
1986-87	Dave Poulin, Philadelphia
1987-88	Guy Carbonneau, Montréal
1988-89	Guy Carbonneau, Montréal
1989-90	Rick Meagher, St Louis
1990-91	Dirk Graham, Chicago
1991-92	Guy Carbonneau, Montréal
1992-93	Doug Gilmour, Toronto

HART MEMORIAL TROPHY

Long considered the most prestigious of all NHL awards, the trophy is awarded to the player judged the most valuable to his team during the season. The trophy was first presented to the league in 1923 by the father of Cecil Hart, the former manager-coach of the Montréal Canadiens. It was retired to the Hockey Hall of Fame in 1960 after Hart's death and was immediately replaced by the Hart Memorial Trophy. The trophy today is presented by the NHL, and the recipient is selected by the Professional Hockey Writers' Association. The winner receives $10,000, with $6000 and $4000 going to the runners-up.

1923-24	Frank Nighbor, Ottawa
1924-25	Billy Burch, Hamilton
1925-26	Nels Stewart, Montréal Maroons
1926-27	Herb Gardiner, Montréal Canadiens
1927-28	Howie Morenz, Montréal Canadiens
1928-29	Roy Worters, New York Americans
1929-30	Nels Stewart, Montréal Maroons
1930-31	Howie Morenz, Montréal Canadiens
1931-32	Howie Morenz, Montréal Canadiens
1932-33	Eddie Shore, Boston
1933-34	Aurel Joliat, Montréal Canadiens
1934-35	Eddie Shore, Boston
1935-36	Eddie Shore, Boston
1936-37	Babe Siebert, Montréal Canadiens
1937-38	Eddie Shore, Boston
1938-39	Toe Blake, Montréal Canadiens
1939-40	Ebbie Goodfellow, Detroit
1940-41	Bill Cowley, Boston
1941-42	Tom Anderson, New York Americans
1942-43	Bill Cowley, Boston
1943-44	Walter Pratt, Toronto
1944-45	Elmer Lach, Montréal Canadiens
1945-46	Max Bentley, Chicago
1946-47	Maurice Richard, Montréal Canadiens
1947-48	Herb O'Connor, New York Rangers
1948-49	Sid Abel, Detroit
1949-50	Chuck Rayner, New York Rangers
1950-51	Milt Schmidt, Boston
1951-52	Gordie Howe, Detroit
1952-53	Gordie Howe, Detroit
1953-54	Al Rollins, Chicago
1954-55	Ted Kennedy, Toronto
1955-56	Jean Béliveau, Montréal Canadiens
1956-57	Gordie Howe, Detroit
1957-58	Gordie Howe, Detroit
1958-59	Andy Bathgate, New York Rangers
1959-60	Gordie Howe, Detroit
1960-61	Bernie Geoffrion, Montréal Canadiens
1961-62	Jacques Plante, Montréal Canadiens
1962-63	Gordie Howe, Detroit
1963-64	Jean Béliveau, Montréal Canadiens
1964-65	Bobby Hull, Chicago
1965-66	Bobby Hull, Chicago
1966-67	Stan Mikita, Chicago
1967-68	Stan Mikita, Chicago
1968-69	Phil Esposito, Boston
1969-70	Bobby Orr, Boston
1970-71	Bobby Orr, Boston
1971-72	Bobby Orr, Boston
1972-73	Bobby Clarke, Philadelphia
1973-74	Phil Esposito, Boston
1974-75	Bobby Clarke, Philadelphia
1975-76	Bobby Clarke, Philadelphia
1976-77	Guy Lafleur, Montréal Canadiens
1977-78	Guy Lafleur, Montréal Canadiens

1978-79	Bryan Trottier, New York Islanders
1979-80	Wayne Gretzky, Edmonton
1980-81	Wayne Gretzky, Edmonton
1981-82	Wayne Gretzky, Edmonton
1982-83	Wayne Gretzky, Edmonton
1983-84	Wayne Gretzky, Edmonton
1984-85	Wayne Gretzky, Edmonton
1985-86	Wayne Gretzky, Edmonton
1986-87	Wayne Gretzky, Edmonton
1987-88	Mario Lemiuex, Pittsburgh
1988-89	Wayne Gretzky, Los Angeles
1989-90	Mark Messier, Edmonton
1990-91	Brett Hull, St Louis
1991-92	Mark Messier, New York Rangers
1992-93	Mario Lemieux, Pittsburgh

Below: Hall of Fame right wing Andy Bathgate of the New York Rangers.

JACK ADAMS AWARD

Established in 1974 in memory of the late coach and general manager of the Detroit Red Wings, the award is presented by the National Hockey League Broadcasters' Association to the coach of the year — the coach who, in the wording of the award, has contributed the most to his team's success. The winner receives $10,000 once selected by the Broadcasters' Association.

1973-74	Fred Shero, Philadelphia
1974-75	Bob Pulford, Los Angeles
1975-76	Don Cherry, Boston
1976-77	Scotty Bowman, Montréal Canadiens
1977-78	Bobby Kromm, Detroit
1978-79	Al Arbour, New York Islanders
1979-80	Pat Quinn, Philadelphia
1980-81	Red Berenson, St Louis
1981-82	Tom Watt, Winnipeg
1982-83	Orval Tessier, Chicago
1983-84	Bryan Murray, Washington
1984-85	Mike Keenan, Philadelphia
1985-86	Glen Sather, Edmonton
1986-87	Jacques Demers, Detroit
1987-88	Jacques Demers, Detroit
1988-89	Pat Burns, Montréal
1989-90	Bob Murdoch, Winnipeg
1990-91	Brian Sutter, St Louis
1991-92	Pat Quinn, Vancouver
1992-93	Pat Burns, Toronto

Top right: Hall of Fame defenseman Doug Harvey of the Montréal Canadiens.

Right: Ready to go into action.

JAMES NORRIS MEMORIAL TROPHY

Donated to the NHL in 1953 by the four children of James Norris Sr, the longtime owner of the Detroit Red Wings, the award recognizes the season's best all-around defenseman. Each season's winner is selected by the Professional Hockey Writers' Association and receives $10,000. The runners-up are awarded $6000 and $4000 respectively.

1953-54	Red Kelly, Detroit
1954-55	Doug Harvey, Montréal Canadiens
1955-56	Doug Harvey, Montréal Canadiens
1956-57	Doug Harvey, Montréal Canadiens
1957-58	Doug Harvey, Montréal Canadiens
1958-59	Tom Johnson, Montréal Canadiens
1959-60	Doug Harvey, Montréal Canadiens
1960-61	Doug Harvey, Montréal Canadiens
1962-63	Pierre Pilote, Chicago
1963-64	Pierre Pilote, Chicago
1964-65	Pierre Pilote, Chicago
1965-66	Jacques Laperriére, Montréal Canadiens
1966-67	Harry Howell, New York Rangers
1967-68	Bobby Orr, Boston
1968-69	Bobby Orr, Boston
1969-70	Bobby Orr, Boston
1970-71	Bobby Orr, Boston
1971-72	Bobby Orr, Boston
1972-73	Bobby Orr, Boston
1973-74	Bobby Orr, Boston
1974-75	Bobby Orr, Boston
1975-76	Denis Potvin, New York Islanders
1976-77	Larry Robinson, Montréal Canadiens
1977-78	Denis Potvin, New York Islanders
1978-79	Denis Potvin, New York Islanders
1979-80	Larry Robinson, Montréal Canadiens
1980-81	Randy Carlyle, Pittsburgh
1981-82	Doug Wilson, Chicago
1982-83	Rod Langway, Washington
1983-84	Rod Langway, Washington
1984-85	Paul Coffey, Edmonton
1985-86	Paul Coffey, Edmonton
1986-87	Ray Bourque, Boston
1987-88	Ray Bourque, Boston
1988-89	Chris Chelios, Montréal
1989-90	Ray Bourque, Boston
1990-91	Ray Bourque, Boston
1991-92	Brian Leetch, New York Rangers
1992-93	Chris Chelios, Chicago

LADY BYNG MEMORIAL TROPHY

Seen by many hockey fans as anything from ironic to downright funny because of the game's roughness, the Lady Byng Trophy is awarded annually to the player who demonstrates the best type of sportsmanship and gentlemanly conduct on the ice while simultaneously maintaining a high standard of playing ability. The award was first presented in 1925 by Lady Byng, the wife of Canada's then governor-general. In the eight-year span between 1927-28 and 1934-35, Frank Boucher of the New York Rangers claimed the award seven times, a triumph in good manners and skill that resulted in the trophy being given to him to keep. Lady Byng then presented another trophy in its place. After her death in 1949, the NHL replaced the award with the Lady Byng Memorial Trophy. On being selected by the PHWA, the winner receives $10,000 and the runners-up $6000 and $4000.

Season	Player, Team
1924-25	Frank Nighbor, Ottawa
1925-26	Frank Nighbor, Ottawa
1926-27	Billy Burch, New York Americans
1927-28	Frank Boucher, New York Rangers
1928-29	Frank Boucher, New York Rangers
1929-30	Frank Boucher, New York Rangers
1930-31	Frank Boucher, New York Rangers
1931-32	Joe Primeau, Toronto
1932-33	Frank Boucher, New York Rangers
1933-34	Frank Boucher, New York Rangers
1934-35	Frank Boucher, New York Rangers
1935-36	Doc Romnes, Chicago
1936-37	Marty Barry, Detroit
1937-38	Gordie Drillon, Toronto
1938-39	Clint Smith, New York Rangers
1939-40	Bobby Bauer, Boston
1940-41	Bobby Bauer, Boston
1941-42	Syl Apps, Toronto
1942-43	Max Bentley, Chicago
1943-44	Clint Smith, Chicago
1944-45	Bill Mosienko, Chicago

Below: Hall of Fame left wing Doug Bentley of the Chicago Black Hawks.

Above: Hall of Fame center Jean Ratelle of the New York Rangers is all smiles after scoring a goal against the Toronto Maple Leafs

Right: Center Alex Delvecchio of the Detroit Red Wings was elected to the Hall of Fame in 1977.

1945-46	Toe Blake, Montréal Canadiens
1946-47	Bobby Bauer, Boston
1947-48	Herb O'Connor, New York Rangers
1948-49	Bill Quackenbush, Detroit
1949-50	Edgar Laprade, New York Rangers
1950-51	Red Kelly, Detroit
1951-52	Sid Smith, Toronto
1952-53	Red Kelly, Detroit
1953-54	Red Kelly, Detroit
1954-55	Sid Smith, Toronto
1955-56	Earl Reibel, Detroit
1956-57	Andy Hebenton, New York Rangers
1957-58	Camille Henry, New York Rangers
1958-59	Alex Delvecchio, Detroit
1959-60	Don McKenney, Boston
1960-61	Red Kelly, Toronto
1961-62	Dave Keon, Toronto
1962-63	Dave Keon, Toronto
1963-64	Kenny Wharram, Chicago
1964-65	Bobby Hull, Chicago
1965-66	Alex Delvecchio, Detroit
1966-67	Stan Mikita, Chicago
1967-68	Stan Mikita, Chicago
1968-69	Alex Delvecchio, Detroit
1969-70	Phil Goyette, St. Louis
1970-71	John Bucyk, Boston
1971-72	Jean Ratelle, New York Rangers
1972-73	Gil Perreault, Buffalo
1973-74	John Bucyk, Boston
1974-75	Marcel Dionne, Detroit
1975-76	Jean Ratelle, New York Rangers
1976-77	Marcel Dionne, Los Angeles
1977-78	Butch Goring, Los Angeles
1978-79	Bob MacMillan, Atlanta
1979-80	Wayne Gretzky, Edmonton

1980-81	Rick Kehoe, Pittsburgh
1981-82	Rick Middleton, Boston
1982-83	Mike Bossy, New York Islanders
1983-84	Mike Bossy, New York Islanders
1984-85	Jari Kurri, Edmonton
1985-86	Mike Bossy, New York Islanders
1986-87	Joe Mullin, Calgary
1987-88	Mats Naslund, Montréal
1988-89	Joe Mullen, Calgary
1989-90	Brett Hull, St. Louis
1990-91	Wayne Gretzky, Los Angeles
1991-92	Wayne Gretzky, Los Angeles
1992-93	Pierre Turgeon, New York Islanders

LESTER PATRICK TROPHY

Named in honor of the hockey pioneer and guiding force of the early-day New York Rangers, the trophy was presented to the league by the Rangers in 1966 and has been awarded annually ever since for outstanding service to the game in the United States. Eligible for the honor are players, coaches, officials, team executives and referees. The recipients are chosen by a committee whose membership includes the NHL president, a member of the league's Board of Governors, sport writers and a sports representative of a US national radio-television network. With the exception of the league president, the committee's membership is rotated annually. The award can be given to more than one person each year. Each winner receives a miniature of the trophy.

1966	Jack Adams	1975	Donald M Clark
1967	Gordie Howe		Bill Chadwick
	Charles F Adams		Thomas N Ivan
	James Norris Sr	1976	Stan Mikita
1968	Gen. John R Kilpatrick		George A Leader
	Walter A Brown		Bruce A Norris
	Thomas F Lockhart	1977	John Bucyk
1969	Bobby Hull		Murray Armstrong
	Edward J Jeremiah		John Mariucci
1970	Eddie Shore	1978	Phil Esposito
	James C V Hendy		Tom Fitzgerald
1971	William M Jennings		William T Tutt
	John B Sollenberger		William W Wirtz
	Terry Sawchuk	1979	Bobby Orr
1972	Clarence Campbell	1980	Bobby Clarke
	John Kelly		Edward M Snider
	Cooney Weiland		Fred Shero
	James D Norris		US Olympic Hockey Team
1973	Walter L Bush Jr	1981	Charles M Schulz
1974	Alex Delvecchio	1982	Emile Francis
	Murray Murdoch	1983	Bill Torrey
	Weston W Adams Sr	1984	John A Ziegler Jr
	Charles L Crovat		Arthur Howie Ross

1985	Jack Butterfield
	Arthur M Wirtz
1986	John Macinnes
	Jack Riley
1987	Hobey Baker
	Frank Mathers
1988	Keith Allen
	Fred Cusick
	Bob Johnson
1989	Dan Kelly
	Lou Nanne
	Lynn Patrick
	Bud Poile
1990	Len Ceglarski
1991	Rod Gilbert
	Mike Illitch
1992	Al Arbour
	Art Berglund
	Lou Lamoriello
1993	Frank Boucher
	Red Dutton
	Bruce McNall
	Gil Stein

Below: Emile Francis, who made the Hall of Fame as a builder, once played for the Chicago Black Hawks.

WILLIAM M JENNINGS TROPHY

One of the newest of NHL honors (a year older than the Emery Edge Award), the trophy is awarded to the goalkeeper or goalkeepers who played a minimum of 25 games for the team with the fewest goals scored against it during regular season action. The trophy, which was first presented in the 1981-82 season, is a gift of the NHL's Board of Governors and is named for the late governor and president of the New York Rangers. The overall winner receives $10,000; the runners-up receive $6000 and $4000.

Right: Hall of Fame goalie Ken Dryden of the Montréal Canadiens won the Vezina Trophy five times.

Below: A trio of New York Islander goalies.

1981-82	Denis Herron and Rick Wamsley, Montréal Canadiens
1982-83	Billy Smith and Rollie Melanson, New York Islanders
1983-84	Pat Riggin and Al Jensen, Washington
1984-85	Tom Barrasso and Bob Sauve, Buffalo
1985-86	Bob Froese and Darren Jensen, Philadelphia
1986-87	Brian Hayward and Patrick Roy, Montréal Canadiens
1987-88	Patrick Roy and Brian Hayward, Montréal
1988-89	Patrick Roy and Brian Hayward, Montréal

1989-90	Andy Moog and Rejean Lemelin, Boston
1990-91	Ed Belfour, Chicago
1991-92	Patrick Roy, Montréal
1992-93	Ed Belfour, Chicago

VEZINA TROPHY

This award is linked to the Jennings Trophy in several ways. It goes to a goalkeeper and honors the memory of the leading goalie of the early 1920s – the superb Georges (The Chicoutimi Cucumber) Vezina of the Montréal Canadiens. The trophy was presented to the league in the 1926-27 season after Vezina died of tuberculosis. Presenting the trophy were three former owners of the Canadiens – Leo Dandurand, Louis Letourneau and Joe Cattarinich. Until 1981, it was awarded to the goalkeeper or goalkeepers who permitted the fewest goals during the regular season, an accomplishment that has since then been recognized by the Jennings Trophy. The Vezina winner today is the goalkeeper who is judged best at his position by a vote of the league's general managers. The winner receives $10,000 and $6000 and $4000 is awarded to the runners-up.

1926-27	George Hainsworth, Montréal Canadiens
1927-28	George Hainsworth, Montréal Canadiens
1928-29	George Hainsworth, Montréal Canadiens
1929-30	Tiny Thompson, Boston
1930-31	Roy Worters, New York Americans

1931-32 Charlie Gardiner, Chicago	1966-67 Glenn Hall and Denis Dejordy, Chicago
1932-33 Tiny Thompson, Boston	1967-68 Gump Worsley and Rogie Vachon,
1933-34 Charlie Gardiner, Chicago	Montréal Canadiens
1934-35 Lorne Chabot, Chicago	1968-69 Jacques Plante and Glenn Hall,
1935-36 Tiny Thompson, Boston	St Louis
1936-37 Normie Smith, Detroit	1969-70 Tony Esposito, Chicago
1937-38 Tiny Thompson, Boston	1970-71 Ed Giacomin and Gilles Villemure, New
1938-39 Frank Brimsek, Boston	York Rangers
1939-40 Davie Kerr, New York Rangers	1971-72 Tony Esposito and Gary Smith, Chicago
1040-41 Turk Broda, Toronto	1972-73 Ken Dryden, Montréal Canadiens
1941-42 Frank Brimsek, Boston	1973-74 Bernie Parent, Philadelphia
1942-43 Johnny Mowers, Detroit	Tony Esposito, Chicago
1943-44 Bill Durnan, Montréal Canadiens	1974-75 Bernie Parent, Philadelphia
1944-45 Bill Durnan, Montréal Canadiens	1975-76 Ken Dryden, Montréal Canadiens
1945-46 Bill Durnan, Montréal Canadiens	1976-77 Ken Dryden and Bunny Larocque,
1946-47 Bill Durnan, Montréal Canadiens	Montréal Canadiens
1947-48 Turk Broda, Toronto	1977-78 Ken Dryden and Bunny Larocque,
1948-49 Bill Durnan, Montréal Canadiens	Montréal Canadiens
1949-50 Bill Durnan, Montréal Canadiens	1978-79 Ken Dryden and Bunny Larocque,
1950-51 Al Rollins, Toronto	Montréal Canadiens
1951-52 Terry Sawchuk, Detroit	1979-80 Bob Sauvé and Don Edwards, Buffalo
1952-53 Terry Sawchuk, Detroit	1980-81 Richard Sevigny, Denis Herron and
1953-54 Harry Lumley, Toronto	Bunny Larocque, Montréal Canadiens
1954-55 Terry Sawchuk, Detroit	1981-82 Billy Smith, New York Islanders
1955-56 Jacques Plante, Montréal Canadiens	1982-83 Pete Peeters, Boston
1956-57 Jacques Plante, Montréal Canadiens	1983-84 Tom Barrasso, Buffalo
1957-58 Jacques Plante, Montréal Canadiens	1984-85 Pelle Lindbergh, Philadelphia
1958-59 Jacques Plante, Montréal Canadiens	1985-86 John Vanbiesbrouck, New York Rangers
1959-60 Jacques Plante, Montréal Canadiens	1986-87 Ron Hextall, Philadelphia
1960-61 Johnny Bower, Toronto	1987-88 Grant Fuhr, Edmonton
1961-62 Jacques Plante, Montréal Canadiens	1988-89 Patrick Roy, Montréal
1962-63 Glenn Hall, Chicago	1989-90 Patrick Roy, Montréal
1963-64 Charlie Hodge, Montréal Canadiens	1990-91 Ed Belfour, Chicago
1964-65 Terry Sawchuk and Johnny Bower,	1991-92 Patrick Roy, Montréal
Toronto	1992-93 Ed Belfour, Chicago
1965-66 Gump Worsley and Charlie Hodge,	
Montréal Canadiens	

Below: Tony
Esposito, Chicago
Black Hawk goalie,
won the Vezina
Trophy twice.

ALL-STAR GAMES

Ever since 1947, the league has honored its top players with an annual All-Star game. From 1947 through 1965, the game was played just prior to the beginning of each new season and, with two exceptions, pitted the All-Star crew against the team that had won the Stanley Cup in the preceding season. The exceptions were the games of 1951 and 1952 when the competition featured the first and second All-Star units.

To date, there have been two years in which the game has not been staged. It was not played within the calendar year in 1966, the reason being that its date was switched at that time from the start of the season to mid-season. In 1979, the Challenge Cup series between Team NHL and the Soviet Union replaced the game.

From 1969 through 1973, the game saw representative players from the East and West Divisions in competition. Since 1975, it has involved players selected from the two conferences — the Wales and the Campbell.

The game is played in the league's various venues.

THE HOCKEY HALL OF FAME

The NHL maintains a Hall of Fame with two branches — a Canadian branch at Toronto, and an American branch at Eveleth, Minnesota. The Canadian Hall was the first to take shape. Construction of the Hall in 1960-61 was made possible by contributions from the six teams then in the league — the Boston Bruins, the Chicago Black Hawks, the Detroit Red Wings, the Montréal Canadiens, the New York Rangers, and the Toronto Maple Leafs. The Hall was completed on 1 May 1961, and was officially opened on the following 26 August, with the inaugural ceremonies conducted by Canadian Prime Minister John G Diefenbaker and US Ambassador Livingston T Merchant.

The Hockey Hall of Fame opened a new, modern state-of-the-art facility on 18 June 1993 in downtown Toronto in the prestigious Bank of Montreal Building. The new museum contains 50,000 feet of display space, a complete library including rare photo collections and

Below: The 1976 All-Star team.

Above: The All-Star team poses for a picture.

ALL-STAR RESULTS

YEAR	WINNER	LOSER			
1947	All-Stars, 4	Toronto, 3	1970	East, 4	West, 1
1948	All-Stars, 3	Toronto, 1	1971	West, 2	East, 1
1949	All-Stars, 3	Toronto, 1	1972	East, 3	West, 2
1950	Detroit, 7	All-Stars, 1	1973	East, 5	West, 4
1951 (tie)	First Team, 2	Second Team, 2	1974	West, 6	East, 4
1952 (tie)	First Team, 1	Second Team, 1	1975	Wales, 7	Campbell, 1
1953	All-Stars, 3	Montréal, 1	1976	Wales, 7	Campbell, 5
1954	All-Stars, 3	Detroit, 2	1977	Wales, 4	Campbell, 3
1955	Detroit, 3	All-Stars, 1	1978	Wales, 3	Campbell, 2
1956 (tie)	All-Stars, 1	Montréal, 1	1980	Wales, 6	Campbell, 3
1957	All-Stars, 5	Montréal, 3	1981	Campbell, 4	Wales, 1
1958	Montréal, 6	All-Stars, 3	1982	Wales, 4	Campbell, 2
1959	Montréal, 6	All-Stars, 1	1983	Campbell, 9	Wales, 3
1960	All-Stars, 2	Montréal, 1	1984	Wales, 7	Campbell, 6
1961	All-Stars, 3	Chicago, 1	1985	Wales, 6	Campbell, 4
1962	Toronto, 4	All-Stars, 1	1986	Wales, 4	Campbell, 3
1963 (tie)	All-Stars, 3	Toronto, 3	1987	Wales, 4	Campbell, 3
1964	All-Stars, 3	Toronto, 2	1988	Wales, 6	Campbell, 5
1965	All-Stars, 5	Montréal, 2	1989	Campbell, 9	Wales, 5
1967	Montréal, 3	All-Stars, 0	1990	Wales, 12	Campbell, 7
1968	Toronto, 4	All-Stars, 3	1991	Campbell, 11	Wales, 5
1969 (tie)	East, 3	West, 3	1992	Campbell, 10	Wales, 6
			1993	Wales, 16	Campbell, 6

Above: A Buffalo Sabre high-sticks a Chicago Black Hawk.

research material, meeting rooms, two theatres and one of the largest retail gift shops in the country. Thanks to corporate support from Imperial Oil, Molson's, Bell Canada, Coca Cola, The Sports Network and the *Toronto Sun*, among others, the new Hall of Fame is an intricate mixture of memorabilia, display areas and hands-on participatory games for hockey fans of all ages.

Attempts to establish the Hall date back to 1945 when there was talk of founding it at Kingston, Ontario, the city that many hockey historians believe to have been the game's birthplace.

Though the Hall was not erected until the start of the 1960s, hockey greats have been named to it since the 1945 talk of a Kingston site. Inductees to the Hall are of three types –

players, executives and referees. Executives are known as Builders. Players and referees normally have completed their active careers three years prior to nomination and election, but this period may be shortened by a decision made by the Hall of Fame Governing Committee. Candidates are chosen on the basis of playing ability, character, integrity and contributions to the game.

The members are listed below in alphabetical order, along with the dates of their induction. Though award winners have been hitherto listed according to the first names by which they were best known to the public, the Hall of Fame listings give their formal names, with nicknames (other than such obvious abbreviations as 'Bill' for 'William') in parentheses. The same is done in the list which follows.

PLAYERS

A.
Sidney (Sid) Abel, 69
John (Jack) Adams, 59
Charles (Syl) Apps, 61
George Armstrong, 75
B.
Irvine (Ace) Bailey, 75
Donald Bain, 45
Hobart (Hobey) Baker, 45
Bill Barber, 90
Martin (Marty) Barry, 65
Andrew (Andy) Bathgate, 78
Jean Béliveau, 71
Clinton Benedict, 65
Douglas Bentley, 64
Maxwell Bentley, 66
Hector (Toe) Blake, 66
Leo Joseph Boivin, 86
Richard (Dickie) Boon, 52
Mike Bossy, 91
Emile (Butch) Bouchard, 66
Frank Boucher, 58
George (Buck) Boucher, 60
John Bower, 76
Russell Bowie, 45
Francis Brimsek, 66
Harry (Punch) Broadbent, 62
Walter (Turk) Broda, 67
John Bucyk, 81
Billy Burch, 74
C.
Harold Cameron, 62
Gerald Cheevers, 85
Francis (King) Clancy, 58
Aubrey (Dit) Clapper, 45
Robert (Bobby) Clarke, 87
Sprague Cleghorn, 58
Neil Colville, 67
Charles Conacher, 61
Alex Connell, 58
William Cook, 52
Arthur Coulter, 74
Yvan Cournoyer, 82
William Cowley, 68
Samuel (Rusty) Crawford, 62
D.
John Darragh, 62
Allan (Scotty) Davidson, 50
Clarence (Hap) Day, 61
Alex Delvecchio, 77
Cyril Denneny, 59
Marcel Dionne, 92
Gordon Drillon, 75
Charles Drinkwater, 50
Kenneth Dryden, 83
Woodrow (Woody) Dumart, 92
Thomas Dunderdale, 74
William Durnan, 64
Mervyn (Red) Dutton, 58
Cecil (Babe) Dye, 70
E.
Philip Esposito, 84
Tony Esposito, 88
F.
Arthur Farrell, 65
Fern Flaman, 90
Frank Foyston, 58
Frank Fredickson, 58
G.
William Gadsby, 70

Left: Hall of Fame goalie Gerry Cheevers of the Boston Bruins.

Below: Phil Esposito (facing camera) scores his first goal as a Ranger after being traded by the Boston Bruins.

Above: Hall of Fame Philadelphia Flyer goalie Bernie Parent.

Above right: Hall of Fame left wing Ted Lindsay of the Detroit Red Wings prepares for a game.

Bob Gainey, 92
Charles (Chuck) Gardiner, 45
Herbert Gardner, 58
James Gardiner, 62
Joseph (Bernie/Boom Boom) Geoffrion, 72
Eddie Gerard, 45
Edward (Eddie) Giacomin, 87
Rodrigue (Rod) Gilbert, 82
Hamilton (Billy) Gilmour, 62
Frank (Moose) Goheen, 52
Ebenezer (Ebbie) Goodfellow, 63
Michael Grant, 50
Wilfred (Shorty) Green, 62
Silas Griffis, 50
H.
George Hainsworth, 61
Glenn Hall, 75
Joseph Hall, 61
Douglas Harvey, 73
George Hay, 58
William (Riley) Hern, 62
Bryan Hextall, 69
Harry (Hap) Holmes, 72
Charles (Tom) Hooper, 62
George (Red) Horner, 65

Miles (Tim) Horton, 77
Gordon Howe, 72
Sydney Howe, 65
Henry (Harry) Howell, 79
Robert Hull, 83
John (Bouse) Hutton, 62
Harry Hyland, 62
I.
James (Dick) Irvin, 58
J.
Harvey (Busher) Jackson, 71
Ernest (Moose) Johnson, 52
Ivan (Ching) Johnson, 58
Thomas Johnson, 70
Aurel Joliat, 45
K.
Gordon (Duke) Keats, 58
Leonard (Red) Kelly, 69
Theodore (Teeder/Terrible) Kennedy, 66
David Michael Keon, 86
L.
Elmer Lach, 66
Guy Lafleur, 88
Edouard (Newsy) Lalonde, 50
Jacques Laperriére, 87

Guy Lapointe, 93
Jean (Jack) Laviolette, 62
Hugh Lehman, 58
Jacques Lemaire, 84
Percy LeSueur, 61
Robert (Ted) Lindsay, 66
Harry (Apple Cheeks) Lumley, 80
M.
Duncan (Mickey) MacKay, 52
Frank (Big M) Mahovlich, 81
Joseph Malone, 50
Sylvio Mantha, 60
John Marshall, 65
Fred (Steamer) Maxwell, 62
Lanny McDonald, 92
Frank McGee, 45
William McGimsie, 62
George McNamara, 58
Stanley Mikita, 83
Richard Moore, 74
Patrick (Paddy) Moran, 58
Howie Morenz, 45
William Mosienko, 65
N.
Frank Nighbor, 45
Edward (Reg) Noble, 62

Buddy O'Connor, 88
Harry Oliver, 67
Murray (Bert) Olmstead, 85
Robert Orr, 79
P.
Bernard Parent, 84
Brad Park, 88
Joseph Patrick, 80
Lester Patrick, 45
Gil Perreault, 90
Tommy Philips, 45
Joseph (Pierre) Pilote, 75
Didier (Pit) Pitre, 62
Joseph (Jacques) Plante, 78
Denis Potvin, 91
Walter (Babe) Pratt, 66
Joseph Primeau, 63
Joseph Pronovost, 78
Bob Pulford, 91
Harvey Pulford, 45
Q.
Hubert (Bill) Quackenbush, 76
R.
Frank Rankin, 61
Joseph (Jean) Ratelle, 85
Claude (Chuck) Rayner, 73

Kenneth Reardon, 66
Henri (Pocket Rocket) Richard, 79
Maurice (Rocket) Richard, 61
George Richardson, 50
Gordon Roberts, 71
Arthur Ross, 45
Blair Russell, 65
Ernest Russell, 65
J D (Jack) Ruttan, 62
S.
Serge A Savard, 86
Terrance (Terry) Sawchuk, 71
Fred Scanlan, 65
Milton Schmidt, 61
David (Sweeney) Schriner, 62
Earl Seibert, 63
Oliver Seibert, 61
Edward Shore, 45
Steve Shutt, 93
Albert (Babe) Siebert, 64
Harold (Bullet Joe) Simpson, 62
Darryl Sittler, 89
Alfred Smith, 62
Billy Smith, 93
Reginald (Hooley) Smith, 72
Thomas Smith, 73

Allan Stanley, 81
Russell (Barney) Stanley, 62
John (Black Jack) Stewart, 64
Nelson Stewart, 62
Bruce Stuart, 61
Hod Stuart, 45
T.
Frederic (Cyclone) Taylor, 45
Cecil (Tiny) Thompson, 59
Vladislav Tretiak, 89
Col. Harry Trihey, 50
U.
Norman Ullman, 82
V.
Georges (Chicoutimi Cucumber)
    Vezina, 45
W.
John Walker, 60
Martin Walsh, 62
Harry Watson, 62
Ralph (Cooney) Weiland, 71
Harry Westwick, 62
Fred Whitcroft, 62
Gordon (Phat) Wilson, 62
Lorne (Gump) Worsley, 80
Roy Worters, 69

Above: A reunion of two Hall of Famers – Fred 'Cyclone' Taylor and Francis 'King' Clancy.

177

Above: Harold Ballard, elected to the Hall of Fame in 1977 as a builder.

Above right: Another builder, Foster Hewitt, elected to the Hall in 1965.

BUILDERS

A.
Charles Adams, 60
Weston Adams, 72
Thomas (Frank) Aheam, 62
John (Bunny) Aherne, 77
Sir Montague Allan, 45
Keith Allen, 92

B.
Harold Ballard, 77
Father David Bauer, 89
John Bicknell, 78
Scotty Bowman, 91
George Brown, 61
Walter Brown, 62
Frank Buckland, 75
Jack Butterfield, 80

C.
Frank Calder, 45
Angus Campbell, 64
Clarence Campbell, 66
Joseph Cattarinich, 77

D.
Joseph (Leo) Dandurand, 63
Francis Dilio, 64
George Dudley, 58
James Dunn, 68

E.
Alan Eagleson, 89

F.
Emile Francis, 82

G.
Dr John Gibson, 76
Thomas Gorman, 63
Frank Griffiths, 93

H.
William Hanley, 86
Charles Hay, 74
James Hendy, 68
Foster Hewitt, 65
William Hewitt, 45
Fred Hume, 62

I.
George (Punch) Imlach, 84
Thomas Ivan, 74

J.
William Jennings, 75
Bob Johnson, 92
Gordon Juckes, 79

K.
Gen. John Kilpatrick, 60
Seymour Knox III, 93

L.
George Leader, 69
Robert LeBel, 70
Thomas Lockhart, 65
Paul Loicq, 61

M.
Major Frederic MacLaughlin, 63
John Mariucci, 85
Frank Mathers, 92
John (Jake) Milford, 84
Hon. Hartland Molson, 73

Left: Harry Sinden played for Whitby — 1958-1959.

N.
Francis Nelson, 45
Bruce Norris, 69
James Norris, 58
James D Norris, 62
Willliam Northey, 45

O.
John O'Brien, 62

P.
Fred Page, 93
Frank Patrick, 58
Matt Pavelich, 87
Allan Pickard, 58
Rudy Pilous, 85
Norman (Bud) Poile, 90
Samuel Pollock, 78

R.
Sen. Donat Raymond, 58
John Robertson, 45
Claude Robinson, 45
Philip Ross, 76

S.
Frank J Selke, 60
Harry Sinden, 83
Frank Smith, 62
Conn Smythe, 58
Ed Snider, 88
Lord Stanley of Preston, 45
Gil Stein, 93
James Sutherland, 45

T.
Anatoli Tarasov, 74
Lloyd Turner, 58
William Tutt, 78

V.
Carl Voss, 74

W.
Fred Waghorner, 61
Arthur Wirtz, 71
William Wirtz, 76

Z.
John A Ziegler, Jr 87

Top right: L-r: Bruce Norris, Frank Selke, Conn Smythe.

Above: Chaucer Elliott.

REFEREES
Neil Armstrong, 91
John Ashley, 81
William Chadwick, 64
John D'Amico, 93
Chaucer Elliott, 61
George Hayes, 88

Robert Hewitson, 63
Fred (Mickey) Ion, 61
Michael Rodden, 62
J Cooper Smeaton, 61
Roy (Red) Storey, 67
Frank Udvari, 73

THE UNITED STATES HOCKEY HALL OF FAME

Located some 60 miles to the north of Duluth, the US Hall is the work of the Eveleth Civic Association's Project H Committee, the group that, under the special leadership of chairman D Kelly Campbell, spearheaded the drive for the facility.

The National Hockey League contributed $100,000 toward the Hall's construction. The Hall, which is open Mondays through Sundays throughout the year, was dedicated and opened on 21 June 1973.

Inductees are drawn from the ranks of players, coaches and referees. Eligibility for induction requires a significant career contribution toward hockey in the United States. At the time this book is being written, there are 80 enshrinees in the Hall, consisting of 48 players, 17 coaches, 14 administrators and 1 referee.

Below: Bill Chadwick, the only referee to be elected to both Halls of Fame.

PLAYERS

A.
Clarence (Taffy) Abel

B.
Robert (Hobey) Baker
Earl Bartholome
Peter Bessone
Robert Blake
Frank Brimsek

C.
Rae Chaisson
John Chase
Roger Christian
William Christian
Robert Cleary
William Cleary
Anthony Conroy

D.
Carl (Cully) Dahlstrom
Victor DesJardins
Richard Desmond
Robert Dill

E.
Doug Everett

G.
John Garrison
Jack Garrity
Frank (Moose) Goheen

H.
Austin Harding

I.
Stewart Inglehart

J.
Virgil Johnson

K.
Mike Karakas
Jack Kirrane

L.
Myles Lane
Joseph Linder
Sam LoPresti

M.
John Mariucci
John Matchefts
John Mayasich
Jack McCartan
William Moe
Fred Moseley
Hugh (Muzz) Murray, Sr

N.
Hubert (Hub) Nelson

O.
Eddie Olson
George Owen, Jr.

P.
Winthrop Palmer
Robert Paradise
Clifford (Fido) Purpur

R.
William Riley
Elwin (Doc) Romnes
Richard Rondeau

W.
Thomas Williams
Frank (Coddy) Winters

Y.
Ken Yackel

COACHES

Oscar Almquist
Amo Bessone
Herb Brooks
Len Ceglarski
James Fullerton
Malcolm Gordon
Victor Heyliger
Willard Ikola
Edward Jeremiah
Bob Johnson
John (Snooks) Kelley
John Pleban
Jack Riley
Larry Ross
Clifford Thompson
William Stewart
Alfred (Ralph) Winsor

ADMINISTRATORS

George Brown
Walter Brown
Walter Bush
Donald Clark
J C (Doc) Gibson
William Jennings
Nick Kahler
Thomas Lockhart
Cal Marvin
Robert Ridder
Harold Trumble
William Tutt
William Wirtz
Lyle Wright

REFEREE

William Chadwick

Above: A young Bobby Hull scores a goal for the Chicago Black Hawks against the Toronto Maple Leafs.

Left: Hall of Famer Frank 'Big M' Mahovlich in action at left wing for the Detroit Red Wings.

CHAPTER EIGHT

RECORD
PERFORMANCES

In common with all organized sports bodies, the NHL has seen many record performances, by both individuals and teams. Here now, at the time of this book's writing, is a representative list of those performances. Some are so complete that they will undoubtedly remain intact for years to come, while others are currently being so closely pursued that they may well fall at some near date in the future. With the game being what it is — and the caliber of players entering the league being what it is — all the records can be expected to change hands at some time to come.

INDIVIDUAL RECORDS

CAREER

MOST SEASONS
26. Gordon (Gordie) Howe, Detroit, 1946-47 through 1970-71; Hartford Whalers, 1979-80.

MOST GAMES:
1767. Gordie Howe.

MOST GOALS:
801. Gordie Howe.

MOST ASSISTS:
1563. Wayne Gretzky.

MOST POINTS:
2328. Wayne Gretzky.

Page 183: Waiting to skate.

Far right: Mark Howe of the Philadelphia Flyers won the Emery Edge Trophy in 1985-86.

Below: Gordie Howe holds several NHL records, including most seasons, most games and most goals.

CAREER

MOST GAMES, INCLUDING PLAYOFFS:
1924. Gordie Howe. 1767 regular-season games, 157 playoff games.

MOST GOALS, INCLUDING PLAYOFFS
875. Wayne Gretzky. 765 regular-season games, 110 playoff games.

MOST ASSISTS, INCLUDING PLAYOFFS
1799. Wayne Gretzky. 1563 regular-season games, 236 playoff games.

MOST POINTS, INCLUDING PLAYOFFS
2674. Wayne Gretzky. 2328 regular-season games, 346 playoff games.

CAREER

MOST CONSECUTIVE GAMES:
962. Doug Jarvis. From 8 October 1975 through 5 April 1987, with Montréal, Washington and Hartford.

MOST GAMES APPEARED IN BY A GOALTENDER:
971. Terry Sawchuk. From 1949-50 through 1969-70, with Detroit, Boston, Toronto, Los Angeles and NY Rangers.

MOST CONSECUTIVE COMPLETE GAMES BY A GOALTENDER:
502. Glenn Hall. From beginning of 1955-56 season through twelfth game of 1962-63 season.

MOST SHUTOUTS BY GOALTENDER:
103. Terry Sawchuk.

MOST GAMES SCORING 3 OR MORE GOALS:
49. Wayne Gretzky. In 14 seasons with Edmonton and Los Angeles.

MOST 20-OR-MORE-GOAL SEASONS:
22. Gordie Howe. In 26 seasons.

MOST 30-OR-MORE-GOAL SEASONS:
14. Gordie Howe, in 26 seasons with Detroit and Hartford; Marcel Dionne, in 18 seasons with Detroit, Los Angeles and NY Rangers; Mike Gartner, in 14 seasons with Washington, Minnesota and NY Rangers.

MOST 40-OR-MORE-GOAL SEASONS:
12. Wayne Gretzky, in 14 seasons with Edmonton and Los Angeles.

MOST 50-OR-MORE-GOAL SEASONS:
9. Mike Bossy, in 10 seasons with NY Islanders; Wayne Gretzky, in 14 seasons with Edmonton and Los Angeles.

MOST 100-OR-MORE-POINT SEASONS:
13. Wayne Gretzky, in 14 seasons with Edmonton and Los Angeles.

SEASON

MOST GOALS:
92. Wayne Gretzky, Edmonton Oilers, 1981-82.

MOST ASSISTS:
163. Wayne Gretzky, 1985-86.

MOST POINTS:
215. Wayne Gretzky, 1985-86.

MOST GOALS, INCLUDING PLAYOFFS:
100. Wayne Gretzky, 1983-84, 87 in regular-season games; 13 in playoffs.

MOST ASSISTS, INCLUDING PLAYOFFS:
174. Wayne Gretzky, 1985-86, 163 in regular-season games; 11 in playoffs.

MOST POINTS, INCLUDING PLAYOFFS:
255. Wayne Gretzky, 1984-85, 208 in regular-season games; 47 in playoffs.

Left: The Calder Memorial Trophy winner for 1985-86, Gary Suter of the Calgary Flames stands ready on the ice.

Below: Goalie Terry Sawchuk slaps away another shot for the Detroit Red Wings. Sawchuk was elected to the Hall of Fame in 1971.

SEASON

SEASON

MOST GOALS BY A ROOKIE.
76. Teemu Selanne, Winnipeg Jets, 1992-93.

MOST GOALS BY A DEFENSEMAN.
48. Paul Coffey, Edmonton, 1985-86.

MOST ASSISTS BY A DEFENSEMAN.
102. Bobby Orr, 1970-71.

MOST ASSISTS BY A GOALTENDER.
14. Grant Fuhr, Edmonton, 1983-84.

MOST SHUTOUTS:
22. George Hainsworth, Montreal, 1928-29, in 44 games.

LONGEST UNDEFEATED STREAK BY A
   GOALTENDER.
32 Games. Gerry Cheever, Boston, 1971-72, 24 wins
   and 8 ties.

LONGEST SHUTOUT SEQUENCE BY A
   GOALTENDER:
461 Minutes, 29 Seconds, Alex Connell, Ottawa
   Senators, 1927-28.

LONGEST CONSECUTIVE GOAL-SCORING
   STREAK:
16 Games. Harry (Punch) Broadbent, Ottawa
   Senators, 1921-22; 25 during streak.

LONGEST CONSECUTIVE POINT-SCORING
   STREAK:
51 Games. Wayne Gretzky, 1983-84, with 61 goals
   and 92 assists for 153 points, from 5 October
   1983 through 27 January 1984.

LONGEST CONSECUTIVE ASSIST-SCORING
   STREAK.
23 Games. Wayne Gretzky, Los Angeles, 1990-91.

MOST GOALS, 50 GAMES FROM START OF
   SEASON:
61. Wayne Gretzky, 1981-82, from 7 October 1981
   through 22 January 1982.

MOST GOALS:
7. Joe Malone, Québec Bulldogs, 31 January 1920,
   against Toronto; Wayne Gretzky, in 1980, 1986
   and 1986.

MOST ASSISTS:
7. Billy Taylor, Detroit; 16 March 1947; against
   Chicago.

MOST POINTS:
10. Darryl Sittler, Toronto; 7 February 1976;
   against Boston.

Below: The Edmonton Oilers in action against the New York Islanders in the 1980s.

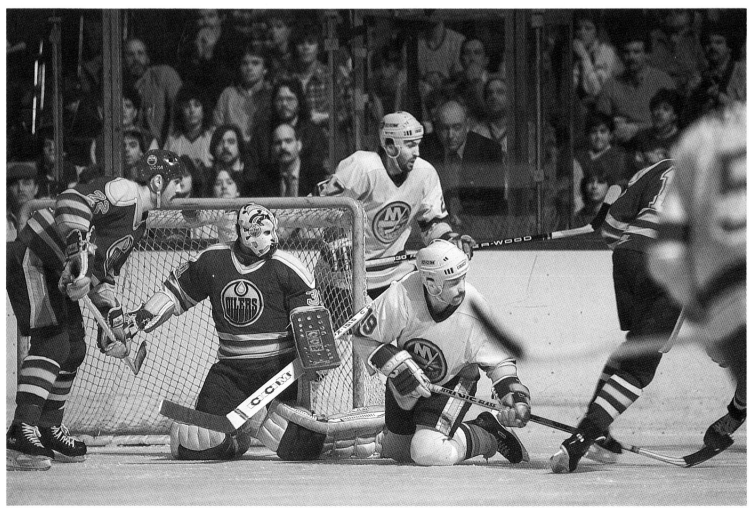

SEASON

MOST GOALS BY A DEFENSEMAN:
5. Ian Trumbull, Toronto; 2 February 1977; against Detroit.

MOST POINTS BY A DEFENSEMAN:
8. Tom Bladon, Philadelphia; 11 December 1977; against Cleveland Barons.

MOST ASSISTS, ONE PERIOD:
5. Dale Hawerchuk, Winnipeg; 6 March 1984; against Los Angeles.

MOST POINTS, ONE PERIOD:
6. Bryan Trottier, NY Islanders; 23 December 1978; against NY Rangers.

FASTEST GOAL FROM START OF GAME:
5 Seconds. Bryan Trottier, NY Islanders; 22 March 1984; against Boston.

FASTEST GOAL FROM START OF A PERIOD:
4 Seconds. Claude Provost, Montréal Canadiens; 9 November 1957; second period; against Boston; Denis Savard, Chicago Black Hawks, 12 January 1986.

FASTEST 2 GOALS:
4 Seconds. Nels Stewart, Montréal Maroons; 3 January 1931; 8:24 and 8:28, third period; against Boston.

FASTEST 3 GOALS:
21 Seconds. Bill Mosienko, Chicago; 23 March 1952; 6:09, 6:20 and 6:30, third period; against NY Rangers.

FASTEST 3 ASSISTS:
21 Seconds. Gus Bodnar, Chicago; 23 March 1952; assists to Bill Mosienko at 6:09, 6:20 and 6:30, third period; against NY Rangers.

TEAM RECORDS

SEASON

BEST WINNING PERCENTAGE:
875. Boston, 1929-30; 44-game season; won 38, lost 5, tied 1.

MOST WINS:
60. Montréal Canadiens, 1976-77; 80-game season.

MOST GOALS:
446. Edmonton, 1983-84; 80-game season.

MOST ASSISTS:
737. Edmonton, 1985-86.

MOST POINTS:
132. Montréal Canadiens, 1976-77; 80-game season; won 60, lost 8, tied 12.

MOST HOME WINS:
36. Philadelphia, 1975-76; 40 home games.

SEASON

MOST ROAD WINS:
27. Montréal Canadiens, 1976-77; 40 road games.

LONGEST WINNING STREAK:
17 Games. Pittsburgh Penguins, 9 March to 10 April 1993.

LONGEST WINNING STREAK FROM START OF SEASON:
8 Games. (Tie) Toronto, 1934-35; Buffalo, 1975-76.

LONGEST WINNING STREAK, INCLUDING PLAYOFFS:
15 Games. Detroit, 27 February 1955 through 5 April 1955; 9 regular-season games, 6 playoff games.

LONGEST HOME WINNING STREAK:
20 Games. (Tie) Boston and Philadelphia; Boston, 3 December 1929 through 8 March 1930; Philadelphia, 4 January 1976 through 3 April 1976.

Above: New York Rangers' goalie John Vandiesbrouck celebrates a score.

SEASON

MOST POINTS, ONE PERIOD:
23. NY Rangers, 21 November 1971; 8 goals and 15

MOST POINTS:
40. Buffalo, 21 December 1975; 14 goals and 26
    assists; 14-2 win over Washington.

MOST SHOTS:
83. Boston, 4 March 1941; against goaltender Sam
    LoPresti; 3-2 win over Chicago.

MOST GOALS, ONE PERIOD:
9. Buffalo, 19 March 1981; 14-4 win over Toronto.

MOST SHOTS, BOTH TEAMS:
141. NY Americans and Pittsburgh Pirates, 26
     December 1925; 73 shots by Americans, 68 by
     Pittsburgh; 3-1 win for NY.

MOST GOALS, BOTH TEAMS, ONE PERIOD:
12. Buffalo and Toronto, 19 March 1981; second
    period; 9 goals for Buffalo, 3 for Toronto; 14-3
    win for Buffalo; Edmonton and Chicago, 11
    December 1985; second period; 6 goals for
    Edmonton, 6 goals for Chicago in 12-9 victory by
    Edmonton.

MOST POINTS, BOTH TEAMS, ONE PERIOD:
35. Edmonton and Chicago, 11 December 1985;
    second period; Edmonton 6 goals and 12 assists,
    Chicago 6 goals and 11 assists; 12-9 win for
    Edmonton.

Opposite: Doug Gilmour's popularity has helped breathe new life into the Toronto Maple Leafs.

Below: Troy Murray of the Chicago Black Hawks handles the puck. Murray was the 1985-86 Frank J Selke Trophy winner.

Page numbers in italics refer to illustrations

Photo Credits

Bruce Bennett Studios: Bruce Bennett: 1, 2-3, 4-5, 19, 36, 53, 78, 87 (top), 109, 110, 112, 113 (top), 114, 115, 116, 117, 118, 119 (top), 120, 121 (both), 123 (both), 124, 125, 126, 127, 128 (both), 131, 132 (bottom), 134 (right), 136 (top), 137, 138 (top left, top right), 139 (both), 141, 142, 142-143, 144, 145, 146-147, 148, 149, 151, 153, 155 (both), 161, 163 (left), 164, 166 (left), 170 (left), 171, 174, 183, 184, 185 (top), 186, 187, 188; Tony Biegun: 133 (top), C. Covatta: 122; J. DiMaggio 105, 170 (right), 173; J. Giamundo: 127 (bottom), 135 (top); Scott Levy: 125 (top), 129, 156; J. Michaud: 133 (bottom); G. Tickles: 135 (bottom); B. Winkler: 134 (left).

FPG: 10-11, 13 (left), 15, 17, 50-51, 54, 55 (top), 59, 60, 62, 63, 71, 72, 84 (top), 93 (bottom), 102, 102-103, 108 (bottom), 113 (bottom), 167, 175 (bottom).

Hockey Hall of Fame and Museum: 16, 20, 21, 22, 23, 24, 25, 26-27, 28, 29, 30, 31, 32, 33, 34, 35, 38, 39, 40, 42, 43, 44, 45, 46, 47, 48, 49, 55 (bottom), 56, 57, 58, 61, 64, 65, 66, 67, 68-69, 70, 73, 74, 75, 76, 77, 80, 81, 82, 83, 84 (bottom), 85, 86, 87 (bottom), 88, 89, 90, 91, 92, 93 (top), 94, 95, 96, 98, 99, 100, 101, 111, 133 (bottom), 150, 152, 160 (right), 162, 163 (right), 165, 166 (right), 167, 168 (bottom), 169, 172, 175 (top), 176, 177, 178, 179, 180, 181, 185 (bottom); Doug MacLellan 132 (top), 138 (bottom right), 189.

The Ice Age: Tony Biegun: 136 (bottom).

New York Public Library Picture Collection: 6, 9 (bottom), 11, 13 (right).

Mike Tamborrino 106-107 (bottom).